D1568471

Evangelists
in
Chains

Cover design by
Marie Schapansky

All other illustrations
by the author

Evangelists in Chains

by *Elizabeth Wagler*

Rod and Staff Publishers, Inc.
P.O. Box 3, Hwy. 172
Crockett, Kentucky 41413
Telephone: (606) 522-4348

Printed in U.S.A.

ISBN 0-7399-0156-7

Catalog no. 2228

10   11   12   13   14   —   16   15   14   13   12   11   10   09   08   07

This book is written
in memory of
the faithful saints
of ages past
who sacrificed all
to follow Christ
and
to challenge
the saints of today
and those who will be
to a life
of selfless consecration
to God.

TABLE OF CONTENTS

THE HAPSBURG EMPIRE (AUSTRIA) in 1539

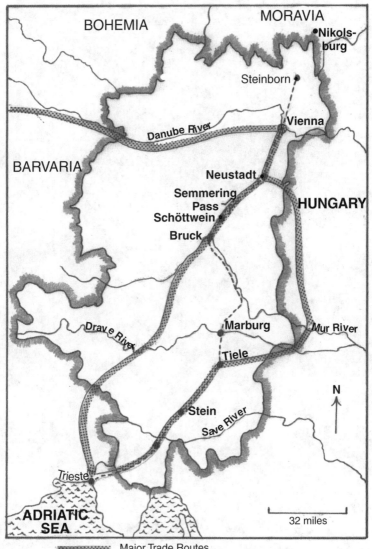

BOHEMIA

MORAVIA

•Nikols-
burg

Steinborn •

Danube River

Vienna

BARVARIA

Neustadt •

Semmering
Pass
Schöttwein •

HUNGARY

Bruck

Drave River

Marburg •

Mur River

Tiele

Stein •

Save River

N
↑

Trieste

ADRIATIC
SEA

32 miles

━━━━━ Major Trade Routes
------ Route Of The Evangelists in Chains

1

In the Cabinet Shop

A cloud of fine dust particles danced in the subdued light that filtered through the large, multi-paned window in the front of the small cabinet shop of Steinborn. The clean fragrant odour of freshly cut wood and pungent aroma of melted glue permeated the dim atmosphere. An intermittent, dull *thunk! thunk!* of hammers striking wood rose above the steady rasping drone and gentle rubbing sound of files and sanding stones.

In the centre of the room, on a low stool, sat a young man, industriously rubbing a pumice stone back and forth over a slender chair rung. A disorderly collection of rungs, legs, and armrests lay strewn at his feet, awaiting their final sanding.

Young Peter Hans, the occupant of the stool, lifted his head, and, holding the rung to the light, swivelled it this way and that. He ran the index finger of his free hand along the smooth surface. Satisfied, he rose from his stool, stepped gingerly over the pile of chair parts and carried the finished rung over to where two older men were assembling chairs.

"Here's another," he said, laying the piece on a bench alongside several others of its kind.

"Good," mumbled one of the men, Cornelius by name, taking a short piece of doweling from the row he held in his mouth. He tapped the dowel neatly into a hole on the chair bottom and reached for another.

Peter stood watching for a moment as Jacob, the older of the two men, carefully drilled tiny holes along the chair back and his companion followed quickly with the little dowels. Before his eyes, a chair was taking shape. Beside the men stood a finished product—useful and simple, with every piece shaped and sanded to perfection. To Peter, who knew the tedious hours of labour that went into the fashioning of each piece, it was a work of art. He looked forward to the day when he would be permitted to assemble the fine, sturdy chairs, tables, cabinets, and benches that were the trademark of his father's cabinet shop. But in the meantime . . .

Jacob glanced at Peter, who was running his hand lingeringly over the carving on the back of the completed chair. "Better get to work. We're going to be waiting on you soon."

With a resigned sigh, Peter returned to his stool and stooped to pick up another rung. As he rubbed, his eyes wandered to the area in front of the window. There his father, known as Big Peter Hans, to distinguish him from his son and also because of his tall, broad-shouldered frame, bent over the homemade lathe. Under his skillful fingers, a plain, chestnut pole was rapidly being transformed into a beautiful bedpost. A young lad of about fourteen years stood at one end of the lathe, endlessly turning the handle round and round.

"At least," Peter consoled himself, "I've graduated from that task." And he attacked his sanding with renewed enthusiasm.

For a time, the only sounds to be heard were the buzzing and tapping of the tools, broken occasionally by the low murmur of voices.

At the tinkling of the bell over the door, announcing the arrival of a customer, all hands paused in their work and all eyes turned inquisitively to the open doorway, where stood a middle-aged man in outdoor clothing. Big Peter laid down his tools and turned from the lathe to meet the new arrival. The young apprentice gratefully dropped his hands from the lathe handle and sank wearily onto a nearby stool, glad for the unexpected reprieve.

"Good afternoon, Mr. Blötter." Big Peter's voice was congenial.

"Good day to you, sir," responded the other man, stamping some wet snow from his boots. "Sure is damp weather we're having lately."

"Yes, the clouds are hanging in low these days," agreed Big Peter.

"Maybe if it'd snow properly for a day or two, the clouds would lift and we could see the sun again," Mr. Blötter complained. "When a man has to work outside all day, this damp cold air just chills him through and through." He shivered slightly in his thin coat.

"Well," Big Peter remonstrated. "It's typical weather for the beginning of December in this northeast corner of Austria, isn't it? And God knows what is best for us. He sends the clouds so we can appreciate the sun more when it shines."

"Yes, yes, I suppose so," muttered Mr. Blötter. "But what I came for," he hastened on to say, "was to pay for the cabinet you made for me."

The other occupants of the shop, having recognized Mr. Blötter as a woodcutter who lived in Steinborn, took up their tasks again, but their ears continued to follow the conversation at the front of the room.

"My wife was delighted with the cabinet," Mr. Blötter was saying as he counted out coins. "I must commend you for your high-quality workmanship."

"Thank you," Big Peter humbly acknowledged the compliment.

"You know," Mr. Blötter said, lowering his voice, "when you

people settled here in Steinborn three years ago, the priest warned us emphatically to have no dealings with you."

"He did?" Big Peter feigned mild surprise, although the revelation was not news to him.

"Yes," the townsman said, nodding his head. "He maintained that you were infidels, unbelievers, enemies of the true church and he was convinced that you harboured some heinous plot against the king!"

Young Peter and the other workers let their hands fall idle as they strained their ears to better hear this interesting conversation.

A faint smile played around the corners of Big Peter's mouth as he asked, "And do you believe all this about us?"

"Well," the other admitted, "of course I accepted it at first. We all did. After all, when the priest says something, it is to be believed. But"—his voice sounded almost puzzled—"three years have gone by and I haven't seen any attacks on the king. Some of my neighbours told me that you people did good work for a fair price. My own brother, who is bolder than most of us, dared to approach your blacksmith for a new plowshare. He was so well satisfied with the results that the rest of us saw no harm in dealing with you either—of course, the priest wasn't too pleased at first, but he hasn't been saying much lately."

"Christ taught that we should live at peace with God and our fellow men," Big Peter replied. "We have no desire to harm anyone and are loyal to the king, wherever his laws don't contradict the laws of God."

"I'll be sure to recommend your work to my neighbours," Mr. Blötter assured him, buttoning up his cloak.

Big Peter escorted him to the door. "My friend," he said, laying a hand on the man's arm, "wouldn't you like to read the words of Jesus for yourself? I have some papers here . . ."

Mr. Blötter's head jerked up to meet the large man's compassionate gaze. A look of fear was in his eyes. He stepped away from Big Peter and held up a hand in protest. "Eh, no, no. The priest is the only one who can interpret God's Holy Book. It would be wicked for me, an unlearned man, to read the Scriptures." He reached hastily for the door catch.

"But how do you know that what the priest tells you is true?" persisted Big Peter.

"Oh, I'm sure he knows what he is talking about," stammered the man. "No, no. I have no desire to read any of your books." Then Mr. Blötter hurried from the shop, leaving Big Peter standing in the open doorway, staring after the retreating figure.

Shaking his head, Big Peter closed the door and walked heavily back to the lathe. The apprentice jumped from his stool, and at a nod from his master, began to crank the handle round and round. Big Peter picked up the tool he had been using and held it against the wood. White curls of wood shavings fell to the floor as the design took shape.

"None of the villagers have ever accepted a pamphlet from us, have they?" asked Jacob above the buzzing and scraping.

"Not to my knowledge," Big Peter replied, not lifting his eyes from his work.

"More and more they are coming to our craftsmen to buy and have things mended," Jacob continued. "But they are afraid to listen to the Gospel message."

"The priest holds firm sway over them," Cornelius added. "They are fearful of the consequences should they listen to our message."

"I'm sure if any of them would read the Scriptures or listen to our teaching, they would quickly realise that much of their religion is corrupt and un-Scriptural. They are held in darkness and Christ came to bring them from darkness into light," Jacob said.

Peter too wished that the villagers of Steinborn would embrace the true faith and find the peace that passes all understanding. At the same time, he hoped that his father's offer of a pamphlet to Mr. Blötter would not spoil the brethren's growing reputation in this place.

For the first year or two of their stay here, all their efforts in the cabinet shop had been concentrated on providing furnishings for the use of their community of over two hundred souls.

The group had been able to bring very little with them on their flight from Moravia. They had rented several buildings at the west end of Steinborn from Lord Fünfkirchen, the baron who controlled this valley; then all the men had joined the carpenters and woodworkers in erecting more buildings and renovating the existing ones.

A large, sunny, street-level room had been allocated to Big Peter Hans. Here he, Jacob, Cornelius, and a dozen volunteers had worked steadily through the whole first winter, turning out tables, benches, chests, and cupboards.

Another year had gone by in which the cabinetmakers had focused their skills on producing bedsteads, cradles, chairs, wardrobes, and rockers for individual families.

During these years, other members of the bruderhof* had contributed their varied skills to the formation of the well-ordered community. Weavers, tailors, shoemakers, watchmakers, wagon makers, potters, teachers, and doctors all laboured to provide the equipment necessary for the daily functioning of the group. Farmers raised crops and tended stock to supply the pantries located beneath the large community kitchen.

Because of their reputation as heretics and the incriminating label of "Anabaptists" that had accompanied the large group of refugees, the villagers had kept a wary distance. In spite of the

*community of believers

lenient attitude of Lord Fünfkirchen, who seemed glad to have the thrifty, hard-working, progressive Moravians in his territory, the fact that the newcomers never darkened the door of the small church whose steeple rose above the low roofs of the village lent credibility to the rumours concerning their perverse activities and created an invisible barrier that the villagers dared not cross.

Only in the past few months, as Mr. Blötter had said, had the natives of Steinborn felt free to place their orders with the newcomers.

Once the community was self-supporting, the craftsmen had hoped to attract local customers so that they would have funds to share with other needy brethren. Although they were pleased with the recent growing contact with their neighbours, they were not satisfied to be of service to them only in material affairs. Being possessed with great missionary zeal, they were eager to share with them their faith in the saving merits of the blood of Christ, which is able to lift men from ignorance, superstition, and dependence on the caprices of the corrupt established church system of the day.

Peter's rambling thoughts were brought back to reality by the tinkling of the bell. He gave a last rub to the piece he was sanding and looked up in time to see a tall, slender young man shrugging his coat from his shoulders.

Good. Andreas had come. The time would pass more quickly now with someone to talk to. Andreas was twenty-two, three years older than Peter, but the two were fast friends.

The other men greeted Andreas briefly as he made his way to Peter's stool. As his arrival was a daily occurrence, they soon returned their attention to their respective tasks. The young man propped his hands on his knees and bent to study Peter's work.

"Still making sawdust?" he asked with a friendly grin.

"Oh, yes. If someone would pay me for producing sawdust, I'd be a rich man by now," Peter replied, moving the toe of his shoe and making a circular trail through the dust that lay thick at his feet.

"Someday you'll be a master woodworker like your father," encouraged Andreas, turning a carved chair leg over and over in his hands, his fingers tracing the smooth curves of the design. "I expect he did his share of turning lathes, sweeping shavings, and sanding chair rungs in his younger days."

Peter nodded his acknowledgment of the truth of that statement. "I don't really mind this job. It is satisfying to feel the roughness become a smooth satiny surface. But it does get monotonous," he added ruefully, glancing down at the pile of pieces still to be finished.

"I'll bring my chest over near you, and then we can visit," Andreas offered, stepping to the rear of the shop. He returned, dragging a large wooden chest behind him.

Peter swivelled on his stool to admire the ornately carved article. "Bridgit had better appreciate it," he said. "All that work you've put into it."

Andreas studied the pattern of leaves and rosebuds carved on the heavy lid. "The finest young lady in the world deserves the finest of wedding gifts," he excused himself. He tested the blade of his chisel before touching it to the wood. Near the bottom on the centre front, he had carved the inscription *ANDREAS—BRIDGIT* and below the names, *1539.* With meticulous care, he chipped away at the scroll work around the lettering.

Peter watched for a while. Then he suddenly thought of something. "What if you don't get married before the end of the year? You shouldn't have been in such a hurry to carve the date."

A slight flush spread over Andreas's finely chiselled features. "I wondered about that myself," he said, sitting back on his heels to study his handiwork. "But now I think everything will work out."

"How do you know?"

"You're aware of the conference that is planned for this weekend with the group of Philippite brethren from Moravia?"

Peter nodded.

"Word came today that Bishop Peter Riedemann is expected to be present as well."

"Bishop Riedemann?" Peter's voice held a note of excitement. "You mean the man who wrote our Confession of Faith from prison? The man who has travelled through the Empire, preaching the Word and conducting many Christians to safety in Moravia?"

Andreas nodded his head in answer to Peter's rapid questions. His fingers continued to wield the knife, but his own eyes held an animated glow.

Peter's voice rattled on, "Why, I never expected to meet Peter Riedemann so soon. I've always admired . . . say—" He suddenly stopped in his rush of words and stared at Andreas. The older boy turned so that his face was partly hidden by his shoulder.

"Now I understand. If a bishop is coming, that means you and Bridgit can get married. No wonder you want to finish that chest. Why, by this time next week, you'll be a married man!"

Peter's amazed exclamations had attracted the attention of the other men. News of the imminent arrival of a bishop at the bruderhof caused no small stir of anticipation. The small group at Steinborn had four deacons who led out in spiritual matters, but such solemn ordinances as Communion, Baptism, and Marriage were postponed until such a time as a travelling bishop paid a visit.

Jacob wished the bridegroom the Lord's blessing, and from his lathe, Big Peter assured Andreas that he shared his joy and would remember them in prayer.

Andreas and his chosen bride, Bridgit, had several months previously announced their plans to marry and had been eagerly awaiting the arrival of a bishop to preside over the ceremony. Now the long-awaited day was almost upon them.

Peter was aware that Andreas had spent many afternoons and lonely evenings in the cabinet shop, fashioning two chairs, a small cupboard, and a bedstead for his future home. The brotherhood normally supplied these furnishings to a newly wedded couple, but Andreas had wanted to make them himself. The chest was his own special gift to Bridgit, and he had laboured painstakingly over every joint and carved curlicue, pouring his love into the work of his fingers.

Peter was full of questions. "Do you have an apartment? Where will you live? Does Bridgit have her things ready?"

"We will live with my family for the present. Then, in the spring, when the new tannery is built, we have been promised one of the apartments above it. As to Bridgit, she has been weaving sheets and knotting quilts. I have seen some of her embroidered linens, and they are fit for a king."

"This is all very nice for you but too bad for me," Peter stated, pretending to sulk.

"Why?"

"With Bridgit's chest finished and you happily married, you won't come here to work anymore, and I shall not enjoy your company."

Andreas chuckled. He stood back to squint critically at the carved piece he had just finished. "On the contrary, I will have to make a table and some bookshelves for us to put in our new apartment. Bridgit will be busy all day in the kitchens or weaving barn or laundry, so I can still spend my afternoons here. But . . . I suspect you might not find me here after supper anymore, unless I bring Bridgit along."

"Sure." Peter flourished his rung. "She could sand chair rungs for you."

"I'm sure she'd do an excellent job of sanding," agreed Andreas, who thought all of Bridgit's accomplishments superior.

So Andreas would soon be married. Peter was happy for him, but he sensed that their relationship might not be the same. Andreas had been like an older brother to him. He was always kind and considerate. He took an interest in the younger boy's affairs and did not shake off Peter's many questions with impatience as some young men might have done.

Several times Peter had taken his spiritual problems to Andreas. He thought of the time that Martin Blöcher had accused him of not doing his share of the work during harvesttime. Peter had just recovered from a bout of fever and was not feeling very energetic yet. Martin and the other boys knew this, and yet every time Martin cornered Peter at the water bucket, he would hiss some disparaging remark like, "Dry again? You sure dry up fast when there's work to be done." Or, as Peter struggled to keep up to the others in binding sheaves, Martin would call out, "Better grease your shoes; you could maybe go faster."

A deep resentment had built up in Peter. Martin himself had always been a shirker. For Peter, who strove to do his best in any assigned task, to be accused of laziness was an insult. Several times a sarcastic retort had been on his lips, but he had pressed them tightly together and turned the other cheek. Having just recently become a follower of Jesus Christ, he knew that "an eye for an eye" was no way for a Christian to act. And yet, the bitterness building up inside him had robbed him of his usually cheerful disposition.

Andreas had been the one to notice his predicament. He had helped Peter to see his own part in the affair and had prayed with him, encouraging him to love those "which despitefully use you."

Peter suspected too that Andreas had had a talk with Martin, because the little annoyances had stopped. Peter had asked the Lord to give him a love for the sullen Martin, and now his attitude towards him had become more sympathetic.

Martin's father, Leonhardt Blöcher, was a complainer; a vacillating, unsettled man. At times he spoke out emphatically in favour of some suggestion offered by one of the other brethren. More often he argued hotly against it. If there was an easier or less painful way to accomplish a matter, you could be sure Leonhardt Blöcher would find it. When Peter considered his own father—steadfast, well-grounded in the faith, reliable, and acting always in the best interest of everyone involved—he could only pity Martin.

"The coming of the bishop will mean something to you too." Andreas's statement was almost a question.

Peter looked at him uncomprehendingly.

"Won't you be baptised then?"

"Baptised?" Peter lowered his hands slowly. Yes, he supposed that he and the other applicants for baptism could be accepted into the brotherhood at this time. "I don't know," he answered thoughtfully. "I suppose that the deacons will decide whether we have had enough instruction in the doctrines of the faith, and then Brother Riedemann will have to question us concerning our profession. Isn't that so?"

"That's right."

"I have looked forward to baptism, but . . ."

"But what?"

"I'm . . . I'm not sure I'm ready to take on the responsibilities of church membership. Am I worthy to be named among the people of God?"

" 'Not by works of righteousness which we have done, but according to his mercy he saved us, by the washing of regeneration, and renewing of the Holy Ghost,' "[1] quoted Andreas. "No, you are not worthy. None of us are. But through the blood of Christ, we can be counted worthy to bear His standard."

Bong! Bong! Bong! The dull clang of the supper gong announced the end of the working day for the bruderhof. Big Peter laid down his tools. The lathe slowly rolled to a stop. Jacob and Cornelius laid down their hammers. Then the latter reached to remove the glue kettle from the fire. All the workers made their way towards the door, bending forward to slap the shavings and sawdust from their breeches. Peter brushed his hands smartly over the sleeves of his shirt. Lifting their coats from the pegs near the door, the men filed out into the street.

Big Peter lingered, his hand on the door, to take a last glance around his cozy workshop. Satisfied that the fire was under control and the tools were all accounted for, he let himself out, pulling the door shut behind him. Peter was waiting for him in the street.

The two stood for a moment, gazing past the few houses lining the street to the west. Heavy grey clouds veiled the tops of the low mountains that compassed the valley. In the cultivated fields beyond the town, black splotches of bare earth stood out against the thin layer of white snow. On the slopes, dark spruces stood silhouetted against the grey haze of the leafless hardwoods.

Peter pulled his coat tighter across his chest and hunched his shoulders against the cold wind. "Mr. Blötter was right. The air is damp and chilly."

"No need to stand here," his father replied, and they moved off down the street, which was rapidly filling with men and boys.

They streamed from every doorway up and down the short, narrow street. Doors clanged, feet stamped, and voices rang out in greeting as the crowd converged to one large open doorway from which bright rays of light and delicious odours were streaming.

Following closely behind his father, Peter stretched his neck to see if he could spot any of his friends. He was reminded again that he could not even see over his father's shoulder without standing on his toes. When he was a little boy, his aspiration had been to grow as large as his father. Now, at nineteen, he had abandoned that goal; and he felt that if he could attain to Big Peter's stature of character, he would be content.

11

Swords or Ploughshares?

Inside the door of the brightly lit dining hall, the men and boys removed their coats and hats, stamping their boots on the rag mats covering the wooden floor.

Peter scanned the garment-festooned wall to his right for an empty peg on which to hang his own coat. There was a space on the top row. He reached and . . . *Wham!* Peter staggered into the wall as something hit him between the shoulder blades.

"Need a hand, Shorty?" a hearty voice accompanied the harsh greeting.

Peter whirled to face his cousin and best friend, Caspar, whose blue eyes twinkled merrily from beneath bushy, fair eyebrows.

"Here, let me," Caspar offered, and his long arms set the garment on the high peg without strain.

"You needn't be so violent in your greetings," Peter complained, wriggling his tingling shoulders. "Those bulging muscles of yours might get you into trouble someday."

Caspar chuckled as he bent to brush some straw from his woollen trousers. "I can tell you one thing," he asserted. "They come in mighty handy for chopping wood or making hay."

Peter led the way through the cluster of men towards the tables.

The large dining room was furnished with four long wooden tables, along either side of which rows of round, pewter soup bowls waited in orderly formation. Benches running the length of each table were rapidly filling with hungry men and boys. Young girls with flushed cheeks and snowy white aprons billowing about them, scurried between the rows of tables, bearing pitchers of milk and platters heaped with slices of dark bread.

As they moved along the wall, Peter glanced through the open doorway of the kitchen at the right. Steam rose from iron caldrons, swirling around the heads of the women who presided over them. At a long table, more women were slicing bread. Peter hopped quickly out of the path of a young girl as she hurried into the kitchen for another load.

The cousins made their way between the benches to where two other young men were already seated. One, a sullen-faced boy with slightly hunched shoulders, was picking at a wart on his finger with a small knife and did not look up at their arrival. The other, a thin, pale-faced lad, smiled a welcome at his friends as they swung their legs over the bench across from him. But before he could speak, his gaunt features tightened suddenly and, turning his head, he coughed harshly several times into his handkerchief.

"Cough no better, George?" Peter asked with concern when the spell had passed.

Clearing his throat and wiping his eyes, George shook his head. "It's the cold weather. I hope by summer it will clear up."

Caspar and Peter exchanged a private glance. They too hoped George's cough would be relieved with the return of warm weather, but it was doubtful. He had had that dry, rasping cough for several years. Each summer it seemed to improve, but with the recurrence of winter dampness and cold, it returned, more persistent than ever. His slender body seemed to grow thinner and his skin more transparent each year.

In spite of his frailty, George was well liked by his companions. His steadfast faith and consistent optimism challenged them.

"Where's your big brother, George?" Caspar asked.

While George searched the faces of the few men still stamping their boots by the door, Peter answered for him, "Oh, he was the first one out of the door tonight. I suspect he wanted to sneak into the laundry and see Bridgit for a few minutes before supper."

Caspar shook his head in mock solicitude. "That poor fellow. Think the day will ever come when we'll get so taken up with a girl that we'd risk missing a meal just to spend a few minutes with her?"

"I suppose it will," Peter admitted honestly.

"I think I'll keep my freedom for a while," decided Caspar.

"Maybe your time will come sooner than you think," George predicted. "After all, you are almost twenty."

Caspar's protests were interrupted by the arrival of Andreas and a dark-complexioned youth.

Scarcely had the two seated themselves when the buzz of conversation in the room faded and a hush settled over the assembly. All heads turned to one corner where a stooped, grey-bearded man stood at the head of the first table. Raising his arm, he said solemnly, "Let us pray."

Every man bowed his head reverently over his bowl while the aged deacon, Michel Blauer, gave thanks for God's presence and invoked His blessing on their evening meal.

At the "amen," all heads were raised. The hum of amicable conversation again rose and fell amidst the rattling of spoons and the squeaking of benches as the fragrant chicken soup was ladled into bowls and the bread disappeared from the platters. The serving girls scurried back and forth between the kitchen and the tables, bringing full vessels to replace those being rapidly emptied by the hungry crowd.

The six young men ate in silence for a time.

"This soup is plenty weak," complained Martin Blöcher, the boy with the wart.

"Tastes all right to me," Andreas replied, tipping his bowl to scrape the last drops of broth into his spoon.

"Likely a fellow who's going to be married in a few days has lost his sense of taste," Peter suggested.

"Married?"

"A few days?"

The other boys paused, their spoons in midair, to look from Peter to Andreas and back again.

"How's this?" Caspar asked for all of them.

"It's true." Andreas pushed back his bowl and rested his forearms on the table. "Peter Riedemann is planning to be present at the conference this weekend, and then we will be married."

"Oh-h-h-h," groaned Caspar as if in sympathy.

"Now, Caspar," chided the bridegroom. "Who was it that I saw talking to Hulda Reimer just outside the kitchen door last night?"

Caspar's face reddened. "Oh, oh, that?" he stammered. "Well, can't a fellow even exchange a few words with an old friend without being accused of . . ."

The laughter of the other boys added to his embarrassment. Andreas came to the rescue by changing the subject. "How did the watchmaking go today?"

"Oh-h-h-h," moaned the stalwart youth again, clutching his head between his large hands. "All those tiny screws and springs!" He shook his head in despair. "I can scarcely pick them up, let alone get them into place." He spread his large calloused hands open before him. "Watchmaking is for people like George there with his long, slender fingers. Me, I'd rather be plowing or falling trees. I'm always so glad when Father pokes his head through the doorway and says, 'Time for milking.' "

A general chuckle was the only sympathy he earned from his companions. They were accustomed to the blond giant's struggles with any task involving faculties other than muscle power. Caspar, with his gangling arms and legs and clumsy fingers, endured much badgering from the other boys; but he took it all in good spirits and enjoyed nothing better than a good joke, even if it was at his own expense.

The boys wanted to hear about Andreas's wedding plans; however, since the bishop had not arrived, he was unable to supply many details. The ceremony would likely take place immediately after a preaching service and be followed by a wedding supper.

Martin and Caspar wondered what special dishes would be served at the meal, but Andreas only replied that he would leave that business up to Bridgit and her mother.

Lukas, the blacksmith's son, who up to this point had been occupied with his supper, set down his empty glass and stated, "We had an unusual visitor at the shop today."

"Who was that?" Peter asked as they all turned to the speaker.

"The castellan of Falkenstein," Lukas announced grandly, glancing from face to face to observe their reactions.

Caspar's glass stopped halfway to his mouth, Andreas swallowed his last bite of bread with a gulp, George set down his spoon suddenly, and even the moody Martin looked interested.

"You mean the castellan from Falkenstein—the man who is in charge of the affairs of the castle in Lord Fünfkirchen's absence?" Peter probed disbelievingly.

"That's the man," affirmed Lukas with a nod. "He was dressed in a long, rich, black cloak trimmed with silver braid. His whip was . . ."

"But what did he want?" they all asked simultaneously, not interested in the man's attire.

"He came to order a score of axe heads."

"What does he want so many axes for?" George wondered.

"If you'll just let me finish," Lukas replied with a frown.

"Sorry," George apologized.

"He said Lord Fünfkirchen wants him to cut down several hundred fir trees from the mountain behind the castle."

Caspar whistled softly.

"For firewood?" asked Peter.

"I don't know." Lukas shrugged his shoulders. "It sounds like a tremendous amount of firewood."

"The castle usually purchases firewood from local woodcutters," Andreas pointed out.

"Must be they want to reinforce the battlements or build some new structures inside the castle," Peter suggested.

"Who's to do all this cutting?" Caspar wanted to know.

"That was another thing," Lukas hurried on. "The man asked father whether any of our men would be willing to fell the trees and saw them into timbers."

"That's the job for me!" Caspar thumped his fist down on the table, causing his spoon to rattle in his soup bowl. "No more invisible wheels and screws for me—give me a man's job."

"What if your father doesn't give you permission to go?" Martin tried to quench his enthusiasm.

"Oh, I'll persuade him." Caspar was ever the optimist.

"I can't say I'd enjoy swinging an axe all day," admitted Lukas, "but that castle on the hill has always fascinated me. Maybe the woodcutters would have the opportunity to work inside the walls. I'd sure like a chance to walk across that drawbridge and through that iron grill gate.

"I wouldn't," George disagreed, shivering.

"Why not?"

"They say there are dungeons beneath the towers . . ." George's thin shoulders heaved as a coughing fit cut off his words.

"We aren't criminals. What fear need we have of dungeons?" demanded Lukas.

Andreas spoke then, choosing his words carefully. "It is rather a puzzle. Why does Lord Fünfkirchen want so much wood, and why did he ask our men to work when there are other men in Steinborn who would be glad for the extra wages? I wonder if he's trying to spy on us."

Martin lifted a querulous voice in protest, but Andreas continued, "The lord seemed happy enough to allow us to settle here three years ago, but King Ferdinand is becoming increasingly suspicious of those who fail to embrace the state church and to support his campaigns against the Turks."

"What do the king's suspicions have to do with the Falkenstein castle?" Caspar did not see the connection.

"The landowning nobles must curry favour with the king you know, or they stand in danger of losing their holdings," Andreas explained. "The priests in Vienna have been putting pressure on the king to deal more severely with heretics and enemies of the church. In other countries of Europe, the authority of the church is being threatened. Since the king is the theoretical head of the church, he fears for the safety of his own throne. The priests have been encouraging him to force the barons to weed out dissenters in their domains. It just puzzles me why the castellan would suddenly want to hire our men."

"Why should they bother us here? We aren't causing any trouble, are we?" Martin asked irritably.

"No, we aren't troublemakers," Andreas agreed, "but our very peacefulness and lack of allegiance to the church brings us under suspicion. Because we won't confess to the priest, accept Communion from their hands, or permit them to baptise our infants, rulers are afraid we may be secretly plotting against their authority. They just don't understand us."

"Just as Christ's contemporaries misunderstood Him," mused Peter.

Martin answered in his high-pitched voice, "My father says that we have nothing to fear from the priests. He says if we keep to ourselves and don't go around looking for trouble, trouble will stay out of our way."

"None of us is looking for trouble," Andreas assured him, "but remember that brethren in other cities are imprisoned and tortured for their faith in such castles as Falkenstein."

Lukas, who had listened gravely to Andreas's discourse, now spoke up. "I think I understand now why Father and the other men looked so serious after the castellan left. It hardly registered with me at the time, but just before he stepped out of the door, he made the casual remark that Lord Fünfkirchen would be requiring new swords in the near future and that if the axes provided were of good quality, he would most assuredly place his order with us."

"Swords?" Peter questioned. "We wouldn't make swords, would we?"

"No," Lukas replied, shaking his head along with the other four. "I knew we wouldn't consider such a thing, so I dismissed the matter from my mind. Before Father was able to reply, the man had closed the door and was gone, so he wasn't able to explain that we do not believe in fashioning weapons for the use of destroying human life."

"Swords," Andreas repeated in an undertone. "Why swords?"

"Swords," Peter echoed. "When he returns to order swords, we may find ourselves in a predicament."

The scraping of benches and shuffling of feet from the first table announced that the older men had finished their meal and were vacating their places so that the women and girls could eat.

The young men swung their legs over the benches and stood, stretching their arms and tucking their shirts into their waistbands.

Some men, their duties over for the day, were making their way through a doorway on the left that led into a small sitting room. Here they would share the experiences of the day, seek advice on various aspects of the community's work, or plan for future activities, while they waited for their wives to eat supper and finish their kitchen work.

Andreas strode off in the direction of the door, weaving his way between the tables and milling men.

"Is Andreas off to see Bridgit again?" Caspar asked dubiously.

"He's likely going to work on his chest. He has to finish it before the wedding," Peter guessed.

The boys stood in a huddle at the end of the row, waiting for some men to file past.

"Have any chores?" George asked Lukas.

"No, we cleaned up the shop early tonight."

"Shall we go sit with the men? I'd like to hear more about the castellan's visit."

"Me too," Lukas agreed. "I wonder if the men read any trouble in it, or if Andreas just has an overactive imagination since he's getting married so soon and has his head in the clouds."

"Andreas is pretty levelheaded," Peter defended him.

"Yes, he usually is," Lukas agreed. "But I'd still like to hear the men discuss it. Anyone else coming?"

"I have to bed down the sheep," Martin complained. "Sheep are such stupid creatures. If you don't watch them constantly, they're sure to get into trouble." He moved reluctantly towards the door.

Peter nudged Caspar as they moved slowly along the wall. "Let's go out to our rock," he whispered. "I'd like to talk to you."

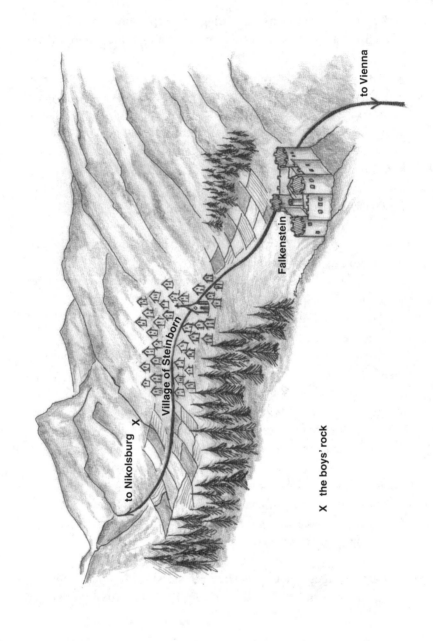

to Vienna

Falkenstein

Village of Steinborn

to Nikolsburg X

X the boys' rock

111

Peter's Dreams of the Future

The cousins stepped from the warmth and light of the dining hall into the damp dusk of the street, buttoning their coats and pulling their collars up around their ears. They made their way between the rows of darkened, closely set houses and on past the stables where feeble lantern glows reached out through open doorways to cast circles of light on the brown slush that covered the cobblestone street. Caspar paused at one doorway to reach inside and take a lantern from a nail. They would need it to guide them back in the darkness.

Beyond the shelter of the houses, the raw north wind bit at their exposed faces and they quickened their pace. Before them, the road wound in ascending curves around the low mountains and disappeared into the grey mist. They hurried past the barren fields and snow-speckled croplands. Where the road veered to follow the lowest route around an obstructing knoll, Caspar turned to the right, following a narrow footpath that led up the hillside. The hill sheltered them from the chill wind, and they trudged in silence up the slope and over the rounded top. In front of them rose a high outcropping of giant boulders, looking as though some giant had dropped them there in a jumbled heap.

Sliding the lantern handle over his arm, Caspar started up the rocks, using his hands to hoist himself from boulder to boulder. Peter followed, his feet threatening to slip out from under him on the snow-crusted rocks. At last they heaved themselves, panting, up onto the flat surface of a projecting rock. Caspar brushed the snow from their perch, and they both sank down, propping their backs against the cliff behind them. From this vantage point, they had a panoramic view of the whole valley.

Below them, the dark strand of road wound into the village and disappeared among the steep-roofed houses, which huddled close together as if for mutual encouragement. Thin ribbons of smoke spiraled from the chimney tops and spread out into a blanket of grey that hovered protectingly over the buildings. At the far end of the village, the peaked church steeple poked through the veil of smoke to pierce the grey sky. Beyond the houses, the road reappeared, twisting and winding past more meadows and ploughed fields.

A third of the way up the highest mountain, on the far side of the valley, perched the Falkenstein castle. The approach followed the crest of a hill and then led across a chasm on a wooden trestle bridge. A sheer cliff dropped away from the rambling stone bailey, or outer wall, which defended the northwestern exposure. The forest-clad hillside rose steeply directly behind the structure so that it seemed almost a part of the landscape itself. The castle's four crenulated towers and high machicolated walls commanded a clear view of the highroad, which curved below it to the south.

"Do you think the visit of the castellan holds any threat to us?" Peter asked, breaking the silence.

"I don't know," Caspar sighed. "It could just be that the castle needs some simple domestic repairs, like new stairways and doors. And the inquiry concerning swords may have been made in innocence. Perhaps the band of resident soldiers has worn out their old ones in mock sword fights. Seems like there couldn't be much for a soldier to do in a quiet secluded place like this."

"I thought Lord Fünfkirchen was sympathetic to our beliefs. I guess I always hoped he'd protect us from any malicious heretic hunters."

"He's not exactly sympathetic to our beliefs. At least he hasn't indicated any desire to know anything about them," Caspar pointed out.

"But he was only too glad to rent us land and allow us to settle here."

"That is because of our reputation for being good farmers and skilled craftsmen. It was to his advantage to have occupants who could raise more grain per acre and utilise some of his marginal land. I think he granted his favour only for selfish motives and not because he felt any great attraction to our religion."

"I suppose you're right," Peter agreed. "And, as Andreas said, if the king puts pressure on the barons to deal with dissenters, there is little Lord Fünfkirchen could do about it."

"Who said, 'Some trust in chariots, and some in horses'?"[2] Caspar asked.

" 'But we will remember the name of the LORD our God,' "[3] Peter finished. "That was David. He lived in an age when God allowed His people to use the sword against their enemies, yet he still felt more security in the Lord's hands than in a great army of soldiers."

The boys stared thoughtfully across the valley at the brooding towers of Falkenstein. The light was fading rapidly.

"Father said that the king is known to have said that the only effective way to deal with rebaptisers is to give them a third baptism," Caspar offered.

"Meaning?"

"Meaning, drowning."

The boys contemplated this harsh sentence for a few minutes. Peter shifted uneasily and thrust his hands into his pockets. "They are burning Anabaptists in Vienna and other centres south of here."

"Death by burning must be a horrible way to die," Casper shuddered.

"It is."

Caspar turned his face sharply to face his cousin. "You saw a burning once, didn't you?"

"Yes, two years ago at Nikolsburg."

"You never told me about it."

"I didn't want to talk about it. I tried to forget it," Peter replied shortly.

"Was it so bad?"

"It was awful."

"Was that the reason you held back from baptism for so long?"

Peter nodded briefly. "I was about to confess the faith," he recalled, "and join the class of applicants for baptism. But then Father took me along to Nikolsburg to buy supplies for the shop. When we left the city, six men were being burned at the stake just outside the gate. It was a fearful sight." He buried his face in his hands as if to hide the scene that haunted his memory still. "The prisoners struggled and writhed against their chains and screamed in agony. They sounded like wild animals caught in a trap. I can still hear those shrieks."

"They weren't Anabaptists, were they?"

"No," admitted Peter, lifting his head and dropping his hands between his knees. "They were common criminals who had been justly condemned. But when I learned that believers are often burned for their faith, I was terrified. I decided I had to avoid that fate at any cost. I tried to console myself that I had been baptised as a baby before my parents became Christians, so that should be good enough."

"But now?" Caspar prodded.

"Now, in the strength of the Lord, I am ready to face whatever He brings into my experience. 'For I am persuaded, that neither death, nor life, nor angels, nor principalities, nor powers, nor things present, nor things to come, nor height, nor depth, nor any other creature, shall be able to separate us from the love of God, which is in Christ Jesus our Lord,' "4 Peter quoted softly.

"Do you no longer fear burning?"

"I can't honestly say that I have conquered that fear. But He has promised that He will not suffer us to be tempted above that which we are able to bear, and I am resting in that promise."

"I'm glad you are to be baptised soon," Caspar encouraged Peter. His own vows had been spoken several years ago, before the group left Moravia. "Of course, baptism is only the outward token of the inner commitment you have already made to Christ, but as such it identifies you in a tangible way with the body of Christ."

Darkness had settled over the valley, and a few fine flakes of snow drifted gently around them.

Caspar spoke again. "I sometimes wonder why it is that our people have to be hounded from one country to the next, never able to remain long in any one place. You'd think that as disciples of the God of Peace, we ought to be permitted to live peacefully."

"Jesus said, 'If the world hate you, ye know that it hated me before it hated you. If ye were of the world, the world would love his own: but because ye are not of the world, but I have chosen you out of the world, therefore the world hateth you,' "5 Peter quoted.

"And 'if they have persecuted me, they will also persecute you,' "[6] Caspar added.

"There will always be enmity between the seed of the woman and the seed of the serpent, until Christ returns and claims the souls of the faithful for His kingdom," Peter explained.

"Sometimes, though," Caspar confided, drawing his knees up to his chin and twining his long arms around them, "I get to wondering what it would be like to be an ordinary citizen, living without the cloud of disapproval and animosity from fellow countrymen and authorities. To be able to map out my future and expect each day and year to go on much the same as they always have."

Peter was alarmed. "Do you mean to give up the faith?"

"No, no," Caspar protested. "I just mean—oh, I don't know. Here we are, young men in the prime of life. What do we have to look forward to? Can we plan to become a skilled carpenter or blacksmith or"—he grimaced—"a watchmaker, and hope to marry and raise a family here in this lovely valley?" He swung his arm towards the village and surrounding fields. "Or will we have to disrupt our ordered lives and move on as our own parents have done several times?"

"The people of Steinborn may have no fear of persecution, but would you like to be at the mercy of the priest, doing penance for every little sin, buying indulgences and paying for every small office he performs while he holds the threat of eternal punishment over your head if you dare to contradict him? And what of their hope for the future? They may have a relatively unmolested lifetime here, but we have a hope that is eternal."

"I know; I know," Caspar hastened to say, "and I would rather die in Christ than live without Him. It's just that, sometimes, these other thoughts get in the way," he finished lamely.

"If you could map out your future, what sort of life would you plan?"

Caspar reflected for a moment before answering. "I don't have any great ambitions," he admitted. "If I had my preference, I think I'd be content to stay right here in this valley. I'm a simple person. I don't fancy changes. I'd like to work in the fields in the summer—to follow the plough, to plant seeds and watch them grow into green plants, to breathe the fresh air and feel close to nature. I can't really explain how I feel, but I just enjoy those things," he finished simply.

"I think I understand," Peter assured him. "But what will you do all winter? Make watches maybe?"

"Ha!" snorted the bigger boy. "Not if I can help it. I'd like to learn blacksmithing or some trade that takes brawn and bulk. As long as there is wood to chop, I'd gladly do that. It is so peaceful out in the forest."

"It's cold work."

"If you swing your axe hard enough, it isn't cold. Hard labour warms your blood. Making firewood warms a person twice, you know—once when you chop it, and again when you burn it."

Peter smiled. "So you'll farm in the summer and cut wood all winter, and be a bachelor?"

"I didn't say that."

"What then?" Peter prompted.

"I'd like to get married—now don't ask me to whom—for if I knew, I wouldn't tell you anyway," he injected hastily. "I'd have a family and take my sons to the fields and forests and teach them to work and enjoy the outdoors. In the evenings I'd teach them the truths of God's Word. And I'd try to be a faithful example of the believers," he finished. "Now that I've told you my dreams, you have to tell yours." He leaned back against the rock, stretched his long legs before him, and folded his arms.

"I used to think like you," Peter began in a low voice. "I thought I'd like to be a cabinetmaker like Father. I enjoy working with wood. The various kinds have their own characteristics. Some are soft; some are harder; some are lighter in colour. And the grains are all different. To choose wood of different grains and form them together into a pleasing design on a chest or cupboard front—that is satisfying. I suppose if God should choose to let us live here in peace, I could be content with such a life."

"What other alternative would there be for us?" Caspar asked.

"What I'd really like is to travel."

"Travel?"

"Yes, to see what lies over that hilltop and around the next bend in the road. I'd like to see the peaks of rugged mountains, follow the course of mighty rivers, walk through the marketplaces of large towns, hear the sound of strange tongues, visit Italy where the sun shines all year, and the Netherlands where the sea is higher than the land—maybe even travel by ship on the wide ocean." Peter's voice rose with excitement while his cousin's eyes widened in astonishment at the scope of these grand aspirations.

"Whew! Where do you get such ideas?"

Peter chuckled. "I don't know. Mostly from people I talk to who've been there, and from my maps."

"Oh, yes, your maps. I never could understand how anyone could spend hours drawing little wiggly lines on paper."

"To me the wiggly lines appear as foaming rivers, snowcapped mountains, and highways leading past turreted castles and through picturesque, walled towns. It gives me travel fever to study my maps."

"Seems pointless to me."

"It would be pointless just to travel for the sake of travel," Peter readily admitted. "But lately I've felt a longing to share the peace and joy of serving Christ with others. Here we all are, in this little village. Once in a while, we exchange a few words with our neighbours. But so far, none of them have come to the knowledge of the truth. Besides, there are many of us here to tell them the Good News. But what about out there?" He waved his arm towards the rest of the world. "There are hundreds and thousands of people out there who have never heard that Christ died for their sins and that they needn't do weekly penance to atone for their wrongs. I'd like to go and tell them."

"To be a travelling evangelist, you mean?"

"Yes. Like Peter Riedemann."

"Many of the brethren do just that," Caspar encouraged Peter. "But the majority of them never return."

"I know."

"Remember Brother Zacharias, and George and Andreas's two older brothers who left here a year and a half ago to travel through Bavaria and Bohemia?"

Peter nodded. "I remember the stirring service at which they were commissioned to go with the Gospel."

"They haven't been heard of since," Caspar said with finality.

"I realise that. But it may be they have travelled far and have not been able to send word."

"More likely, they are rotting away in some filthy dungeon."

"That's highly possible. But I'm sure they are still serving the Lord and even rejoicing that they are counted worthy to suffer for His sake. If they have led souls to the truth, they are well rewarded for their trials."

Peter continued enthusiastically, "I am looking forward to this coming conference and to seeing Peter Riedemann. I hope he relates some of his experiences. If I could choose my own destiny, I would desire to have a life like his. He has travelled in many countries, baptised hundreds of converts, written many edifying pamphlets and letters, led groups of believers to safety in Moravia, and overseen the organization of bruderhofs there."

"He has also been dragged before magistrates, flogged out of various towns, spent several sieges in prisons, and been hunted from one country to another," Caspar reminded him.

"Yes, I realise that the life of a travelling evangelist would be perilous, but if God leads in that way, I want to be ready to give my life in His service."

"I do too," Caspar said solemnly. "Even though I'd much prefer to stay right here, I have a feeling that your aspiration is more likely to be realised than mine."

"How so?"

"Even if we are never sent to foreign lands as travelling evangelists, in all probability, we will have to leave this place someday. The children of God have no abiding city here. With every new mandate issued by the king, our peaceful existence here is threatened anew."

" 'They wandered in deserts, and in mountains, and in dens and caves of the earth.' "[7]

"Yes, you may someday see your raging rivers, snowcapped mountains, and wide oceans, one way or another; but for now, I think my warm bed would feel good," Caspar said, unfolding his long limbs and standing upright. Peter scrambled to his feet while his cousin lit the lantern.

They groped their way down the slippery cliff trail and proceeded in silence back to the village.

At the stables they parted. Caspar entered to return the lantern and to see that the stock was comfortable, and Peter lengthened his stride in the direction of home.

As he passed the cabinet shop, he noticed a faint gleam of light from inside. Was Andreas still working at his chest? He would investigate.

The door swung inward at his touch, and he stepped quietly into the semidarkness of the work area. A dark figure, its back to Peter, was crouching on the floor near the back workbench. One hand held a sputtering candle while the other groped through a pile of shavings as though searching for something.

Peter held his breath. The figure obviously had not heard him enter. Was it a thief? What should he do?

"Hello," he said finally.

The figure turned inquisitively, and Peter relaxed. It was Brother Jacob.

"I almost thought you were a thief," Peter said in a shaky voice.

Brother Jacob rose stiffly. "I suppose I am sneaking around like a thief." A worried frown creased his forehead into wrinkles. "I'm looking for my herb bag," he explained. "A man from the other end of town just came to say that his baby fell into the fire and is badly burned. I told him I would come immediately, and he gave me directions and disappeared, expecting me to follow shortly. When I went to get my herb bag, it wasn't in its usual place. Then I remembered that I had stopped at the nursery school this morning on the way to the shop, to show the teacher how to concoct a potion for some of the children who were coughing. I think my bag is here somewhere, but I can't seem to find it." He rummaged through the tools on his workbench and bent to search under it.

"I'll help you look," Peter offered. Lighting another candle, he joined the search.

Brother Jacob was not only a woodworker, but also an able physician. Many were the bones he had set, wounds he had cleansed, and fevers he had staunched with his skillful fingers and the concoctions he brewed from his little brown leather bag of herbs. On summer evenings, the old man could often be found wandering through the fields or on the periphery of the woods, searching for the healing roots and leaves that grew there. Brother Jacob's living area was always fragrant with the smell of the bundles of dried herbs that hung from the ceiling. Even the townspeople called on the kindly old gentleman in their distresses.

"Here it is!" Peter triumphantly retrieved the lost article from under Andreas's chest. "Andreas dragged his chest over here to be near me this afternoon," he explained.

"I remember now—I had set it on the chest so I'd be sure to remember it." Brother Jacob gratefully tucked the bag into an inner pocket. "Now I must hurry and attend to that poor child. I want to serve the people of Steinborn while the door is still open." And he hurried from the shop.

Peter stood in the empty room, the candle in his hand creating grotesque shadows on the familiar walls. "Now what did he mean by that?"

IV

Maria's Bedtime Story

Peter opened the door to his family's second-floor living quarters on a comfortable domestic scene. His father sat at the table in the centre of the room, his head propped between his great hands, the large leather-bound family Bible open before him. He dropped a hand to mark his place in his reading and looked up to smile at his son.

"I was out with Caspar," Peter explained, shrugging off his coat.

"I know. I saw you go out." Father did not mind the many long walks and heart-to-heart conversations the two boys enjoyed. Caspar was an unsophisticated, steady, realistic, cheerful sort of person—a good complement to Peter's grand flights of fancy and serious demeanor.

Mother smiled a welcome from the rocking chair by the fire, where her hands were busy at the endless task of knitting socks. With one foot she gently rocked the wooden cradle that held Johann, the baby of the family. The sight of Mother's placid face, framed by brown wisps that usually escaped from under her crisp, white head covering, always caused a cozy glow around Peter's heart. How good it was to have a mother who cared about him. When he was little, his mother had kissed away his scratches and bruises and held him on her lap when he came with his childish fears and squabbles. Now she was always interested in his friendships, his interests, and his spiritual struggles. He knew too that she supported him with her prayers.

Five-year-old Maria knelt on the hearth rug, piling wooden blocks—scraps salvaged from the shop—into a big tower. One block too many and *crash!* The whole pile clattered to the floor.

"Oh!" Maria exclaimed in dismay. Then, jumping up, she ran to her big brother, calling, "Throw me up, Peter."

Peter scooped her up and tossed her towards the ceiling. Maria squealed and kicked with pleasure. He caught her just before she hit the floor and threw her again. They played the game over and over. Then, breathless and panting, they both sank onto the rug.

"Make me a castle, Peter," Maria wheedled. "Mine always fall down." She pushed the pile of blocks towards him.

Peter stretched himself on his stomach on the floor and proceeded to give his sister a lesson in building block towers. "You take the biggest blocks first. See? Like this . . ."

While they worked, Maria chattered excitedly about her day in the kindergarten. "Sister Barbara gave all of us a nasty potion today," she related, screwing up her mouth and making a wry face. "Some of the children were coughing, so we all had to take medicine. It was *ugh!*" She made a choking noise.

"Better to take medicine than have a bad cough," Peter consoled her.

Maria prattled on about the cookies they had had, the new song they were learning, and how one little boy had pulled her hair and had been made to stand in the corner. "That wasn't very nice of him, was it?" She pursed her lips and frowned disapprovingly.

"No, it wasn't," Mother said from the rocker. "But what did you do to him?"

"Nothing," Maria insisted indignantly. "I was just counting

my little sticks, and he pulled my hair."

"Did you tell him to pull it again?" Peter asked mischievously.

"Of course not."

"That's what the Bible says you should do."

Maria sat back on her heels and stared at him incredulously. "It doesn't say that." She jumped up and ran to Father. Crawling under his arm and pushing her small face in front of his big one, she questioned, "Father, Peter says that the Bible says if somebody pulls your hair, you're supposed to tell him to pull it again. It doesn't say that, does it?"

Father laughed heartily, pushed back his chair, and lifted the child onto his lap. "No, it doesn't say exactly that." Over her father's arm, Maria flashed Peter an I-told-you-so glance. "But it does say something like that." Father turned the pages of the big Bible.

"Here," he said, taking Maria's small hand and placing her finger halfway down one page. "Here it says, 'Whosoever shall smite thee on thy right cheek, turn to him the other also.'[8] Jesus meant that when someone hurts us or says mean things to us, we shouldn't hit back but rather let them hurt us again. Jesus wants us never to fight or treat other people badly."

"I don't fight," Maria assured him.

"Good," Father approved. "You must try not to quarrel with your friends. Remember to always treat them kindly."

"I think I hear Ursula on the landing." There was a sound of stamping feet outside the door, and Maria slipped from her father's knee to open the door for her older sister.

Ursula came in, rubbing her hands briskly. Her blue eyes sparkled in her round, rosy face. She stopped to kiss Maria lightly on the cheek. "Br-r-r-r, it's getting colder outside," she remarked, untying her dark blue shawl. "I went with Anna to see her new baby sister after we had finished drying dishes."

She hurried to the fire and stopped there, warming her hands near the flame. "Playing blocks, Peter?" she teased, a dimple showing in her right cheek.

Peter finished the tower he was building and sat up. "Just giving Maria a little lesson in engineering," he explained.

Ursula rummaged in the work basket by Mother's rocker until she found her knitting, and then, settling herself in the rocker on the other side of the fire, she unwound her yarn and began to click her needles.

"Everyone is excited about the coming conference," she related. "The women in the kitchen were planning meals. They decided to ask the householder if they could butcher a dozen old hens and maybe a pig. It seems no one is sure how many of these Philippite brethren will be coming.

"Who are the Philippites, anyway?" she went on without pausing. "What do they represent? Are they Christians like we are?"

Father closed the big Bible with a thud and pulled his chair closer to the fire. "Yes, they are Christians," he assured her. "They follow the Biblical teachings of one, Philipp Plener. He preached and taught in Moravia before most of our people arrived.

He established churches and several Christian communities around the same time as Hutter and Riedemann, our spiritual leaders, did. But they were separated from us by geography and also differed a bit on a few points of doctrine and practise. But their leader was burnt at the stake several years ago, and his unfortunate followers have been so persecuted and scattered that they are like sheep without a shepherd. Bishop Peter Riedemann had been in contact with some of them and has encouraged them to find a refuge among our bruderhofs. He feels that our differences can be reconciled by charitable discussion, and so he suggested that some of them come here to observe our faith and practise and together we can enjoy the Lord's blessing."

"Brother Riedemann himself will be here too, won't he?" asked Peter.

"Yes, but he may be a few days late. He sent word to Brother Michel that he will try to make his way to Nikolsburg. Someone will have to go and meet him there. He has a price on his head, so he must move carefully," Father answered.

Mother spoke from her rocker. "It will be good to see him again."

"You've seen him before?" Peter sat up, surprised.

Both parents nodded. Mother went on, "Several times. He travelled from one bruderhof to another in Moravia. Before we had our own bishop at Auspitz, we depended on travelling bishops to conduct baptism and hold Communion services. Brother Riedemann was one of them. At that time, he was a large, vigourous man with a heavy black beard. I wonder if his experiences since have aged him?"

"What experiences?" Ursula wondered.

"He has been twice in prison," Father explained. "With a burden for the churches, he travelled throughout Austria, inviting persecuted believers to come to the relatively tolerant land of Moravia. The heretic hunters were anxious to get their hands on such an influential man, and twice they succeeded. He spent two years incarcerated at Nürnburg, where the chief warden was so impressed with his trustworthiness that he gave him freedom within the castle and eventually released him."

"From prison he wrote letters of encouragement to the churches," added Mother.

"His present concern is to help the leaderless Philippites find their place among the established churches of God. He chose Steinborn for this conference because it is secluded and authorities are not likely to disrupt us here."

"You think there is real danger of persecution then?" Peter asked the question that had been bothering him all evening.

"I don't know." Father thoughtfully ran a hand over his hair. "For myself, I really don't see any new threats on the horizon. One reason we settled here was that it is out of the way. There are no other bruderhofs nearby. Our closest brethren are at Nikolsburg, across the border in Moravia. This valley is not on a main highway, and few travellers pass this way. The villagers are losing their suspicions of us, and Lord Fünfkirchen is pleased with the way we have farmed his lands. Yet, some of the brethren feel that we should be making plans to move on should it become necessary."

"Where would we go?" Peter and Ursula asked together.

"That is a difficult question," Father replied. "Moravia's doors are closing, and the persecution is heavy in countries west of us. I suppose the only direction to move would be east."

"East?" echoed Peter. "You mean into Hungary?"

"Yes."

"But Hungary is full of Turks," Ursula protested.

The Turks were feared by everyone. Stories of their fierceness and their ruthless cruelty had been widely circulated in Europe. Their strange religion along with their ungodly customs made their name a byword of terror. These adherents of the Moslem faith had pushed northwestward from their homelands in southern Asia in an attempt to convert the rest of the world, by force, to their faith. They had succeeded in recent years in forcing their way up through Italy, and ten years ago, they had reached the very gates of Vienna. But the Austrian armies had repelled them, and they had been forced back to the sea. Their ships still plied the Mediterranean, raiding and looting along the coastline. To the east, they occupied most of Hungary, and invasion from that direction was an ever-present threat.

"We may have to throw ourselves on the mercy of the Turks," Father said. "Who knows? They may be more tolerant than the authorities here. And moreover, they have souls to save too. Perhaps God will lead us into Hungary to offer salvation to the heathen Turks."

Maria had been following this adult discussion in bewilderment. She turned to tug at Father's ear. "Are we going to move? Where will we live?"

Father glanced at Mother over the small brown head. "I think this subject is too deep for little ears. Let's postpone our discussion until some other time."

"Are we going to move?" Maria persisted.

"Not now," Father assured her.

"We moved before, didn't we?"

"Yes, but I don't think you remember. You were only two."

"Did I move too?"

"Yes, we brought you along."

"Tell me the story about when we moved here," urged the child.

Father looked inquiringly at Mother and the two older children.

"Tell the story, Father," Ursula urged also. "It's been a long time since I heard it myself."

"Where shall I start?"

"Start back in the Tyrol before you became believers," suggested Peter.

Father shifted the contented child in his lap and gazed thoughtfully into the fire. Then he began, "Long ago, when Peter and Ursula were about your age, Maria, Mother and I lived in a little cottage in a mountain village of the Tyrol."

Maria looked doubtfully at her big brother and sister as if she could not imagine them being little.

"We were happy there," Father continued. "Every day I walked across the street to my father's cabinet shop and made chairs and tables and benches just like I do now. My father was your grandfather," he explained to Maria.

"I don't have a grandfather now," she interrupted.

"No, your grandfather isn't living now. He's in heaven. Someday you can go there and see him."

Maria wriggled happily at this prospect.

"Peter and I used to go over to Grandfathers and climb the stairs to their house above the cabinet shop," Ursula told Maria. "Peter would stand on his toes to bang the big door knocker, and Grandmother would let us in. Then she'd give us ginger cookies and milk."

"I wish I had a grandmother to give me cookies," Maria said wistfully.

"You get cookies in kindergarten," reminded Mother. To Father she added, "Peter, you'd better get on with the story. It will soon be someone's bedtime."

"Yes," agreed Father. "In this town, there was a church with a high pointed steeple, just like the one here in Steinborn. Every Sunday morning, we all went to mass."

"What's that?" demanded Maria.

"A kind of church service," Peter supplied briefly.

Father went on. "There we would pray in Latin, tell our sins to the priest, and maybe light a candle and put it in front of a statue of Mary or one of the disciples."

"Why did you do that?" Maria sat up, startled.

"We didn't know better," Father admitted. "That was the way Grandfather and his father and grandfather had always worshipped God. We never read the Bible. We didn't have one in our house. The priest would read from the Bible, but it was written in Latin so we didn't know what he was reading.

"Sometimes when kneeling before a statue of one of the saints, I would wonder if this lifeless thing could really hear and answer prayer. Then I would feel guilty and pray harder for forgiveness for my evil thoughts.

"We had some very pleasant neighbours living beside us. The man had been my friend from the time I was a little boy. Suddenly, one summer, this friend and his wife stopped coming to church. Some other families stayed home too. We were worried. The priest was alarmed. From the cabinet shop, I saw him go into my friend's house. He came out later, looking very upset.

"After that, he warned us in the services, not to have anything to do with those bad people. He said they were worshipping Satan and were possessed with devils. If we even went near them, he said, we must come to him to be sprinkled with holy water.

"Well, I didn't want to be possessed with devils, but this neighbour had been my good friend. So I watched him closely after that. He was a hatter, but no one came to his house anymore. I saw him go and come back with loads of firewood. I watched him working with his wife in the garden. He didn't act like he was possessed with devils. Instead, he seemed to be especially happy. He whistled as he worked and called friendly greetings to me when he passed.

"I found out from other townspeople that my friend and his wife had been rebaptised." To Maria he explained, "At that time, all the tiny babies were baptised by the priest. Then they were supposed to be Christians. But these people had been baptised over again. There had been some Anabaptists, or rebaptisers, travelling through the country, preaching and calling people to repent of their sins and be baptised.

"I watched my neighbour for a time. I saw him go out at night, several times, and not return until morning. My curiosity got the best of me. One night I followed him. He joined a group of about two dozen people—some were men from our village—in an abandoned quarry. I stood in the shadows, near enough to hear what went on. A man read from a book—part of the Bible, I learned later—in our own language. I listened, fascinated. He was reading the teachings of Jesus from the Sermon on the Mount—words I had never heard before.

" 'For I say unto you, That except your righteousness shall exceed the righteousness of the scribes and Pharisees, ye shall in no case enter into the kingdom of heaven. Ye have heard that it was said by them of old time, Thou shalt not kill; and whosoever shall kill shall be in danger of the judgment: but I say unto you, That whosoever is angry with his brother without a cause shall be in danger of the judgment.'[9]

"This was new to me. We were taught to hate the Turks who threatened to invade Europe and to spit on those who no longer attended mass.

"The man read on, and another verse spoke to me: 'But when ye pray, use not vain repetitions, as the heathen do: for they think that they shall be heard for their much speaking.'[10]

"I thought of my rosary and how I would repeat the same prayer over and over. The oftener I said it, I thought, the more likely that God would hear me.

"I came away from that secret meeting with many new thoughts in my head. And that was not the last time I followed him. Each time I learned more of the New Testament teachings, and I realised more and more that our religion was empty and vain.

"To make a long story short for a little girl"—Father squeezed Maria—"after several months of searching the Scriptures and talking with my friend, Mother and I were baptised. At first Grandfather was angry, but then he began to read the Bible, and he and Grandmother confessed the faith and received baptism too. My younger brother also joined the believers."

"That was Uncle Guttenhann," Peter pointed out for Maria's benefit.

"Caspar's father?"

"Yes."

Father continued his story. "But then hard times came. No one came to Grandfather's shop anymore. He had to sell his cow, and there were no more cookies and milk for Peter and Ursula. "About this time God sent a new little baby girl into our home."

"Was it me?" Maria asked eagerly.

"No, it wasn't you." Father's voice was soft. "Her name was Betkin.

"The priest came to our house to baptise the baby, as was the custom. We told him we did not want her baptised—that she was innocent and safe in the Saviour's care and she would be baptised when she was old enough to serve the Lord with understanding.

"The priest was displeased and threatened to take the baby away, saying we were unfit to be parents. Finally, he left us alone.

"Not long after that, our neighbours who had led us to the true faith, disappeared. One morning we found their two children sitting on the floor of their kitchen, crying and crying. The mother and father just were not there. We took the children home to our house. For a week I searched the countryside and asked questions, but I never found my friend. Then another of our Anabaptist families was arrested and thrown into prison in a nearby town. We knew our turn would come soon.

"But before anything happened to us, a preacher named Jacob Hutter passed through our area. He told us that in Moravia there were certain rich landowners who were allowing Anabaptists to settle on their lands. He said he was planning to lead a band of refugees there and invited us to go along.

"So we prepared to leave. It was a long journey, and we couldn't carry much with us. I packed my tools and the portions of Scripture I had copied, along with some food. I begged my parents to come too, but Grandfather said he was too old for such a trip. He hoped to go to heaven soon, and he said he did not fear the soldiers. He was ready to die. So we said 'good-bye' to them and left one dark night, taking our children and the two little orphans who were with us."

Father brushed a hand over his eyes. "Your grandparents were arrested and thrown into prison, where they died soon after.

"We walked at night, and hid in forests or caves by day. Other refugees joined us until we numbered over a hundred souls. Jacob Hutter was our guide. He kept us divided into smaller groups, travelling a day or two apart. He rode a horse and would make his rounds from one group to the other, supplying us with food and telling us which trails to follow and where to hide each day. He conducted worship services and encouraged us when we grew weary.

"It was not an easy journey. The route lay over some very steep mountains. Mother carried the baby, and I carried Peter and Ursula by turns. Their little legs got tired, and they would often sit down in the middle of the road and cry. Some young men helped to carry the other two children.

"For three days and nights, we had to sit in a damp cave, and our little baby got sick. Jacob Hutter led our family to a farmhouse on the edge of the village. Here a good farm woman hid us in a back bedroom. The next day three men came to her door. They said they were looking for Anabaptists and had seen lights in her house the night before. We felt sure that we would be discovered. We prayed for safety. The farm woman began to talk very fast.

'Lights?' she said crossly. 'Yes, you saw lights. I was up all night with some sick sheep. Back and forth to the barn I ran, heating medicine and pouring it into them. I am so weary. I don't know what to do with the sheep. My husband is away. What would you do?' She talked so fast, she soon had the men begging to leave so they wouldn't have to help her with her sick sheep." Father smiled at the memory. "It was true, she had two lambs that were ailing and she had made several trips to the barn to see to them.

"And so God preserved us, but in spite of all Mother and the good woman could do, our little Betkin died."

Mother lifted Baby Johann from the cradle and held him tightly. Several tears fell on the little round head.

"Then Mother didn't have a little baby to carry." Maria shook her head sadly.

"No. Mother was sad," Father said huskily. "But we had to go on. There were many orphans in the group, and one young mother died, so her little baby boy was given to Mother to carry. Then she had a baby again.

"Finally we arrived in Moravia, at a place called Auspitz. Here the brethren had built a large bruderhof. They lived and worked together. Each family had a house to sleep in, but we all ate in one room just as we do here. When we arrived, we gave the little money we had to the householder and, in turn, we were given clothing and everything else we needed to live comfortably. I soon was working in the cabinet shop there. Mother helped in the kitchen or laundry with the other women. Peter and Ursula went to school."

"What happened to the baby?" Maria asked.

"Oh, the baby's father got married, and then he had a new mother."

"Good," Maria said with satisfaction. "But then"—her head jerked up again—"Mother had no baby to look after."

"Then God sent us *you*," Mother said warmly.

Maria squirmed happily. "But then we had to move again, didn't we?" she prompted her father to finish his story.

"Yes. For a number of years, we lived in peace in Moravia. Then, when you were about two and just learning to talk, the king sent new orders that we must leave the country. The barons that we worked for didn't like it, but they had to obey the king.

"The congregation at Auspitz was divided into four smaller groups, and we each went to a different place. This time we left in carts carrying food, clothing, tools, and supplies with which to start a new community. This time our little baby girl didn't die along the way." Father squeezed Maria fondly.

"And now we live here," finished the little girl with a sigh of contentment.

"I see one little girl who looks sleepy," Mother suggested.

"Oh, no, I'm not sleepy," Maria opened her eyes wide to prove her point. "We have to read from the Bible and pray now," she reminded them.

Father moved his chair back to the table and leafed through the volume until he came to the story of the wanderings of the children of Israel in the wilderness. The family listened intently as his voice rose and fell. They thought about their own wanderings and the way God had miraculously led them through dangers and privations.

At last, Father closed the book. "We are wanderers too," he said. "And as the children of Israel looked forward to entering the Promised Land, we too hope someday to enter our promised land. Eternity with the Lord will be the reward of all the faithful. When we get to heaven, we'll see Grandfather and Grandmother and our little baby, Betkin," he told Maria.

"I'd like to go there right now," she declared earnestly.

"God will take you there when He is ready for you." After they prayed, Mother handed the baby to Ursula and took Maria by the hand. "Until God takes you to heaven, you are my little girl, and I think it is time for me to put you to bed." She led Maria into the small bedroom she shared with Ursula.

Father looked affectionately at his two almost-grown children. "Are you ready to seal your vows by baptism?" he asked seriously. When neither of them answered, he went on, "You have been instructed in the Christian faith; you have learned the catechism; you understand the doctrines that we hold dear. Are you prepared to submit to the disciplines of the brotherhood and testify to the faith wherever you go? It is one thing to be baptised into the church and obey the church leaders here in the safety of the bruderhof, but would you be willing and ready to witness for your Lord before unbelievers or authorities who might question you?"

"The deacons have required us to memorize large portions of Scripture concerning our beliefs, especially on the subjects of infant baptism, the Lord's Supper, and loving our enemies," Ursula told him.

"That is good," Father replied, nodding his approval. "We should put on the whole armour of God, as the apostle says, that we may be able to stand against the wiles of the devil. For the enemies of the faith are sly. They will try us with enticing words of man's wisdom. The Bible calls it 'spiritual wickedness in high places.'[11] It is not the heathen who persecute us, but those who profess godliness, but deny the power thereof.

"If we have the shield of faith and the sword of the Spirit, Christ has promised that when we are brought before governors and kings for His sake, we should take no thought how or what we shall speak, for it shall be given us in that same hour what we shall speak. It is the Spirit of the Father that speaks through us.

"However," he warned sagely, "the Word also tells us that 'out of the abundance of the heart the mouth speaketh.'[12] If our hearts are full of carnality and evil thoughts, we cannot expect the Spirit to suddenly replace them with appropriate Scriptures in our hour of need. That is why we put much emphasis on memorizing the Scriptures. We do not always have access to printed Bibles; even our little notebooks may be lost or taken from us, but no man can remove those words that we have hidden in our hearts. They are an inspiration to us, a preparation for service to others, and a bulwark against the attacks of the evil one.

"I rejoice to see my children embrace the true faith. As a father, I would wish for you a life of peace and prosperity. But when we accept the way of the cross, we must be prepared to suffer the loss of all things, that we may win Christ. When our sins are forgiven and our old man is put off, we experience the power of His resurrection. Then He expects us to share 'the fellowship of his sufferings, being made conformable unto his death.'[13] Only then can we hope to attain unto the resurrection of the righteous."

Peter and Ursula had listened gravely to this advice. Their young faces were serious as they contemplated the step of faith they had taken and were preparing to seal by water baptism.

"If it were not for the hope of heaven," Ursula confessed, "the Christian life would seem too hard."

Mother had tiptoed quietly into the room, and hearing Ursula's last words, she quoted softly, " 'And God shall wipe away all tears from their eyes; and there shall be no more death, neither sorrow, nor crying, neither shall there be any more pain: for the former things are passed away.' "[14]

Father stood and carried the Bible to its special shelf on the wall opposite the fireplace. This was the signal for retirement. Ursula wrapped up her knitting and with a cheerful "good night" disappeared into her room.

Father and Mother also retired, leaving Peter alone by the fire.

With Father's words weighing heavily on his mind, Peter prayed to his heavenly Father, "Give me strength for whatever the future may bring. Increase my faith and grant me the comforting presence of the Holy Spirit as I am baptised into the body of Christ. Make me worthy to suffer for Thee so that I can hope to reign with Thee. Show me the path for my feet, and lead me therein . . ."

Presently he rose from his mat and walked across the room. From the shelf he took several neatly folded papers. Carrying them to the table, he carefully unfolded each one, spreading them open before him. They were his maps.

He had painstakingly copied them, line by line, dot for dot, from similar ones of Brother Joseph's. Brother Joseph was the schoolmaster at the bruderhof. He was a converted priest who had studied the Latin Bible he had used in conducting mass, and had discovered that much of what he was standing for was not true. When some of his flock joined the new Anabaptist faith, instead of reacting in hostility, he had investigated their new beliefs. This led to his own rebaptism and expulsion from the Church of Rome.

A scholar by profession and nature, Brother Joseph soon found acceptance among the brethren as a schoolmaster. His enthusiasm and love of learning inspired many students, especially those with eager and inquiring minds like Peter had.

Peter had been almost too old for school when Brother Joseph had assumed his duties as schoolmaster. But he and several other older boys had been permitted to attend classes for several months during the first winter at Steinborn.

A special rapport had sprung up between Peter and his teacher, which extended beyond the classroom. Brother Joseph lent Peter his few books on history, and the young lad had spent many evenings in his friend's apartment, discussing the heroes of the early church, the spread of Christianity across Europe, and the deterioration of the Catholic Church. Brother Joseph had also introduced his eager pupil to the intricacies of the Latin language. Peter was impressed with the man's command of Italian, French, and Spanish; and being assured that the basis of all these tongues was Latin, he sweated over its verb forms and seemingly endless declensions.

And then, the good man had shown him his maps. Peter was fascinated by Brother Joseph's descriptions of other countries. He loved to pore over these sheets, tracing the roads with his finger and visualizing unknown scenes and foreign peoples. Now he sat, his own set of maps spread before him. What had Father said? The only direction left for them to migrate might be east. He dropped his forefinger on Vienna, the capital of their country and chief residence of the king. Then, slowly, he traced the Danube River eastward. He followed it across the mountains into Hungary, where it flowed east through fertile valleys. Here it cut through a range of mountains, along whose lower slopes, he had been told, lush vineyards flourished. Soon the line curved southward into the heart of Turkish territory. On and on the river flowed, through level croplands, mountain wildernesses, over rocky cataracts, and across barren deserts until it emptied into the Black Sea.

Up this river highway had come traders, bringing spices, perfumes, exquisite tapestries, silks, and gold and silver trinkets from the exotic East. Up this river also had come the notorious Turks, pillaging, burning, looting, and spreading their strange religion.

Resting his chin on his balled fists, Peter stared at the map. Most of his knowledge of the unknown land to the east had been gleaned from listening to the extravagant tales of Patlo. He smiled to himself as he thought of the wizened, oddly attired, droll old peddler who made his appearance at the bruderhof every few months.

The first time Patlo had come ambling down their street, clad in a ragged, violet-hued hooded cloak, whistling a jaunty tune, and leading a pathetically bony donkey laden with lumpy, brown bundles, the children playing on the doorsteps had run in terror to their mothers. Until then, the village inhabitants and most strangers had avoided their section of Steinborn like the plague. But old Patlo had no compunctions about making himself at home with them. He had gladly accepted their offer of a meal and lodging. He had then ordered the ancient mule to kneel, which the beast obligingly did, in the middle of the street, while his master proceeded to open his many bundles and spread his wares before them.

On that first visit, the men had appreciated the opportunity to purchase some necessary supplies—mainly tools or metal scraps for the fashioning of tools. The gregarious Patlo had elaborated at great length, but to no avail, on the pungency of his spices (dried high in the Caucasus Mountains), the high quality of his brilliant silks (woven by a Chinese princess), the incomparable beauty of his jewelry (belonging originally to the harem of a sultan in Arabia), and the durability of his leather (all the way from Palestine).

Peter and his friends had followed his elaborate gesticulations with amusement while a crowd of children peered wide-eyed from behind the skirts of their mothers, who watched from the edge of the crowd of men.

Later, in the warmth of the crowded sitting room, after a satisfying meal, old Patlo had regaled them with more stories. He had travelled much. He had been down the Danube to the sea and followed the trade routes south to Italy. He told fantastic tales of getting the best of Venetian merchants, being waylaid by robbers (and escaping by threatening to put a curse on them), being lost for weeks in the deserts of Arabia, and being captured by Turks who were about to sell him into slavery until he convinced them that he was a long-lost relative of their chief.

Although most of his tales were preposterous, his wide forehead, dark skin, high cheekbones and short stature lent some credibility to his claim of being part Turk. He seemed to have no fear of anyone, be it Turk or religious authority. He said he partook of mass "when he couldn't find anything better to eat." As for baptism, he had been baptised many times—twice in the Danube, once in Venice . . . , but at this point, the disapproving frowns of his audience had made him switch topics quickly.

At least, he had made it clear that he had no scruples against dealing with them, and his visits had become routine. Through him the men were able to sell watches and woven cloth. He was always willing to carry messages and letters to other bruderhofs he might visit along his route.

Although his escapades were questionable, his descriptions of landscape and people seemed plausible, and Peter always welcomed the arrival of the wandering peddler.

Peter stared at the land of Hungary on his map. Would he ever go there? He saw himself standing in a foreign marketplace, surrounded by savage-looking Turks with fierce black moustaches and gleaming scimitars. As he expounded to them the words of Jesus, the glints of hatred softened and the weapons fell to the ground. Peter shook his head. Foolish dreams. Missionary work was not that easy. But maybe, someday . . .

" 'As my Father hath sent me, even so send I you.' "[15] His lips moved as he folded his maps.

The Conference Begins

The next morning, Peter was back on his familiar stool in his father's shop, sanding chair rungs. As his hands moved, he meditated on the Scripture passage his father had read that morning before the family separated for the day. Matthew 24 it was, the signs pointing to the Second Coming of Christ.

Peter reviewed some of them. "Many shall come in my name, saying, I am Christ; and shall deceive many."[16] That was true of these times. The priests claimed to be true followers of Christ, and the pope in Rome was supposed to be God's representative on the earth. Yet their lives made a mockery of the Gospel, and the general populace was deceived.

"Wars and rumours of wars."[17] There was certainly plenty of that. The Turks had been making forays into Europe for almost a thousand years now. The ruling dynasties of the Germanic, French, and Spanish crowns were constantly squabbling over their boundaries. Ever since the time of Christ, it seemed to Peter, there had been fighting somewhere in the world.

"Then shall many be offended, and shall betray one another."[18] He thought of his grandparents, who had been betrayed by a rival woodworker. And many families in their own community here had lost brothers and sisters, parents, aunts, and uncles because some neighbour, greedy for reward, had informed the authorities against them.

Pestilences had ravaged whole cities, famines had caused much death and suffering, and tales of devastating earthquakes in China had filtered into Austria. Surely the time was ripe for His coming.

"So likewise ye, when ye shall see all these things, know that it is near, even at the doors."[19]

Peter retrieved another piece from the floor. Really, the dreams and plans for the future he and Caspar had made last night were rather foolish. According to the Scriptures, the time was almost ripe for Christ's coming again to take the faithful home. It was a waste of time to be so perturbed about possible persecution and forced flights. And their optimistic ambitions appeared childish in light of end-time events. Surely Christ would return before Peter had had a chance to travel, or Caspar had entered the state of matrimony.

Grandfather Boewen was confident that he would live to see Christ coming in the clouds. No one knew how old Grandfather Boewen was. Having lost his whole family on his flight to Moravia years before, the gentle, understanding old man had become Grandfather to the whole bruderhof.

Crippled with arthritis and bent almost double over his cane, he was a common sight moving at a painfully slow, jerking pace along the street on a sunny day. He would appear unexpectedly in the kindergarten, where the children clustered around him in anticipation of a story, or in one of the shops, where the men listened to his advice with great respect. With a radiant sparkle in his faded blue eyes, he would assure his listeners that he did not expect to die, but that he anticipated a flight to glory. It made Peter's spine tingle to hear him because, by all appearances, Grandfather's old body would not sustain life much longer.

The bell tinkled, and Deacon Mathes Legeder, the general treasurer, or householder, of the bruderhof, stepped into the shop.

Oh, yes. Peter had forgotten. This was reckoning day. Every Friday, Brother Mathes made his rounds with his little leather-bound book and large leather purse to collect revenues and dispense funds for any future expenditures.

This morning, Mathes laid his book and bag on the counter and strolled over to inspect Peter's work. "They're keeping you busy I see?"

"Yes, sir."

"I just came from the tailor's shop, and it seems they are having a hard time finding work for everyone there. I want to talk to your father"—he glanced at Big Peter, who had turned from the lathe and was dusting his breeches—"about taking on another apprentice or two."

He turned towards Jacob and Cornelius, but on seeing Andreas's wedding chest behind Peter, he stopped to run his hand over the carved lid. "Looks like Andreas is almost finished," he commented. "He is a fine young man. I wish him a long and happy married life."

Big Peter joined him then in inspecting the dozen chairs that Jacob and Cornelius had completed.

"These are for the nursery; is that right?" Mathes asked, testing the strength of a back by leaning on it.

"Six are for the nursery; the others are for sale in Nikolsburg," Big Peter corrected.

"Oh, yes. That's good. I want to talk to you about that." The two men moved to the front of the room and sat on Big Peter's workbench.

"Did you have much income this week?" began Mathes.

"A little." Big Peter started to rise.

"No, never mind. I'll collect it later." Mathes laid a restraining hand on Big Peter's arm. His expression became sober as he went on. "The outlook for this winter is not good."

The other workers, including Peter, stopped their work to listen.

"As you know, the harvest was poorer this year than usual. We expect the wheat supply to last another two months; and then, if we want to have any left for seed, we will have to purchase grain for flour and feeding stock. The hay for the animals may reach, if we ration it, and we can always butcher more beasts if we run low. But that would mean fewer calves and piglets for next year. We had a fair crop of potatoes, as you recall, but now," he sighed, "the women in the kitchen report that they must have a blight. They are rotting in the bins. I told them to go heavy on potatoes while they are still eatable," he said, smiling wryly. "So if you men get potato soup once a day for a while, you know why." He glanced at the other men.

"Now," he said, getting back to business, "what this means is that we must have some source of income to supplement our dwindling food supplies. Some of our industries cannot produce their goods without an initial investment. The metalworkers must purchase scrap iron to work with. So that avenue isn't much help. The tailors need orders for garments before they can go ahead. Now you, here, might be the answer. All the raw material you need is wood. My proposal is that we send some men out to fell trees; we give you several semiskilled helpers and as many apprentices as you can handle; we clear some of the other shops that are not so busy; and we start turning out chairs, tables, and benches for sale in Nikolsburg."

Big Peter had been nodding his head in agreement with these suggestions.

"Do you think you could sell that many in Nikolsburg?" Mathes asked.

"There would be market for some," Big Peter replied, thoughtfully. "And if not, possibly we could go to Vienna."

Vienna? Peter's eyes sparkled. Maybe he would get to travel to Vienna. He would see the Danube, the vineyards, the king's palace, the great marketplace . . .

"We'll keep that possibility in mind," Mathes agreed. "Now, I'd best keep going. He rose, and Big Peter followed. The money was transferred from the shop's cashbox to Mathes's leather pouch; then the deacon turned to leave. "Anything you need here?" he asked as he picked up his account book.

Big Peter picked up a plane from his bench and gingerly tested the blade with his thumb. "This could stand sharpening," he decided. "And if we're going to be doing more work as you suggested, we should have several more of these."

"I'll find out whether there is enough steel available to do that for you," Mathes promised. "And could you have those six chairs ready to go to Nikolsburg by next week?"

At Big Peter's affirmative nod, the deacon raised his hand to all of them and departed.

When Andreas made his appearance later that afternoon, Peter was kneeling over a fresh-smelling, white-pine board, wielding a plane.

"So they gave you something else to do, did they?" Andreas teased.

Peter straightened his back. "Yes. I'm not sure whether this is a promotion or a demotion." He rubbed the muscles of his right arm. "I make bigger piles at this job," he said, kicking at the curly shavings on the floor, "but it takes more elbow power."

"If I can find your pumice stone"—Andreas bent to search in the dust around Peter's stool—"I'll try my hand at sanding. Here it is." He secured the article and dragged the stool over to the chest. "What are you making now?" he asked as he applied the stone to a front corner.

"These are boards for a bench." Then Peter told him all about Mathes Legeder's visit and the plan to expand their production of furniture for sale.

"He was in the watch workroom too," Andreas informed him. "We have enough parts to assemble about twenty more watches; and then, depending on how much we are able to make on furniture, we may be able to purchase more steel and maybe not."

"I suppose the local people of Steinborn would find it hard to believe that we aren't wealthy," Peter said with a smile.

"Yes. We have warm dwellings, enough clothing, lots of food, and we're all healthy. They likely think we have large reserves of money, not realizing that we make almost everything we have, and by working together and living simply, we can supply our basic needs."

"But we don't have a whole lot left over."

"If we did, we would send it to aid some other bruderhof that is struggling to make ends meet, or give it to some evangelist to help him on his mission of spreading the Gospel."

Peter thought of something else. "If our potatoes are rotting and our grain supply is dwindling, the other inhabitants of this valley are going to be hungry too."

"Father talked about that after Mathes left," Andreas acknowledged. "He feels that we have a duty to help the poor, as well. So we must all work and plan together in order that we can feed our own people and also help those around us. Perhaps it will soften their hearts and give us an opportunity to preach to them if we share our material goods."

Peter turned his board over and began running the plane over the other side. "Are you going to finish that chest on time?" he demanded.

Andreas cocked his head to study his work. "I hope so. I'm

done with the carving, and it just needs sanding and oiling yet. Besides, Bishop Riedemann may not be here for a few days. He wasn't certain just when he'd get to Nikolsburg." Abruptly he changed the subject. "Did you know that seven of the Philippite brethren arrived this afternoon?"

"Did they?" Peter stopped planing, and the other men looked expectantly at Andreas.

"Yes, they arrived on foot soon after lunchtime."

"Have they been cared for?" Jacob asked.

"Mother came to the workroom to summon Father," Andreas explained. "He left to see that they got fed, and I suspect they are resting now."

"Will there be a service tonight?" asked Peter.

"Probably," Big Peter guessed. "Even if Peter Riedemann isn't here, it is such a privilege to have visitors that we may as well enjoy fellowship together."

"We should give them an opportunity to tell of their experiences," Cornelius suggested.

The men fell to work with a will, and the afternoon passed rapidly as they anticipated the evening meeting.

After the evening meal of potato dumplings, Peter hurried home. He wanted to dress before the women and children finished eating.

The apartment was empty, and Peter selected his good, black, woollen, knee-length breeches from the wardrobe. His dusty work shirt was exchanged for a clean, dark, checked one. Setting the washbasin on the table and filling it from the jug by the door, he scrubbed his face and hands thoroughly. He ran the brush repeatedly through his thick brown hair, bending to squint into the tiny mirror that hung on the wall near the door.

Satisfied with his appearance, he sat on a chair and pulled on the new, closely knitted socks his mother had just finished and tucked them under his breeches. Over these went a pair of sturdy, high-topped leather shoes. He finished lacing them and tied the knots with a flourish. These shoes were new last year, he remembered. If he did not grow any more, they should last several more years. And it was not likely he would grow any more, so he might as well accept it. You would think with such a tall father—but then, Mother was short, so he had only had half a chance of being tall.

Heavy steps on the landing announced Father's arrival. Good. He was almost ready. Now Father would have time to dress too.

"All ready?" Father looked his son over. "Better take an overcoat too," he suggested. "The meeting hall has no fireplace, and the wind is chill again tonight."

Peter obediently felt around in the wardrobe for his heavy coat. Slipping his arms into it, he groped on the top shelf for his good hat.

Father was splashing noisily over the washbasin. "Mother won't be going tonight," he sputtered through his washing.

"Oh, why not?" Peter stood before the mirror, adjusting the round-domed, broad-brimmed, black hat.

"The baby was fretful all day, and with the building as cold as it is, she decided to stay home with him and Maria."

"I think I'll leave now," Peter said, reaching for the door.

"Do you have your notebook?" Father reminded him.

"Oh. No." How could he have forgotten? Peter reached for the thick, six-inch-square notebook that rested on the shelf by the Bible. Printed Bibles were rare and clumsy. Not every household owned one. So every Christian carried his little notebook and copied into it, in small, exquisite script, snatches of sermons, Scripture passages, or points from the notebooks of others. Sometimes they contained personal testimonies or sermonettes. The little books were often the Christians' most precious possessions.

They carried them to town, to visit the sick, to public meetings, to court trials, and to prison cells.

Peter tucked his notebook into his inside breast pocket, made large enough solely for the purpose of accommodating it.

Hurrying down the stairs, he almost collided with Ursula, who was on her way up. "See you at the meeting," he said briefly as he continued on his way.

Peter was one of the first ones at the meeting hall. He hung his hat on a peg inside the door but elected to leave his overcoat on. His breath made little clouds in the air. It felt almost colder inside than out.

Four oil lamps, suspended from the ceiling, cast flickering shadows into the corners of the sparsely furnished room. Peter found himself a place on a bench in the front half of the auditorium. Several men were already seated. Their heads were bowed in prayer or bent to study the close writing in their notebooks.

Shuffling at the back of the room announced the arrival of more worshippers. A row of men, most of them in overcoats that hung to their knees, filed up the aisle and filled the first bench. The repeated opening and closing of the heavy door told Peter that the men were gathering rapidly. He turned to smile at Martin and Lukas, who had slid onto the bench beside him. Where was Caspar? He sneaked a quick glance over his shoulder but failed to see Caspar's blonde head towering over the others.

Here came Jacob up the aisle, with a row of strange men behind him. Their beards were all trimmed short, and their coats were of a slightly different cut than the ones Peter was used to seeing. He sat up with interest. These must be the Philippite brethren. As they took their places on the second bench, he counted them. Ten. Three more must have arrived just recently. Two of the strangers were older men, but the rest appeared to be in their twenties or early thirties.

The men's benches were almost full. Caspar finally strode up the aisle and sat down beside Peter. At the same time, a door on the side near the front of the hall opened, and three men emerged to take their places on the bench behind the lectern.

Peter studied the faces of these three deacons who were their spiritual leaders. Michel Blauer's round face was framed by white hair and a long, grey beard. He had suffered much in his lifetime. Two of his children had never left the state church, and their unredeemed state was a continual sorrow to the old man. Three more children had died of diphtheria during the time he and his family had been forced to live in caves in Moravia for fear of Anabaptist hunters. His wife had passed away since the group arrived at Steinborn, and now he lived with his only remaining daughter and her family, pouring his energies into shepherding the flock. Peter always listened with interest to his sermons because he spoke with the voice of experience and had endured much as a faithful soldier of the cross.

Next to him sat Michel Kramer, father to Andreas and George. Like his sons, he was tall, slender, and thin of face. A quiet-spoken man, he was a deep thinker and sensitive to the needs of his congregation. Besides the four oldest sons, his family included six younger children, ranging in age from two to fifteen.

The last deacon was the young, businesslike, energetic Mathes Legeder. He was a doer, and therefore the duties of organizing and manipulating the finances of the community fell naturally to him.

But Uncle Guttenhann was missing. "Where is your father?" Peter whispered to Caspar.

"He took the horses and cart to Nikolsburg to meet Brother Riedemann," Caspar whispered back. "We weren't sure when Brother Riedemann would arrive, so they decided Father should go and wait there for him. He may be back tonight or not for several days."

Some young sisters seated themselves on the benches against the wall along the right side of the building. Their white head coverings looked like a row of white flowers against the brown wall. Their shawls were all dark but of different hues—some brown, some blue, some green. Andreas, who sat directly in front of Peter, glanced involuntarily to the side and flashed a smile in the direction of the girls. Out of the corner of his eye, Peter noticed a becoming flush spread over the cheeks of one blonde young lady—Bridgit, of course.

More girls, including Ursula, joined the others. Some older women and a few mothers with warmly bundled children occupied the benches along the left wall.

A tenor voice from the front row began to sing in a slow, even rhythm.

"O God to Thee we lift our voice,
Our praise and honour, thanks . . ."

The congregation joined in and sang by memory several verses of praise to God. This hymn was followed by three more. Then Brother Kramer rose and opened the large Bible that lay permanently on the lectern.

"Greetings in the Name of our risen Lord and Saviour, who rejoices to see His children meeting together in the unity of the faith." Brother Kramer's soothing voice included the whole assembly. "I will read Romans, chapter twelve."

There was a rustling of paper as each worshipper thumbed rapidly through his notebook to the chosen passage. As it was a familiar one, most had copied it; and when the stir ceased, the deacon began reading.

" 'I beseech you therefore, brethren, by the mercies of God, that ye present your bodies a living sacrifice, holy, acceptable unto God, which is your reasonable service. And be not conformed to this world: but be ye transformed by the renewing of your mind, that ye may prove what is that good, and acceptable, and perfect, will of God. . . .'[20]

" 'Having then gifts differing according to the grace that is given to us, whether prophecy, let us prophesy according to the . . .' "[21]

"I think I hear Father coming," Caspar hissed in Peter's ear.

Peter took his eyes from the script and turned his head.

Gal-lop, gal-lop. Very faintly he thought he caught the sound of horses' hooves in the distance.

Gal-lop, gal-lop, gal-lop. The sound came closer. They were coming very fast. Uncle Guttenhann must be in a hurry. Several others had lifted their heads at the approaching sound.

Now the street echoed the thuds of many horses' hooves and the unexpected clank of metal on metal. A loud voice sang out, "*Whoa!* They're in here."

To the Castle

The commotion in the street outside the meeting hall grew louder. Members of the audience lifted their heads one by one and cast questioning glances over their shoulders. Horses' hooves stamped, metal clanged, muffled men's voices intermingled with the shrill whinnies of horses.

Brother Michel Kramer's voice faltered in his reading, but he bravely struggled on, raising his voice above the clamour. "'... fervent in spirit; serving the Lord; rejoicing in hope; patient in tribulation; continuing instant in prayer ...'"[22]

Peter had returned his eyes to the page, but he was having difficulty focusing on the words. He sensed rather than saw Caspar glance involuntarily to the rear. With an effort, he concentrated on the words being read. "'Bless them which persecute you: bless, and curse not.'"[23]

Bang! Bang! Bang! Peter jumped in his seat. An audible gasp was heard from the women's benches. Brother Kramer's voice trailed off as he raised his eyes to stare at the door.

BANG! BANG! BANG! "Open in the name of the king!" an imperious voice commanded from outside.

At a gesture from Brother Kramer, one of the ushers seated on the back bench sprang to the door and flung it wide.

A soldier in full armour, who had apparently been about to force the door, stumbled into the room. He was followed by a commanding figure in a plumed helmet.

For a full minute, there was silence. The believers were frozen into shocked immobility, and the soldiers who crowded through the doorway blinked in the sudden light inside.

The marshal in the plumed helmet came to life first. Turning to his band, he ordered, "All right men. We have them. Take your places." Then he began to stride purposefully up the aisle, his sword clanking against his metal-clad leg at every step. Four soldiers followed closely behind him, and several more fanned out across the rear of the auditorium.

The young sisters on the right huddled together in a tight group, clinging to one another in fear as three soldiers stepped in their direction. The frightened wails of small children came from the other side of the room, and Peter saw the women gathering the little ones into a protected circle in their midst while more soldiers stationed themselves at the windows in the wall behind them.

In front of Peter, Andreas, his face suddenly pale, watched anxiously as the soldiers approached the young women. He made as if to rise and go to the rescue of his Bridgit, but seeing the soldiers position themselves at the windows, he thought better of it and slumped onto the bench again. Most of the men sat prayerfully, their heads bowed.

As the marshal neared the front of the room, Brother Kramer stepped from behind the lectern to meet him. The other two deacons rose and took their places beside him. At a nod from their commander, the soldiers at his heels positioned themselves— one behind each man. The fourth soldier covered the side door at the front.

"They're going to be sure nobody gets away," Peter thought as a glance to the rear revealed another half-dozen armed men in front of the door.

"Which of you is Peter Riedemann?" the marshal now demanded of the deacons.

They all shook their heads in denial.

So that was what they had come for. Somehow news of Riedemann's expected arrival had leaked out, and they had come here to apprehend him. Peter felt a surge of relief—relief that the soldiers were not after the rest of them and joy because Peter Riedemann was not to be found here. He prayed that Uncle Guttenhann would be delayed with his distinguished guest.

But the marshal was not to be put off so easily. "We know Riedemann is here. You must be the man," he declared, shifting his attention to Mathes Legeder. "Riedemann is a large, dark-haired man. Own up now," he commanded harshly.

But Mathes shook his head. "No, I am not Riedemann."

"You lie," accused the marshal.

"God is my witness that I tell the truth," was the calm answer.

"Give him a little help." The marshal nodded at the soldier who stood behind Mathes.

The soldier responded by landing a swift kick with a metal-toed boot behind Mathes's knee. Mathes winced and lurched forward. The man then seized his arm and twisted it cruelly behind the deacon's back. Mathes bent over, groaned, and then pressed his lips tightly together.

A muffled sob came from the women's section.

Peter's fists clenched involuntarily. Then he forced himself to relax. What was that last verse Brother Kramer had read? "Bless them which persecute you." Easy to read but difficult to do, Peter now discovered as outrage at this rough treatment to an innocent victim threatened to engulf him. "Oh, Lord, give us strength to endure. Help us to love these men and not be consumed by hatred.

Help us to bear this cross with patient endurance."

"Take this man to the back," the marshal ordered the soldier who still held Mathes's twisted arm in a merciless grip behind his bowed back. "We'll question him later."

He turned his attention to the white-haired Michel Blauer. "You look like a wise old man," he said with an almost-courteous voice. "If you know what's good for you and all these people"—he waved his hand towards the women and children—"you'll tell us quickly which one is Riedemann."

With quiet composure, the old man answered the marshal, "Brother Riedemann is not here."

"Hah!" snorted the marshal. "You probably have him hidden." He whirled to study the quiet congregation seated before him. His lips curled into a sneer. "Looks like we've uncovered a whole nest of troublemakers at any rate. Our orders are to seize Riedemann and any other Anabaptist we may find."

Peter's hopes plummeted. Then they would all be arrested. Every one of them. He looked around unbelievingly at the crying children, the agitated mothers, the trembling young women, and the praying men. All of them? That was impossible. They could not arrest such a large group. Or could they?

Summoning soldiers from the rear, the marshal began moving along the rows of benches, pointing out a man here and there. As Peter watched his approach with mounting apprehension, he realised that all of the chosen men were large and black haired. He let out his breath. They were still looking for Riedemann. Then he stiffened as he saw the officer point to Big Peter. But the man shook his head and muttered, "Big, but not black haired."

The soldiers herded a half-dozen suspects towards the back corner to join Mathes Legeder. "Make them talk." The marshal flung the words after them. He marched to the front and again confronted the two remaining deacons. "You are all under arrest."

"Would you be so kind as to tell us why?" Michel Blauer asked politely.

"For holding an illegal meeting," the marshal returned coldly.

"Is it unlawful for people to gather to worship God?" asked Michel.

"You are aware that there is only one recognised, established church in the empire and that all citizens are obligated to belong to it. To take upon yourselves matters of faith, and influence innocent victims to leave the safety of the church, is a crime punishable by death."

Peter's heart thumped wildly. It was true then. They were all to be arrested. Was there no way to stop this horrible nightmare? That was it! Maybe he was dreaming. Any second now he would wake up and find himself in his own bed at home.

A low moan issued from the back corner. Peter turned his head. In that brief glimpse, he saw the six brethren surrounded by soldiers. One soldier held the tip of his sword against the throat of a suspect who stood with his head flung back, his eyes rolling, his arms pinioned by two more armed men. Peter looked away quickly.

To his left the women huddled around the crying children. One small voice sobbed hysterically, "What will they do? What will they do to us?" and was swiftly hushed by a commanding *shh.*

The marshal now tried a new tack. After moving his eyes disdainfully over the bowed heads of the silent men, he turned to the deacons who still stood patiently before him. "Look at them," he said with a sneer, sweeping his metal-clad arm over the assembly. "A whole unit of able-bodied men who should be serving their king and country in the war against the Turks, and here you all sit in this little town, making yourselves rich off the poorer inhabitants. Don't you think it your duty to rid the land of the heathen Turks?"

Michel Kramer said, "Our Lord commanded us to love our enemies, not to take up the sword against them."

"Do you mean then that we should allow the Turks to overrun the land?"

"God has appointed the king to his throne, and He expects him to maintain peace, but the Christian is commanded not to kill."

"You are just like all the others," stormed the marshal in frustration. "I haven't been apprehending heretics in Vienna for five years for nothing. I know your tricks. You talk in circles. Well, I'll let the priests and judges deal with you. My duty is to arrest you and seize your hoarded funds. If you refuse to serve the king in his army, he can at least make use of your money to equip other soldiers. You could save us much trouble by telling us where your treasury is."

"We have no hoard of wealth," Michel Blauer assured him.

"So you say," the marshal retorted. "You all seem to be well fed and warmly dressed. If you won't tell us where the money is hidden, we'll find it."

Vienna! Peter's gaze met Caspar's when the marshal said that. So this was no local band of soldiers, but a contingent sent all the way from Vienna, probably under orders from the king himself. Their quiet existence at Steinborn had not gone unnoticed after all.

The marshal surveyed the hall as if plotting his next move. "You, and you"—he pointed out six of his men—"stay here in the village tonight. Guard all the exits. See that no one escapes. We'll search the buildings tomorrow. Move in, men, and let's move the rest of these obstinate traitors."

"Stand up!" he bellowed at the seated men.

The harsh command jerked Peter to his feet. The soldiers started prodding the women and girls towards the centre benches.

"Will you not excuse these helpless women and innocent children?" pleaded Michel Kramer.

The marshal hesitated a moment. Then he decided. "Leave the women. You two," he ordered, indicating two soldiers. "Stay here and guard them. Don't let them leave the building."

"They will be cold," thought Peter, "but maybe they are better off than we. Where are they taking us?"

The three soldiers behind the group of young sisters had stopped and now looked inquiringly at their commander. He glanced over the pale but composed faces of the girls. "Take them along. We may have use for them," he decided. The girls were then prodded towards the men.

A woman's voice rang out clearly above the shuffling feet. "I will come too."

Everyone, prisoners and soldiers alike, turned abruptly to see a tall, angular woman in a long, black shawl, stepping purposefully from the women's benches.

"Brave!" thought Peter. The prim and stern spinster, Agathe, who used to frown disapprovingly at their boyish pranks and make opportunities to lecture the girls on subjects of decorum and maidenly virtue, was offering herself as a protector to those same girls. Her courage and selflessness shamed Peter as he recalled some of the uncharitable thoughts he had entertained about this same sister in the past.

Following her example, another matronly woman—mother to one of the girls—rose, and without a word, joined the captives.

The soldiers closed in, creating an armed circle around the believers. Slowly they filed from their benches and turned towards the door. Some soldiers began pushing their way between the closely pressed men. Peter saw that the one nearest him had a coil of rope slung over his arm. He felt the rough hemp circle his right hand; then it was jerked back and secured firmly to his left wrist behind his back. "Tied like a dog," he thought numbly. The soldier used the loose end of rope to bind

Caspar and then moved on to the next man.

Tied together in this manner, they were pushed and prodded into the street.

"Be faithful!" "God go with you!" "God bless you!" The tearful voices of the women rang in their ears.

This was it then. It was really happening. The knotted cord around his wrist convinced Peter that this was no dream.

Out in the dark street, all was confusion. The bound brethren stood in a silent, bewildered cluster as the soldiers struggled in the narrow passage between the buildings to mount their prancing horses and keep the group surrounded at the same time.

Then they were moving slowly down the street—past the kitchen door, past the schoolroom, past the tannery. With a sense of doom, Peter mentally ticked off the doorways. Would he ever step through those familiar openings again? Now they were plodding past the cabinet shop. Peter peered longingly at the multipaned window, but all was dark inside.

Over the bobbing heads in front of them, he picked out his father's large head. At that moment, Big Peter turned and looked upwards to the right. Peter's eyes followed. They were passing their apartment. Of course, the women at home would have heard the commotion. And there at the window, her face framed by frost, was his mother.

She lifted both hands to the pane, clasped in an attitude of prayer. Peter blinked back sudden tears. She was praying for them. Would he ever see that dear face again?

On and on they marched—through the village, past the church with its pointed steeple, past the stables of the villagers, and out onto the highroad. Peter was scarcely aware of where they were going.

The clouds hung low, obstructing the moon. A few fine snowflakes swirled around the column of men as they marched steadily eastward along the snow-packed road. The darkness seemed to shroud Peter's heart too. He stepped along, one of many, yet strangely alone in the world of darkness and cold and despair. *Tramp! Tramp! Tramp!* The marching feet echoed in Peter's dulled mind. Away, away, away from all that was familiar. Away from home, away from the shop, away from Mother and Maria and the baby. Beside him the crisp *tlot, tlot* of horses' hoofs and the protesting squeak of leather emphasized the fact that he was now a prisoner and that there would be no turning back.

Tramp! Tramp! Tramp!

"To the castle." Caspar's voice beside him caused Peter to lift his head. "They're taking us to the castle."

Although the features of the landscape were obscured by the blackness, the line of silent marchers had veered to the right onto a narrower, more rutted road. The incline grew steeper, and the men leaned forward as they plodded up the hill.

"The castle!" George had said there were dungeons beneath the castle. Dungeons were for prisoners . . .

"Looks like Lukas is going to get his wish." Peter heard his cousin's voice as though from a distance. "He wished he could see the inside of Falkenstein. I think he'll get his wish tonight."

Peter did not answer. How could Caspar be so nonchalant about this tragedy? He marched straight ahead, eyes forward. He shivered in the frosty air. His hands strained at the confining ropes. What was the matter with him? he thought irritably. Where was his faith? Had he not just last night assured his father that he was ready to face whatever the Lord had for him in life? Yes, but . . . he had not known it would come so soon. He had not even been baptised yet, had not had a chance to prove his loyalty to the brotherhood, had not had the opportunity to tell one soul about Jesus' saving power. Surely God would not cut him off now, before his life had scarcely begun.

These ropes. They chafed his wrists. Could he get rid of them? His knife. His knife was in his pocket. He twisted his hands and stretched for his right pants pocket.

Thonk! Thonk! Thonk! The marching feet made a hollow noise. Peter looked up. They were crossing the narrow wooden trestle bridge over the chasm. As his feet thudded on the wood and the structure trembled under the combined weight of the men, an idea flashed into Peter's mind. Escape! If only he could reach his knife. He leaned forward, maneuvering his hands under his coat. He could cut himself free and slip off the bridge and hang onto the planks until the soldiers had passed. Bending, twisting, and grunting, he groped with his fingers. There, he had it!

It was very dark. He could not see more than a half-dozen men in front of him. Gingerly he eased himself sideways until he was on the outside edge of the group. A quick glance behind him. No soldier in sight. His elbow almost brushed the flimsy railing of the bridge.

He sawed clumsily at the rope.

Thonk! Thonk! Thonk! They must be halfway across. If he was going to do it, he would have to do it soon.

He sawed frantically. The knife cut through more strands.

Just ahead was another railing support. He would slip off the edge and hang onto the support. He was almost through the rope now.

"Ho-ah!" There was a harsh cry from behind. A horse plunged through the column of men and a soldier leaned from the saddle to swing his sword viciously at the ground near the opposite side of the bridge. For a moment there was confusion, but another soldier urged the milling men forward. Peter was carried along with the rest.

"Someone tried to jump from the bridge," he heard one man say.

Peter's legs felt weak. He had lost his chance. They were off the bridge now. It was a good thing he had not tried. He slipped his knife back into his coat pocket. Now he would have to face whatever was ahead.

He studied the sturdy shoulders of the men before him. At least they were all in this together. There was some comfort in that. He squared his shoulders. He might as well face it like a man. "I will never leave thee, nor forsake thee."[24] The words came to him from his subconscious mind. Peter again chided himself for his lack of faith. Even though his own plans had not included such an untimely episode, he knew that God would supply the necessary fortitude.

The twin towers of the gatehouse of the castle loomed out of the darkness ahead.

Thonk! Thonk! Thonk! They passed over the drawbridge between the towers and into the castle. There they huddled in the semidarkness until the last soldier had entered. Then slowly, with much creaking and groaning of pulleys, the heavy iron gate was lowered. It dropped into place with an emphatic thunderous *THUD!*

Plan of Falkenstein Castle

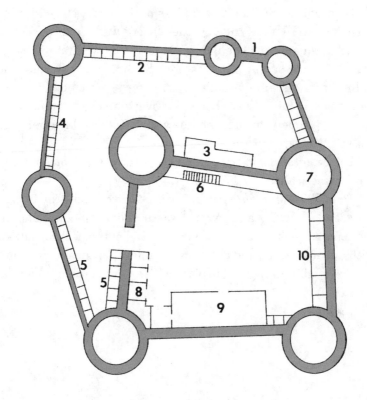

1. Main Gate
2. Stables
3. Kitchens
4. Soldier's barracks
5. Servants' quarters
6. Stairs to dungeon
7. Dungeon Tower
8. Living quarters
9. Great hall
10. Guest chambers

VII

In the Dungeon

Peter, along with one hundred forty of his Christian brothers and sisters, stood forlornly in the shadows of the great stone walls of the Falkenstein castle. The echoes of the closing of the great iron gate reverberated from tower to tower in the darkness.

That decisive thud echoed inside Peter too. It was all over—all his dreams, the missionary vision, the foreign lands he hoped to see, the heathen Turks he might have converted. The scenes flitted in and out of his mind. His future now was nothing but a blank.

A light flared in the darkness, and another, and another. Peter saw the soldiers hang the lanterns on pegs in the wall. The prisoners were standing in a large open space, just inside the outer walls. From his position among the press of prisoners, Peter could see soldiers dismounting their horses and removing their helmets. Stable boys appeared and led the horses towards their stalls along the wall to their right. Beyond the stables, a faint light glowed against the circular wall of a corner tower.

The believers, still bound together, stood motionless, each one wrapped in his own mental ordeal. What were they all thinking? Peter wondered.

A light bobbed towards them from the vicinity of the far tower.

Along with the rest, Peter anxiously followed its steady approach. In the glow from the stable, he recognized the plumed helmet of the marshal. With him were five men, unarmed except for swords dangling from their belts.

The marshal took command. "Untie the women," he ordered the soldiers who were with him.

The soldiers shouldered their way into the crowd, and presently a young woman stepped from the throng, followed by another. Standing on tiptoe to peer over the shoulders of the men in front of him, Peter watched until he saw Ursula join the group.

Poor Ursula. What was she doing in a place like this? The dungeons of a castle were no place for a fresh-faced, tenderhearted girl like his sister. If he felt forsaken and depressed, how must she feel? He wished he could do something about it.

He had often been her protector in the past. Oh, they had had their squabbles, to be sure; but when Ursula had been frightened by a strange dog (as she often was), it was Peter who would come and chase the provoking beast away. When Ursula had twisted her ankle on a mountain hike, it was Peter who had half-carried her home, although it had almost worn him out. When Ursula could not attend a class, or a meeting, Peter had been careful to relate to her afterwards the lessons she had missed.

While the other young men, at times, discussed which of the young ladies was the prettiest, was the best cook, or had the most pleasing personality, Peter usually had nothing to contribute; but personally, he thought his sister ranked among the best. He had often wondered which of his friends would someday claim her as a bride.

Now, there she stood in the hands of rough, ungodly men, facing the most frightening and perilous experience of her young life, and he was powerless to help her.

The sight of the indomitable Sister Agathe beside the young girls comforted him a little. He was sure that if anyone threatened harm to them, they would first have to deal with that worthy woman.

"Take them to the keep," ordered the marshal, and the women were led away.

"The Lord preserve you." Peter recognized Michel Kramer's voice.

"Silence!" roared the marshal, his voice echoing in the gloom.

"Yes," Peter consoled himself. "Not only do they have Sister Agathe to protect them, but the Lord Himself will be their shield and defender."

A verse came to him then. Jesus had told the disciples, "And fear not them which kill the body, but are not able to kill the soul: but rather fear him which is able to destroy both soul and body in hell."[25]

"Untie these men." The marshal directed one soldier to untie the knots on the man nearest him. "You can help," he then ordered the freed man. Raising his voice, he said, "Get free of the ropes, and then form a double line in front of me." To his soldiers, he added, "Keep them surrounded. We'll take no chances."

Someone freed Caspar, who in turn released Peter. Peter flexed his wrists gingerly and stretched his fingers before turning to the man beside him.

"Hurry up," the marshal barked. "Line up here."

All hastened to do his bidding. Caspar and Peter joined the double queue, wondering what was coming next. They waited for several minutes. Were they going somewhere? The soldiers stood at attention on either side of the line.

"Search them," the order came from the head of the line. The soldiers stepped forward.

"Arms up!" A voice from behind him made Peter jump.

"I said, 'Arms up.'" A soldier jabbed at his elbow.

Peter obediently lifted his arms. The soldier put his hands into the pockets of Peter's overcoat. *"My knife!"* The thought flashed into Peter's mind too late as the soldier drew out the valuable item. A knife would have been so useful in prison. He berated himself for not clutching it in his hand quickly.

"Take everything," the marshal directed. "Throw it all on the ground for now."

The soldier's hands groped through Peter's inner pockets, discovering two pen nibs and a small wooden squirrel he had carved for Maria. Peter wished he had given it to her the night before. It was one of the most lifelike things he had ever turned out, and he had wanted to show it to Caspar and Andreas before giving it to his little sister. Now, because of his pride, she would never see it. It would have been something for her to remember him by.

The soldier's hands were moving over his chest. Would he confiscate the little notebook? Peter held his breath as the man drew the book from its ample pocket. He held it up to the light and flipped some pages. Shutting it with a shrug, he tossed it to the ground with the other plunder.

Finally the soldiers stepped back and stood at attention, waiting for further direction.

The marshal spoke briefly to the nearest soldier, who then moved to the end of the line.

The column moved slowly past the stables, escorted by soldiers carrying flickering lanterns. On reaching the tower with the light they had seen from the main gate, they swung to the left. Beyond the circles of light cast by the soldiers' lanterns, Peter could make out another inner wall to their left. Soon they came to an open gateway in this wall, and the soldier led the way inside.

"Another gate to shut us off from the outside world," Peter thought dejectedly.

They turned just inside the gate and made their way along the wall on their left, past another round tower and along another wall. Peter tried to memorize the turns they were taking, just in case he ever had an opportunity to escape; but in the semidarkness, it was difficult to discern any prominent features of the castle.

The men in front of the boys stepped into single file to enter a doorway in the wall. Peter followed Caspar into a corridor. The soldiers spaced themselves between the men as they moved down the narrow hallway.

"Watch the stairs." A soldier stood by an archway, holding a lantern high.

Peter stepped down. "One, two, three . . ." His spirits sank with each step downward. "Nine, ten, eleven . . ." They were to be buried alive. "Twenty-one, twenty-two." He stumbled over a cracked tread. "Thirty-four, thirty-five." His next step carried him forward on the level. "Thirty-five steps!"

A dozen paces along a damp corridor and his progress was stopped by a soldier, his lantern illuminating an open doorway.

"In there," the soldier demanded, jerking his thumb towards the dark aperture.

Peter stumbled forward, and Caspar pushed into him from behind. The boys shouldered their way into the crowd before them as they were pressed forward by others. Peter's feet trod on a soft, spongy carpet; and he stumbled over something hard and lumpy. He shivered in the cold, clammy atmosphere. A stifling, musty odour almost choked him.

The door clanged shut, and the sound of a key grating in a

lock pierced the tomblike silence.

There they stood, in total darkness, twenty feet under the ground. No one moved or spoke. The only sounds to be heard were the rhythmic breathing of the men and a suggestive rustling from under their feet.

A few men began to stir and talk in hushed whispers.

"Let us pray." The quavering voice of Michel Blauer fell like a soothing balm on their ears. Every man bowed his head while the elderly deacon prayed.

"O Lord, Thou who knowest the end from the beginning, Thou who art the God of all comfort, we come to you in our hour of need. Help us, Lord, to bear this tribulation as true soldiers of Jesus Christ. Strengthen our spirits. Help us to commit our lives unto Thy keeping. Calm our troubled souls and grant us that peace which passes understanding.

"We thank Thee that Thou hast redeemed us and called us Thine own. We Thank Thee that we are counted worthy to suffer for Your Name's sake. We thank Thee that we have the privilege of being a solace to one another, that the strong may undergird the weak.

"We pray for our enemies, O Father. Forgive them, for they know not what they do. Help us to be faithful witnesses of Thy grace so that these same captors may see the light. Give us divine compassion for our persecutors.

"Be with our families, O Lord. May they look to Thee in their helplessness. Be with our wives and mothers and little ones. Spare them much tribulation, according to Thy perfect will. Bless also the sisters here in the castle. May they remain true and faithful, conducting themselves in purity and holiness. Keep them in the hollow of Thy hand.

"Preserve Thy Word in us, O Father. Help us to retain those Scriptures we have hidden in our hearts and use them for our own edification and the encouragement of one another. May Thy Spirit be faithful in bringing to our remembrance the precious Word of Life.

"Help us, our Father, to be faithful, even unto death.

" 'Now the God of peace, that brought again from the dead our Lord Jesus, that great shepherd of the sheep, through the blood of the everlasting covenant, make you perfect in every good work to do his will, working in you that which is wellpleasing in his sight, through Jesus Christ; to whom be glory for ever and ever. Amen.' "[26]

The simple, heartfelt prayer brought an element of peace to Peter's troubled mind. The cold chilled him. The darkness oppressed him. His life seemed pointless and the future grim. Yet, with his mind, Peter clung to the certainty that his heavenly Father cared for him and that his present situation was a part of the master plan for his life. He could not yet find it in himself to thank the Lord for the events of the past five hours, but he could submit and patiently endure.

Presently Caspar whispered into his ear, "Are we to stand here all night?"

"I don't know," Peter replied honestly. "I'm not sure I want to lie down on whatever is on this floor." He bounced up and down on the softness underfoot.

"I don't think we're the only living creatures in this place," Caspar guessed.

Other men were conversing in low voices. There was some shuffling in the closely packed mob.

Mathes Legeder's authoritative voice rose above the rest. "I suggest we wait until morning to inspect our surroundings. It's hard to say what vermin and filth we may unearth if we move about. We'll be warmer if we stay close together. Is there anyone without a coat?"

There was no response. Mathes then recommended, "The younger boys and anyone suffering from a cough or cold should move into the centre of the group. Those who are hardier can position themselves along the edges."

"Let's get families together," Michel Kramer spoke up.

"Good idea," Mathes Legeder agreed. "All those fathers with sons here, come and stand by Brother Kramer and myself." After a few moments of shuffling and jostling, he continued, "Brother Kramer, you call your boys first." He had the men one by one call their sons.

Finally Peter heard his own name. "Come with me," he urged Caspar. "Your father isn't here."

He started through the press towards his father's voice. "Oh, excuse me," he murmured as he bumped into an unknown person.

"Ouch," Peter groaned as someone accidentally kicked his ankle.

He continued to grope blindly forward, Caspar in tow. "This is like a game of blindman's buff," he thought. "Father, where are you?"

"Peter, is it you?" He felt his Father's large hand on his face and clutched the familiar arm and, for an instant, leaned with relief against the strong shoulder.

Big Peter guided the two lads through the throng. "We can stay on the edge," he decided.

The boys stood, one on either side of Big Peter while the stirring and calling behind them gradually lessened. Big Peter was not a man of many words, especially when it came to expressing deeper emotions, but his very nearness was a comfort to Peter.

His father had weathered tribulation before. He had never been in prison, but he had forsaken family, friends, and homeland to follow Christ. He had suffered hunger and privation for the sake of the Gospel, yet his faith stood like a rock. Peter was confident that Big Peter would face this trial with his characteristic courage.

Peter strained his eyes to peer into the dark void beyond the circle of men. Try as he might, he could see nothing. The shuffling feet had sent new waves of foul odours into the stale air. Peter shifted his weight restlessly. How long could a person exist in a place like this?

A harsh, rasping coughing came from somewhere behind him. It sounded like George. Poor George. How could he stand the cold and dampness?

Peter had been so busy feeling sorry for himself, he had not taken time to consider what this experience meant to others.

There was Caspar, always optimistic and cheerful. But here he was, all alone. At least he, Peter, had his own father to turn to for encouragement. And George. George, who suffered enough in the Austrian winters, must now face this. What about Andreas? He, who had planned to be married in a few days. If Peter had felt helpless when they led his sister away, how must Andreas have felt to see his bride in the hands of rude soldiers? What a dashing of hopes for him.

He prayed silently for each of his friends, and in bearing the burdens of others, he felt his own heaviness relieved in a measure.

The minutes dragged by slowly. Peter had no way of knowing what time it was. His legs ached. He shifted his weight back and forth on his feet.

From time to time, Big Peter would quote a Scripture to the two young men who leaned up against him.

" 'I will never leave thee, nor forsake thee. So that we may boldly say, The Lord is my helper, and I will not fear what man shall do unto me.'[27]

" 'Let not your heart be troubled: ye believe in God, believe also in me. In my Father's house are many mansions: if it were not so, I would have told you. I go to prepare a place for you. And if I go and prepare a place for you, I will come again, and receive you unto myself; that where I am, there ye may be also.' "[28]

Peter closed his eyes. Those words had always thrilled him. Now they took on new meaning. Here he had been rebelling because his future plans had been swept out from under his feet. Why, he had a whole glorious future before him. His lifetime here was but for a moment, but after that came all eternity. He tried to remember what he had learned of heaven.

"Let's sit down," proposed Big Peter after what seemed an eternity of standing motionless.

"On this?" Peter was dubious.

"If we keep our coattails under us, I don't think we'll be too damp," his father replied. "We can lean up against each other and rest a little."

He didn't say "sleep," Peter noticed. He was sure there would be little sleep for any of them that night. How many hours until morning? Would there be a morning in this cell? He did not know. And if there was a morning, would there be another night for any of them?

A soft rustling in front of him made Peter draw his knees hastily up to his chin.

Low murmurs and quiet breathing, an occasional sneeze or cough. The moments crept by.

Peter stirred uneasily. He was cold, his feet were sleeping, and his neck ached. What time was it by now?

"Still awake?" Big Peter's voice came softly.

"Um-hmmm," Peter grunted.

"The apostle Paul was a prisoner too," his father reflected quietly. "He wrote letters to the churches from prison cells. To Timothy he said, 'Wherein I suffer trouble, as an evil doer, even unto bonds; but the word of God is not bound. Therefore I endure all things for the elect's sakes, that they may also obtain the salvation which is in Christ Jesus with eternal glory. It is a faithful saying: For if we be dead with him, we shall also live with him: if we suffer, we shall also reign with him: if we deny him, he also will deny us.' "[29]

Peter meditated on the life of the apostle. He recalled the time that Paul and Silas had sung songs at midnight, while in bonds. Then there was the time in Philippi that their chains had fallen off and they had been miraculously freed. Would to God that He would deliver them from this noisome dungeon.

What had Paul said? "I endure all things for the elect's sakes." Maybe that applied to the apostle, but Peter could not really see how the incarceration of all the able-bodied men of their congregation was going to be of any benefit, either to the elect or to anyone else.

Yet—"If we deny him, he also will deny us." Even though he could not comprehend the whys and wherefores, Peter was determined not to deny his Lord.

VIII

A Dungeon, a Cathedral

All long nights come to an end—sometime. Peter studied his father's face—his eyes closed in sleep or prayer, his straight nose, firm mouth, and beard. Beside his father sat Caspar, his blond head resting on his knees, his long arms twined about his legs.

With a start, Peter realised that he could also discern the bodies of others, crouching, sitting, or half-lying against one another. The night was almost over. Four feet in front of him was a curved stone wall.

About him now, other men were stirring, standing, stretching, groaning, yawning. His own joints felt rusty, he discovered, as he pulled himself to his feet. He flexed his arms and bent his knees to limber up. He looked about him. There was not much to see. They were in a great round chamber about twenty feet high. Pale light filtered down from four narrow slits near the ceiling in the wall to his left.

"Let's explore." Caspar, also on his feet now, pulled at Peter's sleeve.

"What's to see?"

"Oh, who knows?" Caspar shrugged. "Might find a trap door leading to a tunnel; might find a treasure left here by some former prisoner."

Other men were already circling the stone wall.

"What is this stuff?" Peter kicked at the layer of soft, dark filth on the floor.

"It's decomposed straw and rushes," explained an older man beside him. "I was in prison once for six weeks. They give you this kind of thing for bedding and"—he hesitated—"absorption of body wastes."

Peter's stomach rolled. "Ugh!"

"This layer has probably been here for at least twenty years," the man went on.

"It would make good fertilizer," another commented.

Peter and Caspar made their way along the circular wall. They passed the wooden door through which they had entered the night before. Peering between the bars of the tiny opening cut into the upper half of the door, Peter could see only a short distance along the narrow corridor outside. Out there lay freedom. In here (he turned to follow Caspar along the wall) was thralldom in harsh reality.

Lukas joined them.

"Well," Caspar chided him, "here we are—inside the castle."

"Don't mention it." Lukas held his hands over his ears. "What's this?" They had come to another heavy door in the wall. Several men had already tried the latch, but it was locked.

"Wonder where that leads?" Caspar asked.

"Likely to another dungeon," one man suggested.

"We may never know," another man stated, shrugging his shoulders.

All sorts of interesting possibilities flooded into Peter's mind. An escape tunnel? A stairway to an upper chamber? He had better not waste energy thinking about it.

"We must be under one of the towers," surmised a third individual standing near Peter. "Wonder which side of the castle we're on."

"We'll have to wait until sundown and decide whether the sun shines more directly through those windows in the morning or the evening," another pointed out.

"If the sun doesn't shine any oftener than it has for the past week, we'll have a time of it deciding," returned the first speaker.

"Someone should keep track of the days and nights," a voice spoke up.

Days and nights? Peter shuddered. How could he get through another night like the last, and another, and possibly another— without end?

"We'll have to stage a rat hunt," Caspar was saying.

Peter shot him a withering glance, but it was lost on his cousin's buoyant spirit.

"Wonder when they serve breakfast?" Caspar rubbed his abdomen. "I'm hungry."

"Me too," agreed Lukas.

The boys wandered back to the main group in the centre of the room.

Brother Mathes Legeder raised his voice above the buzz of conversation. "Let us have a time of fellowship and share Scriptures together in this uncertain hour."

The men willingly turned their attention to him.

Michel Blauer led out with the Twenty-third Psalm. One by one, the men joined him in reciting it. " '. . . Yea, though I walk through the valley of the shadow of death, I will fear no evil: for thou art with me . . .' "[31] How significant those words became at this time. " 'And I will dwell in the house of the LORD for ever,' " they finished triumphantly.

The light of day, the familiar faces of the men, and the comforting verses chased away some of the horror and apprehension of the previous night. Michel Kramer then led in prayer, again committing the group into God's keeping and remembering the women in the tower and the loved ones at home.

Someone suggested a time of sharing, so the men by turns quoted Scriptures that had been precious to them through the long hours of the night, or related how the Lord had been their helper in previous trying circumstances.

The testimony meeting was interrupted by footsteps in the corridor outside their door. They all turned expectantly. The door swung slowly inward to admit a broad-shouldered, burly, clean-shaven individual with a bald head and small, close-set eyes.

He was followed by six servants, each bearing a large steaming kettle.

The first man advanced towards the group, muttering to himself, yet loudly enough to be heard, "What a mob to feed. 'Go feed those men,' he says. So I have to hustle about and get the cooks to fix something. 'Never a peaceful moment,' says I. It is, 'Do this, fetch that, go here, go there.'" Mumbling and grumbling, he indicated that the bearers should set down their kettles.

Peter's mouth watered as the smell of warm porridge met his nostrils.

"Thank you kindly, sir." Mathes Legeder spoke for all of them.

"Eh? How's that?" the beady-eyed individual cocked his head to one side.

"Thank you!" Mathes repeated more loudly.

"Oh, eh," the man grunted and turned to go. Before closing the door, he peered again at the group, shook his head, and muttered, "What a mob. Fetch and carry. Do this, do that." The door slammed shut.

The men looked hungrily at the steaming pots of porridge on the floor. "How do we eat?" someone asked for all of them.

They all looked to Mathes Legeder for direction. He did not fail them. "Big Peter, Michel Kramer, Jacob . . ." He named six men. "Each of you take one kettle and nineteen men. We will eat with our fingers. Pass the kettle around the circle, and mind your manners," he finished.

They needed no second invitation, and in spite of the lack of utensils and cream, the thick cereal was surprisingly satisfying.

The hours of that morning and afternoon dragged. From a general inventory, it was learned that all their watches had been confiscated. There were eight pen nibs that had escaped the probing fingers of the soldiers. The man who had attempted to jump from the bridge had had the presence of mind to secrete in his shoe the knife with which he had earlier cut his bonds. So they had that much. He had paid a price for his boldness however, as a painful bruise on his right shoulder rendered his arm almost useless.

Not that there was much chance of digging themselves through eight feet of solid masonry with a knife, Peter reflected.

The men sat about in groups, speculating on future developments, rehearsing the events of the evening before, wondering what was happening to their families, and trying to bolster one another's spirits.

The daylight was beginning to fade when the key grated in the lock again.

Instead of the grumbling jailor and his helpers, an old, bent man, tapping his cane unsteadily before him, shuffled through the doorway.

"Grandfather!" the men cried.

Those nearest the door sprang to the aid of their beloved Grandfather Boewen. Gently two men supported him, and the rest parted to give him a place of honour in their midst. Someone spread a cloak, and he was eased onto it. They almost failed to notice the other two men who had followed him from the corridor. Now they were greeted warmly and conducted to seats of honour beside Grandfather.

Questions flew thick and fast. "Where did you come from?" "How did you get here?" "Did you see my wife?" "What's happening in the village?"

Grandfather and the two others held up their hands in protest. At last the hubbub died down, and the men crouched around the new arrivals, waiting to hear their story.

The youngest man began, "I was at home last night because my wife was feeling poorly and needed help with the children. I heard the commotion in the street when the soldiers arrived. I saw them enter the meeting hall. I crept down the stairs and into the street. But four soldiers had stayed outside with the horses, so there was nothing I could do. I watched helplessly as they led you all away."

Then Grandfather spoke. "I, of course, was in bed with my arthritis. I wanted to attend the meeting, but my daughter wouldn't hear of it, saying it was too cold." He sounded almost regretful that he had missed the arrest.

"And I was home sick with a fever," the third man explained.

The first speaker took up the story. "I stayed in my apartment that night. When morning came, I was about to venture out when the soldiers returned. They went first to the meeting hall. I watched the women and children hurry from the hall and go to their own homes. I hadn't realised they were there all night.

"Then the soldiers disappeared into the tailor shop across the street. They bludgeoned the door down and pushed their way in. Soon bales of cloth were flying into the street. I couldn't see what they did inside, but when they left, a soldier smashed the window with his sword.

"They moved from shop to shop. As they drew nearer our house, I could hear smashing noises from inside the buildings. Furniture, tools, and anything else of value was tossed into the street.

"I realised then that they would soon be searching our apartment. What could I do? Where could we hide? We had caught glimpses of other women peeking from windows, even after the soldiers had left their houses, so apparently they had harmed no one. My wife insisted that the safest place for me was in my bed. Maybe they would think I was sick. And that is where they found me.

"Two soldiers burst into our apartment. They seemed to be searching for something. They threw everything out of the wardrobe, emptied the cupboard and my wife's chest. From the bedroom where we waited in fear, we saw one soldier poke his sword up the chimney. He hammered at the brickwork as if he expected to find some loose bricks."

"They were looking for money and valuables," Brother Kramer surmised.

"They did a thorough job," the speaker averred. He continued his narrative. "When they had ransacked the living room, they came into the bedroom. 'Here's some more,' one soldier said. 'And a man,' he added, seeing me. 'Up with you, you lazy peasant,' he ordered, and I had no choice. They slashed the mattress to shreds and spread the stuffing on the floor. But they didn't find what they were looking for, so they had to give up. My wrists were bound, and I was led away from my wife and helpless children."

"What will become of our wives?" Brother Joseph, the schoolmaster, who had four small children at home, asked the question that was bothering all of them.

The third newcomer spoke up, "We had a similar experience in our house. When I saw that the soldiers were coming and suspected that my turn had come to be taken, I counseled my wife that the women should stay together, possibly in the kitchen and dining hall, and try to carry on as best they could. Some of the young boys that are left can help carry firewood and keep that one room warm. Being together will help them to keep up their courage."

The other men agreed that this was a wise plan. Each hoped fervently that the soldiers would not harm the women.

"Did they rob the food stores?" asked one.

The three men shook their heads. They did not know.

"If they didn't, they likely will." Peter recognized Leonhardt Blöcher's pessimistic voice.

"The women may go hungry," stated Big Peter.

"There is nothing we can do for them at the moment." Mathes Legeder was ever practical.

"Except pray," reminded Michel Blauer.

"Did you have to walk all the way to the castle?" someone asked Grandfather Boewen, who had listened silently, his gnarled hands clasped about the crook of his cane.

The old man shook his head. "No. They had brought carts on which they loaded the tools and valuables they had found. I rode on a pile of woven goods."

"Wouldn't they spare an old man like you?" Big Peter asked.

"My daughter pled and argued." Grandfather smiled a toothless smile. "But the soldiers insisted that they had orders to bring in all the men they found, and that orders were orders. My daughter wrapped several quilts for my comfort into a bundle and marched after the soldiers who led me away. But the quilts were left in the carts when we reached here."

The faint glimmer of light from the four small slits near the ceiling was fading rapidly. The men drew instinctively closer to one another in the darkness.

Peter heard Andreas ask haltingly, "Did you see what they did in the cabinet shop? Did they smash everything?"

"I looked through the window as we went by," answered one. "Yes, it was a complete shambles. I don't think they left one whole piece of furniture . . ."

Oh, poor Andreas. Peter knew he was thinking of his chest. All the loving hours of painstaking work he had put into that chest. No chest, no wedding, no happy married life. Despair again gripped Peter as he crouched there on the filthy, rotted bedding. Why? Why? Why all this misery, this dashing of hopes, this wanton destruction?

"Do not be discouraged, my brethren," Grandfather said in his low, cracked voice. "The Lord knows we are here and, yea, is even here in our midst. I have often been in dark caves deep in the earth, and I have learned that the foulest cavern can be a cathedral if God is there. We have no light here, but Jesus is our Light. Even though the darkness is round about us, no one can eliminate the radiance in our souls.

"You are wondering why this had to happen."

"How did he read my mind?" thought Peter, startled.

"Remember, 'All things work together for good to them that love God, to them who are the called according to his purpose.'[32] Although it is hidden to us now, God does have a purpose in allowing this suffering. Many times I have experienced persecutions. Always, God used our tribulations to His glory. For some, it meant the offering up of their lives, but there was always a harvest. When the seed is sown in suffering, the harvest is bounteous."

"What can he mean?" Peter pondered. "How could the harvest be bounteous when the seed was buried twenty feet below tons of rock?" He must ask Grandfather sometime.

A light flickered through the bars of the tiny aperture in the door. The jailor, bearing a lantern, shuffled into the room, followed by two servants struggling with a great wooden tub.

"What a mob. Soldiers upstairs, prisoners downstairs, ladies in the tower. Fetch and carry, go here, go there, do this, do that," he mumbled grumpily. "Here's yer supper," he said more loudly, directing the servants to set the wooden tub at his feet. "Leftovers for the dogs," he growled. "Come and get 'em."

The men hesitated. Those nearest the tub warily eyed the contents. "Bones," they reported.

"Sure it's bones," the jailor snapped. "Lots o' good meat on 'em yet. What a mob. Soldiers! Bah! No manners! Eat what comes easy and toss the rest. . . ." He shook his lantern impatiently. "Come on now; take 'em or leave 'em. Can't wait all day."

The morning's scanty meal of porridge had long ago lost its effect. Big Peter and another man who stood near the food began picking out bones and handing them one by one to those nearest them. "Move to the right when you have your share," they directed.

After the prayer, Peter stood by the wall with the other boys, chewing the scraps of meat from his bone. He felt more like an animal than a man—a dung heap to lie on, a bone to gnaw.

"If a dungeon can be a cathedral, a bone can be a king's banquet." Caspar flourished his supper and smacked his lips.

"It does hit the spot," George agreed.

The jailor had withdrawn with his light, and they finished their meal in total darkness.

Mathes Legeder repeated the process of joining family members as they prepared to spend another night in their cell.

When all were positioned, Michel Kramer led in prayer and invited others to share Scriptures.

Peter, seated on the refuse and his coat pulled snugly about him, drank in the familiar words. Scriptures that had previously held only surface meaning for him now reached deeper within his being and spoke to his very present need.

" 'We are troubled on every side, yet not distressed; we are perplexed, but not in despair; persecuted, but not forsaken; cast down, but not destroyed; always bearing about in the body the dying of the Lord Jesus, that the life also of Jesus might be made manifest in our body. . . . Knowing that he which raised up the Lord Jesus shall raise up us also by Jesus, and shall present us with you. . . . For which cause we faint not; but though our outward man perish, yet the inward man is renewed day by day. For our light affliction, which is but for a moment, worketh for us a far more exceeding and eternal weight of glory; while we look not at the things which are seen, but at the things which are not seen: for the things which are seen are temporal; but the things which are not seen are eternal.' "[33]

"The apostle Paul again," Peter mused. "That great soldier of the cross. The missionary-traveller-church builder. What tribulations he had suffered, and what glory to God had resulted!

"O Lord," he prayed. "I am troubled and cast down. Help me not to be utterly destroyed. May I willingly bear in my body the dying of the Lord Jesus and share the fellowship of His sufferings. Help me to see beyond this present night and the uncertain tomorrow to that far more exceeding and eternal weight of glory. In this dark place where the temporal things cannot be seen, let me cling to the things that are eternal . . ."

Someone began singing. Others joined him, softly.

Peter's head drooped. The sleepless night, the tension-filled hours of the day, the apprehensions of the morrow had taken their toll. He slept.

IX

Saints in Prison

"And furthermore, consider what the king does for you. If it were not for his protection, highway robbers and bandits would constantly harass you. Your crops and houses would not be safe. The imperial armies, which you persistently scorn, make it possible for you to live in safety." The marshal glowered at the men crouching on the filthy floor in front of him.

One hundred twenty pairs of polite, but unresponsive eyes stared back at him. Their uncompromising silence angered him. He stepped nearer and shook his fist at them. "You . . . you . . . cowards," he stuttered. "Men like myself and these loyal citizens"—he indicated the two soldiers who stood at attention before the cell door—"risk their lives to protect your land from the Turks and to enforce the law while you live comfortably off the fat of the land, storing up riches, never lifting a hand to do your duty to your king and country." He spat contemptuously.

Peter, squatting on his heels, his back against the cold stone wall at the rear of the crowd, shifted his weight restlessly and wondered when the lecture would be over.

This was their fourth day in the dungeon beneath the Falkenstein castle. For the last three of those days, this determined marshal from Vienna had visited the cell and attempted, by appeals

115

to their loyalty, offers of reward, and threats, to enlist them as soldiers in the armies of Austria. The Turkish hordes were threatening his eastern borders, and King Ferdinand was anxious to train more soldiers to defend his domain.

In this sixteenth century, however, a new spirit had sprung up among the common people—it was an age of progress. The advances in medicine and science, improvements in transportation and increasing ease of travel, and the invention of the printing press had lifted the masses from the Dark Ages and placed in them a desire for better things. They questioned the centuries-old institutions and methods. That there existed among the king's citizens an element which rebelled against the supreme authority of the state church and, moreover, refused to take up arms in defense of the country in which they dwelled safely, stirred his ire to the limit. He foresaw this new heresy sweeping the land and possibly knocking his very throne from under him. How could one rule a land full of disobedient, independent thinkers who, according to his religious advisors, also consorted with the devil?

In response to this threat, King Ferdinand redoubled his efforts to stamp out the sect known as Anabaptists. To arrest the leaders and travelling evangelists would strike at the root of the matter, he felt. So he had sent this marshal to the little town of Steinborn near the Moravian border to apprehend Peter Riedemann—a notorious and influential heretic who was supposed to be spending time there.

The marshal had orders to arrest any other Anabaptists he found and bring them in, either as prisoners or as potential soldiers. That there was such a large group of the rascals living in this secluded valley had come as a surprise to the marshal. Now that he had succeeded in arresting all their men, he knew the king would look with favour upon him if he could convince them by persuasion or force to give up their foolish faith and become soldiers.

"Now listen." The marshal's tone softened and became almost conciliatory. He stepped forward and addressed the deacons and older men who crouched near him. "A soldier's life is a good one. The wages are substantial. Your wives would be given a portion so that they could live comfortably while you are on duty. Two months of the year you may return home and do as you please.

"As for fighting," he continued, shrugging his shoulders, "of course, no one enjoys killing. But let me tell you this"—his voice dropped to a confidential whisper—"many soldiers serve in the king's armies for years and never harm a soul. You may be called on merely to guard the palace or even to conduct travellers on the highroads. Now that wouldn't be against your religion, would it?" The marshal lifted his head and smiled expectantly at the men, his hard eyes darting over the crowd for some sign of acceptance. There was none.

Beside Peter, a strangling sound broke the stillness. George hastily drew his handkerchief from his pocket and held it against his mouth in an attempt to smother the coughing spasm that shook him.

The marshal glared over the heads of the men and contemplated the cluster of young men along the wall.

"See." He pointed at the still-choking George. "Look what is happening to you, young men. How do you like sitting here in this damp place? You will rapidly lose your health. You are strong and full of energy. This is no place for you. Wouldn't you like to wear a suit of armour and travel over the empire in service to the king?"

"Travel, yes. Suit of armour, no," thought Peter.

"Come, now," the marshal coaxed. "If any one of you will stand to your feet, I will personally conduct you through that door and up to the great hall, where you can dine tonight a free man. Who will stand to serve your king?"

No one stirred. The marshal's lips tightened, and he drew himself up straight. "All right." The placating tone was gone, and his voice was harsh. "Maybe a few days on bread and water will help you change your minds. Your wives and little ones will starve too while you sit here like a bunch of stubborn sheep. At least you could do your duty like men for their sakes." He turned to leave. At the door he paused. "If you will not volunteer, we have other ways of enlisting men, you know." With this parting threat, he left them.

"Well, Lukas," Caspar began, "you were always talking horses. Wouldn't you like to be part of the king's cavalry?"

"I would like to have a horse," admitted Lukas, "but not under those circumstances."

"We are soldiers already," Andreas reminded them. "Soldiers of a far greater King. The battles we fight are fiercer than an earthly soldier faces." Seeing question marks on the faces of some younger boys, he explained, "Take right now. We are all battling with despair, uncertainty, boredom, fear. If we let these things rob us of our joy and faith, we are losing the battle. Our enemy, Satan, is trying to destroy us. He wants us to give up our service for the King of kings because we find that service too hard."

"What do you think he meant by that last statement?" asked Caspar.

"I don't know."

"Perhaps they intend to drag us bodily into the front line of battle," Peter ventured.

"Wouldn't do them any good," Caspar declared. "They couldn't make us fight."

"Let's go see what the men are saying," Peter suggested.

Brushing their clothing, the knot of young men circled the cell and stood on the edge of a cluster of men.

"Wish we'd know how the women and children are faring."

"Do you think they really are without food, or was he just trying to scare us?"

"I wonder if they have raided the food stores."

"Most likely they've taken everything in sight."

"There are the cattle and fowl."

"They may have seized those too."

"Do you suppose they've discovered the emergency food stores?"

The emergency stores! Peter hoped they were safe. It was probable, as the men said, that the soldiers had confiscated all the available food, but had they discovered the secret trap doors, one in the schoolroom and one under the bedding in the stable, that led to the concealed cellars? It was Grandfather Boewen who had advocated the building of such stores. Many of the brethren had scoffed at the idea, thinking it a waste of time, but in the end the extra cellars had been dug and each fall a sizable portion of the harvest had been stowed there against such a time as this.

"Isn't there some way we could find out how the women are faring?" a young father pleaded.

"I'm sure the Lord is providing His grace, but we would rest easier if we were sure they were unharmed and not in need."

"What about Garth?"

What about Garth? This question had been voiced before. Garth, they had learned, was the name of the shuffling, grumbling jailor who regularly visited their cell with food and water. Aside from the marshal and his soldiers, Garth and his houseboys were the only contacts they had had with the outside world. Although the old man complained at great length about the extra work these prisoners and the soldiers from Vienna were causing him, some of the men felt that his surliness was only a front that concealed a soft heart. Others were not ready to trust him.

Michel Kramer was of the opinion that if he were approached in the right way and at the right time, Garth might be ready to convey a message to the wives at home. "Why don't we just ask Garth if he's heard any news of them?" he suggested now. "If he seems reluctant to talk, we don't have to proceed with attempts at messages."

"Suppose he is sympathetic," another opposed. "The house servants he brings with him might thwart our plans."

"He talked about the girls in the tower," reminded Brother Joseph.

The men smiled at the mental picture of Garth, standing just inside their cell door yesterday, rubbing his hand repeatedly over his bald pate and muttering, "Soldiers! Prisoners! Fetch and carry! Take this; take that! 'Twill be the death of me old bones yet. Ladees? Ladees you say?" His voice rose and his expression became more doleful than ever. "Ladees everywhere you go. Ladees in the kitchen, ladees in the hall, ladees in the chambers, ladees on the stairs. Thick as flies; always in your way. Everywhere I go—ladees. Bah!" Then as though he sensed he had said too much, he growled, "Hurry up. Finish that food. Don't have all day. Get on with it!"

And so they had learned that the girls must have been let out of the tower and were being used as cooks and cleaning women in the castle.

The boys soon tired of the debate concerning whether or not to risk trusting Garth to get a message to either the girls in the castle or the women in Steinborn.

Peter stared at the four rectangles of light on the tower wall. The sun was evidently shining today, because the four spots were brighter than on previous days. He sighed restlessly. The stone wall that surrounded them was so confining. Sometimes he felt the urge to just throw himself bodily against that wooden door and escape into the sunlight again. "For thy sake we are killed all the day long."[34] Well, they were not actually being killed— not yet anyway. The marshal had threatened several times to torture some of the brethren to reveal their supposed hidden treasures and divulge the whereabouts of Peter Riedemann. Peter tried not to think about the instruments of torture that were used on Anabaptist prisoners. Right now, the stifling conditions and boredom of the chamber felt like slow death to him. He shook himself. "Keep your mind active." He remembered the advice of his father when he had expressed his restlessness.

"Let's work on our memory passage," he suggested to Caspar and Lukas, who had been staring at the four notches carved into the frame of the door, as if by staring they could hasten the passage of time.

Brother Joseph had appointed himself schoolmaster of the prison, and had assigned all the young men to learn Paul's letter to the church at Philippi. Since their notebooks had been seized, it was necessary to draw on the memories of the entire group in order to piece together the whole book. Most of the men had joined them in this mental exercise. In the previous days, they had memorized chapter one.

Hearing the boys chanting their verses, Brother Joseph detached himself from a knot of men and joined them.

"Are you ready for chapter two?" he asked.

The other young men gathered around him, and some older men interrupted their various conversations to listen.

"Chapter two begins with instructions of personal relationships," Brother Joseph recalled. " 'If there be therefore any consolation in Christ, if any comfort of love, if any joy of the Spirit.' "[35]

"I believe that should be 'fellowship of the Spirit,' " a grey-bearded man interjected politely.

Brother Joseph looked questioningly about him, and several men agreed that the word was *fellowship,* rather than *joy.*

"I'm sorry," the schoolmaster apologized. "Looks like I need this class too. Now let's begin again . . ."

For an hour, the men prompted each other and recited the passage over and over. Finally Caspar stretched his long arms over his head. "I think it's exercise time." Mathes Legeder took the hint. "You lead out, Caspar."

A little self-consciously, Caspar began trotting around the circumference of the tower dungeon, and others either fell in behind him or else squeezed into the centre of the cell to make room. Soon there was a solid circle of men running, hopping or skipping around the room.

Grandfather Boewen and the dozen other older or sickly men who rested near him chuckled at the ludicrous sight of Big Peter's flapping coattails and short Brother Jacob's pumping knees. Soon others were smiling and even laughing breathlessly as one former soldier led them in a series of arm-flinging, body-bending gymnastics.

These frequent exercise sessions helped the men to pass the time, sent the blood pounding into their unused limbs, and helped to warm their chilled bodies. They also stirred up the dirt and smells. Peter wrinkled his nose as he stooped to touch his toes, over and over again.

Their exertions so absorbed them that Garth and his assistants were through the door before the men were aware of their arrival. They watched, fascinated, while the prisoners sheepishly adjusted their suspenders, buttoned their coats, and tried to smooth their hair.

Finally Garth came to his senses. "Fun and games?" he snorted. "Fun and games on bread and water. 'Give them bread and water,' he says. 'What am I to do with all the table scraps?' I says. 'Give 'em to the dogs,' he tells me. 'All right,' I says, 'I'll give 'em to the dogs.' Here they are."

His helpers had filled the two wooden water containers beside the door and emptied a bag of black bread onto the floor. Now they brought from the hallway the usual tub of leftover meat bones, boiled potatoes, and crumbs.

The men glanced at each other significantly. Those who had held out for using Garth as a message bearer were telegraphing with their eyes: "See, he's going against the marshal's orders and feeding us more than bread and water." They all watched Mathes Legeder. But he hesitated.

At that moment, Brother Jacob stepped towards the jailor. "Sir," he addressed him respectfully. 'We have some men here with severe coughs. I am a physician, but I cannot help them without medicines. If they are not relieved, they may become sicker, and I'm afraid more of us will be taken ill as well."

"What am I supposed to do?" Garth, sidetracked from his habitual line of thinking, forgot to mumble.

"Do you have anyone in the castle who can fix poultices?" Jacob asked. "Or can someone brew some sage tea for us?"

Garth muttered confusedly, "Poultices? Sage tea?"

Becoming bolder, Jacob went on. "And the situation could be improved with fresh bedding. This is wet." He kicked at the ancient refuse. "A small fire would help also," he hinted.

"Fire?" Garth exploded. "Fire! Hah! You think they'll let you have fire? Burn the whole place down, ye would. Fire indeed." He turned and stomped from the room. "Poultices, medicines, fresh straw, fire!" he grumbled down the corridor.

Michel Blauer turned to Brother Jacob. "Maybe you went too far in asking for a fire," he reproved.

"If the marshal hears of our requests, we may be rationed to less than bread and water," another added.

"But will the marshal hear of it?"

"That is the question," agreed Michel Kramer.

Peter, Caspar, and George were licking their fingers after their meal when Andreas approached, along with a stocky young Philippite. Peter had been aware of the ten Philippite brethren, who had been arrested along with their hosts. He had felt sorry for them—travelling so far to escape persecution in their own land to seek out a group with whom to fellowship, and then to be so rudely apprehended. They were all married men, however, and had been engrossed in conversation with the local men their own age. Peter would have liked to meet them personally but had been too shy to take the initiative to walk up and introduce himself.

"This is Johan," Andreas now introduced his friend. Peter saw that, up close, Johan looked rather younger than he had expected, except for the deep furrows in his broad forehead.

Introductions completed, Andreas explained, "Johan and I have much in common. He has, in a sense, lost his bride too."

"Then you aren't married?" George asked.

"Yes," Johan said with a slurred accent. "I am but . . ."

Andreas told it for him. "He has a wife, but she is not a believer." The boys looked curiously at the newcomer. How could this be?

Johan explained. "I was making plans for my marriage when the responsibilities and seriousness of the step struck me. I felt that the church wasn't giving a man much guidance as to how to have a godly home. About that time I was sent to harvest grain on the estate of a man where several Philippite brethren were working. From them I heard the message of the Gospel and learned that I could have Jesus as my personal Saviour. I surrendered my life to the Lord and was blessed with peace and the assurance that He would help me to be a good husband and father.

"I was certain my wife-to-be would eagerly embrace my new faith, but she was not impressed. Oh, she wasn't angry. She smiled sweetly and accepted my explanations so calmly that I was convinced it would only be a matter of time until she too would be a Christian."

"Do you mean you married an unbeliever?"

Johan nodded gravely. "I loved her very much. I thought I couldn't give her up. We were married by the priest at her insistence. I was not yet baptised," he hastened to explain. "So although the brethren advised against it, I married my Lise." He shook his head. "Disobedience to the Word never pays. I soon saw that, under her sweetness, Lise was very determined. She went alone to mass while I met with the brethren. It was a house divided against itself."

"Where is she now?" asked Caspar.

"When the heretic hunters came to our estate two months ago, we were forced to flee to the mountains. My wife returned to her parents' home."

There was a sympathetic silence.

Argh, Argh! George doubled over, coughing violently. He hastily reached for his pocket and stepped away from the group, but not before Peter had seen the dark stains on the handkerchief he pressed to his mouth.

"The truth always brings separation," Andreas mused.

Peter thought about that statement later that night as he lay on the floor beside his father.

Separation. Andreas from Bridgit, Johan from his wife. Himself from Mother, Maria, Ursula, and Baby Johann.

Separation not only from people but also from hopes and aspirations.

Separation from all that had meant so much to him.

Separation, perhaps, from life itself.

Could he say with the apostle Paul, "For to me to live is Christ, and to die is gain"?[36]

It was Garth himself who the next day unexpectedly supplied the means for them to communicate with the women.

The men nearest the door looked up indifferently at the arrival of their morning meal. Their surprised exclamations alerted the others, and they all stared incredulously at the tall, prim woman who followed the serving boys into their dungeon.

"Sister Agathe!" they cried joyously, surging towards her.

Garth held up his hands in alarm. "Heh, Heh! Stop, Stop. Where is that one that wanted the medicines?" His nearsighted eyes darted over the men's faces.

Brother Jacob eased himself forward. "Here I am."

"Here's a nurse. Tell her what ye need—and be quick about it."

Sister Agathe had stood silently peering into the gloomy chamber. Now she stepped forward, one hand to her face. "What a stench. How can they live in this filthy atmosphere?" she demanded of Garth.

He gave her a baleful look. "Woman—I brought you here to look after some sick men—now look. Be quick." He turned to direct his helpers, grumbling under his breath, "Bah! Women! Talk, talk, talk; boss, boss, boss. Can't turn around but what some woman tells you what to do . . ."

Brother Jacob led Sister Agathe to the feverish men who now numbered five. In a loud voice, he said, "These men should have hot mustard poultices to break their cough." And in a whisper, he added rapidly, *"How are you being treated?"*

Sister Agathe caught on quickly. She answered loudly, "I think there may be some mustard in the kitchen. I will have the cook prepare the poultices." And under her breath, she said, *"We are fine. We are cleaning and cooking. All are well and in good spirits."*

"Now this man"—Brother Jacob bent over one invalid—"should have more blankets. *Have you news from the women in town?"*

"I will ask the castellan for blankets. *No word, but several beggar women come regularly to the kitchen. One I'm sure is Sister Boewen."*

"And could you prepare some hot sage tea with honey? *Can you get a message to her?*"

Sister Agathe stepped towards the impatient jailer. "I will send some tea as well." She turned slightly. "*I will try.*"

Then she was gone.

All but those nearest him had been unaware of the second conversation that had gone on between Brother Jacob and Sister Agathe.

"Praise the Lord," Michel Blauer said for all of them. "Now, we must prepare a message."

"I have pen nibs," one man offered, delving into an inner pocket. "Who has paper?"

There were blank faces and dismayed looks as they realised their lack.

"And what about ink?"

"I think I might have some paper." It was one of the Philippite brethren. While they all looked on, he sat down and began to unlace his shoe.

"Is he going to cut up his shoe?" wondered Peter.

The man, having removed his footwear, proceeded to draw from it a thick insole. As he peeled it apart in layers, the onlookers could see that it had been constructed from many sheets of heavy paper. But as he spread the layers one by one across his knees, he shook his head. "They're all damp," he declared.

The other Philippites began removing their shoes. One of them found several sheets of paper in the middle of his insoles that were dryer than the rest.

"Those will do," the men agreed.

"And I have the ink." A tall Philippite waved his hand-knitted sock above his head. "I see that my insoles are all blue from the dye in these new socks. If we soak the socks in water, it may make dark enough ink to use."

Accordingly, the message was written in Brother Joseph's scholarly script, with sock dye ink, on used insole paper. It read simply,

> Sisters,
> We are well. Have you food? Are you well?
> Be faithful.
>
> The Brethren

The letter was folded into a tight square.

Later when Sister Agathe returned with a kettle of hot tea and the poultices, Garth stood by the door, closely watching her every move.

Peter could not be sure, but he thought he saw the note pass from Jacob to his helper as they arranged the poultice on an invalid's chest.

Before leaving, Sister Agathe surveyed the chamber critically. "These men should have fresh straw," she complained to Garth. "Lying on such dampness is unhealthy. There is lots of straw in the stable. You could spare some for them."

Garth glared at her wordlessly.

She went on, "And they are too crowded here. Don't you have more space in this great place?"

Garth's face grew red with indignation. He stuttered, "Woman! Come out of here. Straw indeed. Fetch and carry. Make tea. Get straw. More space. What next?" He practically pushed Agathe into the corridor.

The door closed after them, but the men could still hear Agathe saying, "Some clean straw, a few blankets . . ." and Garth mumbling after her.

Peter smiled to himself. With Sister Agathe on the staff, there was hope that conditions might improve. And maybe they would soon know whether the women were all right. But would the message ever reach them? Would Grandfather Boewen's daughter ever return to beg at the castle kitchen? And would Sister Agathe have an opportunity to slip the note to her?

The owner of the knife was carving the seventh notch into the door when Garth surprised them by requesting a dozen men to accompany him upstairs.

Mathes Legeder quickly pointed out the privileged ones—or was it to be *torture?* Who knew? The remainder waited in suspense.

In a quarter of an hour, the men were back bearing large bundles of fresh straw. They dumped it on the floor before hurrying away for more.

With exclamations of delight, Peter joined in kicking the fresh bedding around, covering up their dung-heap bed with something dry and clean. He was amazed at how high such a simple thing could lift his spirits. He almost looked forward to that night.

The men were a long time coming back the second time. What was happening? Peter kicked his way through the straw to Caspar and Lukas.

"Do you think the marshal's threats were real?" he asked.

Caspar shrugged. "He claims he's raided the village and our women are starving, but we don't know if that is true."

"Wish we'd get a message back from the women." Lukas sounded discouraged.

"Now he's starting to talk about sending priests to investigate our beliefs." Caspar referred to the marshal's lecture of that morning in which he had angrily attacked their disrespect for the church and threatened dire consequences if they would not recant.

He had hinted darkly of "other" ways to persuade people.

Where were the men?

When they did return much later with more straw, they brought good news.

Andreas told the boys, "We had to help clean out stables. The stableboys were all in a bustle, currying horses and mending harnesses. We gathered that the marshal and his soldiers are preparing to return to Vienna."

"What a relief. But what of us?" Martin asked.

Andreas shook his head. "I don't know. Nothing was said about that."

"They'll just leave us here to rot," Martin said bitterly.

"Christ is here with us. Let's leave the future in His hands," Andreas reassured him.

"Did you see Bridgit?" Peter asked.

"No, but I did catch glimpses of some of the girls as we returned. They flashed smiles, so I gather they are in good spirits."

When Sister Agathe returned that night to minister to the sick, who now numbered eight, she was able to whisper to one of them that the note had been safely passed to the "beggar" woman at the kitchen door.

"But my God shall supply all your need according to his riches in glory by Christ Jesus."[37]

Their needs were reduced to the basics here, Peter reflected. And yet the verse was still true. Their needs, not necessarily their wants, were being supplied. They had food. In spite of the marshal's sentence of bread and water, Garth's thrifty soul rebelled at throwing away the food left by the soldiers. They were blessed with the fellowship of one another, and now they might soon be reassured concerning the circumstances of the dear ones left behind. The Lord had provided clean straw and medical help for the sick. Peter fell asleep counting his blessings.

Accepted Into the Brotherhood

"Well, he's left." Caspar idly picked a straw from the floor in front of him and began tearing it into slivers.

"That's a relief," Peter agreed. He stretched his legs out in front of him. The shoes that had looked so new and shiny on that long ago night (was it only eight days ago?) when he had so eagerly dressed for the conference were now dull and shabby-looking. His best suit was filthy and smelly, but there was no means of washing clothes or even hands in this place.

"What now?" Caspar asked bluntly, tossing aside the shredded straw and selecting a new one.

"What do you mean?"

"I mean, what happens to us now that the marshal and his soldiers have left?"

"I wish I knew." Peter crossed one foot over the other. "We thought we lived in uncertainty before, but now—"

"Not knowing what lies ahead is almost worse than knowing we had been condemned."

"Don't be too sure about that. We haven't faced that yet." Peter's mind still retained the memory of that burning in Nikolsburg.

"All we can do is face one day at a time and believe that the Lord is in control of our lives, planning every situation." George spoke for the first time.

"We really can't count on tomorrows anymore," Peter mused.

"I thank the Lord for the grace He gives each day," George said, his voice husky.

Peter was silent. George's cough was so much worse, and his friend's thin face grew paler each day. George likely could not count on too many tomorrows even if they were released from prison, yet he seemed to accept their situation more calmly than Peter.

"I can't help thinking that all of us would be of more use to the Lord outside this prison. Why, we may sit here for ten years. Some have, you know. That marshal may return to Vienna and promptly forget all about us."

"I doubt that," Caspar said with a smile.

"Well, he may be called to duty somewhere else and not have time to attend further to our circumstances."

"On the other hand," Caspar said hopefully, "we may be released tomorrow."

"Or sentenced to death."

"Would that matter?" The boys looked up, startled, to see Brother Jacob standing over them.

"I couldn't help but overhear your conversation," he apologized. He squatted near them and repeated his question, "Would that matter?"

Peter studied the straw between his feet.

" 'For to me . . . to die is gain,' "[38] the older man reminded the boys. "What is the Christian's main purpose in life?"

"To glorify God," Caspar answered promptly.

"If by our death we can bring glory to God, we should earnestly desire it. If, by sitting in this dungeon, we can glorify Him, we should rejoice."

"Grandfather said that when the seed is sown in suffering, the harvest is great. How can there be a harvest when we aren't able to reach souls?" Peter asked.

"Why don't you ask Grandfather?"

Peter's eyes followed Jacob's as they sought out the old man. In spite of the crippling arthritis that caused him much discomfort in the dampness of the dungeon, Grandfather Boewen was almost always surrounded by men. His advice was sought by the deacons; his encouragement sustained them all.

Today there were only one or two other old men engaged in conversation with Grandfather, so the boys followed Jacob to his side and presented Peter's question to him.

Grandfather winced as he used his cane to shift his shoulders into a new position. "So you think the harvest here is rather skimpy?" His faded blue eyes searched Peter's brown ones.

Peter glanced around. "All of us here are already believers. Who is there to witness to?"

"There are Garth and the marshal and the kitchen boys who come with our food."

"But we don't even get a chance to talk to any of them," Peter pointed out.

"There are other ways to witness," the old man reminded Peter.

"You mean by our lives?"

Grandfather nodded. "If we can remain cheerful and optimistic, those who come in contact with us will be attracted to the Spirit that reigns in us."

Peter accepted this rebuke quietly.

"There is another harvest too that I can see developing here." Others had gathered round now and were listening eagerly to Grandfather's words. Peter wrinkled his brow in puzzlement.

"I see a ripening of the virtues and the fruit of the Spirit in the souls of each of you."

The fruit of the Spirit. Galatians 5. Love, joy, peace, longsuffering, gentleness, goodness, faith, . . . Peter turned his attention again to Grandfather.

"Here in this place, your spirit is being tried and tested. Remember that gold and silver are fired in intense heat before they can be free of impurities and fashioned into beautiful vessels. So your souls are being tried and tested in a new way. Can you tell me how?" He looked searchingly into the faces of the youths before him.

"Longsuffering, for sure, is something we have to exercise here," Peter pointed out. "And faith," he added.

"It is certainly an exercise in faith," Caspar agreed. "If we didn't have the faith to believe that Christ is interceding for us every moment, we would be quite miserable."

Grandfather nodded his approval.

"We have peace," George pointed out.

"What about meekness?" Grandfather prompted. "Are you able to accept this situation meekly, without rebelling? What thoughts flooded your minds when the marshal spoke to us?"

The boys were silent. Peter recalled Martin's statement, "I hope the marshal and his soldiers are attacked by bandits on the way to Vienna." He had to admit that, though he knew better, it was hard not to wish some ill on the marshal. He had some cultivation to do in that area of his spirit, he realised.

"How about gentleness and goodness?" Caspar asked.

"We can practise those towards each other," Andreas answered.

"That's right," Brother Jacob spoke up from beside Grandfather. "With so many of us crowded into one room, so much idle time, and so little comfort, it would be easy to become irritated."

"Oh, there is another weeding job that needs to be done," Peter thought. Lukas had a habit of standing and staring for long periods of time at some individual, his arms crossed in front of him and a lofty expression on his face, as though he were judging that person. More than once Peter had found himself irked by what he called Lukas's "kingly stance." One man constantly cleared his throat noisily. This kept Peter awake at night. And even Caspar's occasional attempts at humour annoyed him.

Caspar confessed, "When the food is ladled out, it is difficult not to imagine that others are getting a larger portion."

Several men smiled sympathetically, as Caspar's insatiable appetite was common knowledge.

Grandfather agreed. "Perhaps you will learn temperance as well," he suggested.

Caspar nodded. These lessons were not easy, he felt.

"There is one no one has mentioned."

"Joy," George supplied quietly.

"And if anyone of us has that, it is he," Peter thought, looking fondly at his friend.

George was hardly able to sing. It set off his coughing. But whenever time hung heavy, he would say, "Sing something," and the songs he liked best were those that spoke of heaven, or Christian victory, or songs of praise.

The little session with Grandfather had given Peter much food for thought. As he prayed and meditated in the darkness before falling asleep that night, the Spirit spoke to him about his attitudes. He had suffered much discouragement and even lack of peace at the disruption of his life and the crumbling of his plans. He had felt that his desire to be a missionary was the Lord's will for his life. Now he saw that he had derived a great deal of pleasure from the thought of being well known and popular—like Peter Riedemann. His desires were carnal ambitions that fed his own pride and self-interest. He did have an honest desire to see souls saved, but he had imagined the glory he might receive through this. Now he saw that the Lord was asking him to yield himself to His service unconditionally.

"Use me, Lord," Peter prayed, "when and where and how You will. Mold me into a vessel fit for Your service. Help me to give up my own hopes and selfish desires and desire only that I be found acceptable in Your sight. . . ."

With his surrender, Peter felt the seeds of joy swelling and bursting within him. "Grandfather was right," he thought drowsily. "A dungeon can be a cathedral if God is there."

The next day was Sunday. Although much time had been spent every day of the week in memorizing Scripture, praying, singing, and spiritual discussion, the deacons had agreed that the Lord's Day should be observed in a special way.

So on this morning, the men rose with an expectant air. There was a general attempt to make themselves presentable. Peter tried to brush some lustre into the dull leather of his shoes by rubbing them with his coattail. He arranged his hair as best he could with his fingers and even used some of his precious portion of water to wipe his face with his handkerchief.

The men seated themselves in orderly rows rather than gathering in the usual scattered formation. Brothers Michel Blauer, Michel Kramer, and Mathes Legeder took their places, facing the congregation.

The sisters' voices were conspicuous in their absence, but perhaps the girls in the castle above heard the joyous strains as the dungeon walls rang with the joyful singing of the brethren.

Each of the deacons spoke in turn. They chose topics pertinent to the present circumstances. Peter, his new commitment fresh in his mind, drank in every word. Michel Blauer spoke of Joseph. His story especially appealed to the young men. Joseph had been falsely accused and brought low through no fault of his own. During his prison years, although he had no reason to believe his fate would be altered, he simply continued faithful. "I have faith that we too will be spared for better things after this trial is over."

Peter sat up straight. Had he heard right? Peter wondered. Had Michel really said he felt that they might be delivered? In all their prayers, the men had asked only that the Lord's will be done. No one had ever expressed certainty that they would be released. What had prompted the aged deacon to say what he had?

Michel Kramer's sermon was on consecration. It was a confirmation of what Peter had experienced in his own soul the evening before.

Mathes Legeder then reviewed for them the ordinance of holy baptism.

"Our Lord commanded his disciples in his last instructions to them to go and teach all nations, and baptise them in the Name of the Father, Son, and Holy Ghost. . . .

"Philip told the Ethiopian eunuch that if he would believe with all his heart, he could be baptised. So the applicant for baptism must first believe that Christ has died for his sins. . . .

"This belief in Jesus must be accompanied by genuine repentance. Sorrow for past sin and willingness to turn from his evil works must be evidenced in the life of the one seeking water baptism. . . ."

After briefly discussing the act of baptism as practised by the brotherhood, the young deacon sat down and Michel Blauer rose.

"We regret that we have among us a group of young brethren who have not received this ordinance."

A thrill ran up Peter's spine. He listened eagerly.

"The class of applicants was prepared to receive water baptism as soon as a bishop brother would arrive to conduct the service. Now we find ourselves in unusual circumstances; and after much prayer, we have reached some decisions concerning this matter." Michel Blauer looked around to be certain he had everyone's attention. "If it seems good to you, we are suggesting that these young men be considered one with us, even though their vows have not been sealed by the ordinance of baptism." He paused to give the men time to consider.

Big Peter spoke. "This seems good to me. Our young men may face questioning and persecution. If they are not freely accepted as brethren, it will be easier for them to yield to temptation. In their own minds, they may have questions about their standing in the church of Jesus Christ."

Another father rose. "Would we accept the applicants without an examination or a public testimony from each of them?"

"No," Brother Michel assured him. "We want to question them carefully and cause them to realise that this identification with the believers will doubtless mean greater tribulations for them."

"Will the rest of the bruderhofs and our bishops accept this decision?" someone asked.

"We mean to write a letter explaining our action and asking for the approval of the Christian churches at large."

Following more discussion, the class of applicants was called to stand before the congregation.

How different this was from the ceremony Peter had anticipated.

"The outward baptism with water does not constitute entrance into the kingdom of God; nor does the visible element of water contain any power or holiness; neither is it able to give any grace or salvation; but baptism is the outward sign of the entrance of the Holy Spirit and the regeneration that a man has received already in his heart," Michel Kramer said.

"Although, normally, baptism is the instrument by which a person is recognised as a member of the church and gives one the right to share in Communion, we are willing to accept you as brethren upon confession of your faith with the understanding that you do desire baptism and will submit to it if the Lord sees fit to give the opportunity." Mathes searched the solemn faces before him.

"You are aware that under questioning you will be more severely tried if you say you are an Anabaptist. This step will mean greater hardship for you. But the alternative—to not become a part of the brotherhood now in order to escape persecution—is to have your Lord deny you later. Are you willing to give your word to cast your lot with God's people?" Michel Blauer's eyes filled with tears. In his wisdom, he knew only too well what the commitment might mean, and his heart went out to the young men before him.

One by one the boys gave their testimony. Not one wished to be left out.

The Philippite brethren were also accepted by the brotherhood, and they agreed to share the fate of this group. Two brethren who had fallen into sin confessed their wrongs and were accepted back into fellowship.

After the service, more insole paper was appropriated and Brother Joseph painstakingly recorded their decision. The letter was surreptitiously passed to Sister Agathe later that afternoon.

Peter was skeptical about whether the letter would ever reach the other churches or be acknowledged by a bishop. Suppose it did make it out of the castle gate; it would still have to be sent from Steinborn, and how could that happen? No one knew whether the women were being guarded. Who would there be to carry the message out of the valley?

At least they had done their best, and even though their position was not recognised by the larger brotherhood, Peter was satisfied that the men who shared this imprisonment accepted him as a brother.

Peter lay with his eyes open in the shadowy dawn of Monday morning, wondering what had roused him. There it was again. A low moan from across the room. He sat up, rubbing the sleep from his eyes. The moaning grew louder. Through the gloom he could see the form of Brother Jacob bending over one of the sick men. Peter stood up and maneuvered his way carefully over the slumbering bodies to Jacob's side. "What is wrong?"

The old doctor sighed wearily. "This brother is much worse. His fever is high. I have been sponging him most of the night, but I cannot bring the fever down. I am afraid he will soon go into convulsions."

"Here, let me." Peter took the wet rag from Jacob's hand. The older man showed him how to massage the patient's wrists, forehead, and feet. The man continued to toss and moan while Peter tended him and Brother Jacob ministered to the other sick ones in his care.

It was colder this morning, Peter realised as he refilled a cup from the water bucket. Cold he was acquainted with. Like all small boys, he had often played out in the snow too long and had come home crying to have his mother rub his red hands and feet. He had known the agony of thawing a frozen nose after a day of cutting wood. But this cold was different. It was not so intense, but there was no relief. It was an uncomfortable condition of never being quite warm enough. It lowered the resistance of the men, and a slight cough or head cold quickly became worse. The sick ones suffered the most.

When Sister Agathe came, she was much distressed about the deteriorating health of the men. "Haven't you a dryer place, or at least another cell so these men can have more room?" she badgered Garth.

Garth glared balefully at her. "More room now. Dry place.

Women. Bah! Next you'll want to take over the great hall."

"And these men must have fresh water. This is warm and stale." Sister Agathe swirled a finger through the tepid water in the container by the door.

"Boss, boss, boss," grumbled Garth, but he motioned to his helpers to empty the bucket and refill it with fresh water from the well upstairs.

"That was a good suggestion," Peter overheard Sister Agathe whisper to Brother Jacob. "I shall see whether the worst of these cases can be moved upstairs."

"Will the castellan allow that?"

"The castellan seems to concern himself little with his prisoners. I have the impression that we are here under orders from Vienna, and the castle authorities have no choice but to accommodate us against their wishes. Old Garth has been in service here so long, he does what he pleases. I doubt he's had to work much at all for years and is not too happy about this unexpected duty that has been thrust upon him."

"We can praise the Lord for their leniency, but, dear Sister, don't push your advantage too far, or they may tire of our many demands."

Sister Agathe made no promises.

"She will get her way," Peter thought fondly as he watched her unbending, determined back march through the doorway in front of Garth.

XI

An Inquisition

The next day their morning meal was not delivered until nearly noon. When it did arrive, and the kitchen helpers had hastily retreated, Garth stepped to the side and, bowing obsequiously, motioned four richly attired men into the cell.

The brethren regarded the newcomers with mingled curiosity and apprehension.

The four officials, easily recognised by the display of insignia on their chests, placed their polished boots carefully as they moved into the room. They looked about them disdainfully.

"So, these are the Anabaptists," one sneered.

"A fine-looking lot they are," another mocked.

"Must we conduct our business in this filthy place?" a third one asked, touching a lace-edged handkerchief delicately to his nose.

The first officer was quick to respond. "No, we can interrogate them upstairs. You and you and you"—he pointed rapidly at six men—"come with us immediately." Then he turned and made a hurried exit, followed by his companions.

As the six designated brethren passed into the corridor, those in the cell called after them, "God go with you."

"Be faithful."

"We will pray for you."

Peter's porridge seemed to stick in this throat. The hunger pains that had nagged him all morning had wrapped themselves into a hard knot in his stomach. Big Peter was among the six.

"Not hungry?" Caspar had speedily disposed of his portion and was looking hungrily at Peter's.

"You can have my share."

"You sure?" Caspar hesitated, remembering Brother Joseph's admonition to practise temperance.

"I can't eat for wondering what they will do to Father."

"They probably don't have many instruments of torture here in this castle."

"How do you know they won't take them away to some other place?" Peter returned bleakly. "I might never see Father again." His voice choked on the last words. It was hard enough to be separated from Mother, Ursula, Maria, and Baby Johann. It had been such a comfort to have his father near during these days. He thought of that glimpse through the frost-rimmed windowpane of Mother clasping her hands in prayer. She was still praying for them, he knew. Now he would have to do the same for Father.

"At least you've had your father up until now," Caspar said softly.

Peter glanced sharply at his cousin. "I'm sorry," he faltered. Poor Caspar. He was always optimistic, and his faith that the Lord would work things out in His own time had never wavered. But of course he had missed his father. How could Peter have been so insensible to his hurt?

"I don't know where he is," Casper went on, staring up at the small slits in the wall. "Was he warned not to return to Steinborn? Was he captured, along with Brother Riedemann, in Nikolsburg? Did the soldiers wait and seize them as they entered the valley? I just wish I knew where he was."

"God knows," Peter replied, finding himself in the role of comforter.

Many private and communal prayers went up that day for the safety of those who were under questioning.

When the men had not returned by nightfall, Peter again found himself battling Giant Fear. As he wrestled in prayer, the Comforter gave him the assurance that the angels were watching over his father and all those who put their faith in God.

In the following days, Peter came to appreciate more deeply the passage the boys were committing to memory. It was amazing how these words penned so many centuries ago could meet their need now.

"Yea doubtless, and I count all things but loss for the excellency of the knowledge of Christ Jesus my Lord: for whom I have suffered the loss of all things, and do count them but dung, that I may win Christ."[39]

As they worked on the passage, Brother Joseph directed their thoughts to the life of Christ, who humbled Himself and took upon Him the form of a servant, suffering the death of the cross that He might win their eternal souls. Together they had studied Jesus' teachings, His mode of soul winning, His character and His way of life. It would take a dozen lifetimes to attain the goal of becoming truly Christlike, and then one would still have room to grow, Peter decided.

Peter continued to help Brother Jacob relieve the suffering of the sick among them. He wiped fevered brows, searched for dryer straw, and rubbed Grandfather's arthritic limbs with horse liniment, which was the best Sister Agathe could supply. The poultices had to be placed and removed at intervals so they would not burn. Some of the invalids had no appetite for the coarse prison fare and had to be coaxed to take nourishment. Peter was happy for something to do and, in serving others, he nurtured the seeds of goodness and compassion in his own soul.

When Big Peter and the other five men had been absent for two days, there was much speculation as to their fate. Sister Agathe was not able to alleviate the apprehensions of the other prisoners. She had seen nothing of the men, although she mentioned that the officers and their servants were still in the castle.

The third day she had more information. "Bridgit and Barbel, who peel potatoes in the kitchen, say that food is being carried to one of the towers. They think the men are there. The officers are trying to make us believe they have sent them away. That is all I can tell you."

Sister Agathe handed Peter a pile of new poultices. "Check these carefully before you use them. That houseboy sometimes forgets to put enough paste between the layers." She gave Peter a penetrating look and left him standing there, his hands full of poultices, wondering why she should suddenly be so concerned about their construction. She had been bringing them every day, and they had always been made the same. Maybe there was a new servant preparing them now.

Peter set down the pile and began going through them one by one. Brother Jacob questioned him. "What are you doing?"

"Sister Agathe said I should check these. I thought I might as well do it right away while it is light enough to see."

"Check for what?" Brother Jacob paused with a bottle of liniment in his hand.

"I don't know. She said something about them not being made correctly."

"Only one way to make a poultice." Jacob's voice was impatient. His constant attentions to the sick were draining his energy. Then he turned suddenly and set the bottle on the straw. "Let me help you." He was excited now. He snatched the next cloth from the pile, pulled the layers apart, and set it aside. Another was treated the same. The next— "Here it is!" he cried, waving a yellow-stained poultice in the air.

"What is it?" The men crowded close.

Brother Jacob eagerly tore the cloth layers apart; and there, secured by a thin layer of sticky mustard, lay a letter. He carefully lifted it and wiped the mustard from the back before handing it to Brother Michel Blauer.

Invalids and poultices forgotten, the men waited expectantly as Michel broke the seal and unfolded several sheets of closely written script.

His voice trembling slightly, he read:

> To my dearly beloved brethren in bonds, by the hand of your
> humble servant, Peter Riedemann.

"Riedemann!" the men gasped. "How? . . . What? . . . Where is he?" They quickly fell silent as Mathes continued to read:

> Grace, peace, and mercy from God, the heavenly Father, be
> your portion as you offer daily your sacrifice of praise.
>
> 'Blessed are ye, when men shall revile you, and persecute you,
> and shall say all manner of evil against you falsely, for my sake.
> Rejoice, and be exceeding glad: for great is your reward in heaven:
> for so persecuted they the prophets which were before you.'[40]
>
> 'And every one that hath forsaken houses, or brethren, or sisters,
> or father, or mother, or wife, or children, or lands, for my name's
> sake, shall receive an hundredfold, and shall inherit everlasting life.'[41]
>
> My dear brethren, comfort one another with these words, knowing
> that He who made provision for His own mother, even while in
> the throes of death, has also cared for your mothers, wives, and
> little ones.
>
> I will proceed to inform you of how the Lord graciously led me

to this place and gave His angels charge over us that we were not apprehended by the enemies of the truth.

In His mercy, the Lord delayed my arrival at Nikolsburg. The brethren in Moravia, where I had last ministered, advised against my travelling by public highway, as many officials and soldiers were on the roads for the singular purpose of seizing those who are true soldiers of the cross. I was much distressed at the delay, longing to meet with you and the dear Philippite brethren that we might fellowship together around the Word. Nevertheless, I waited on the Lord, trusting that He would guide my footsteps whither He desired.

At last I was able to make my way by night, with the aid of two sturdy young believers, to a village near Nikolsburg. My guides entered into the city to see if, perchance, anyone from your village had waited for me. They were returning at nightfall, having been unsuccessful in their errand, when a man on a cart drew up beside them and stopped. Fearing that their identity had been discovered and their end had possibly come, the two young men prepared for the worst, but the driver only offered them a ride. When they speedily and courteously refused, the man handed them a pamphlet, chirruped to his horses, and drove on. Glancing at the paper, they discerned that it was written by believers like themselves. They then hastened and overtook the man, whereupon they all greeted each other joyfully.

The Lord, in His goodness, had directed them to your own Brother Guttenhann Hans, who, having waited in vain in Nikolsburg for a week, was returning to Steinborn.

Knowing nothing of what had transpired in his absence, you may imagine our dismay at the scene that awaited us on our arrival.

Driving through the streets, we found them deserted, the shops battered and looted, and the stables empty. We hurried from building to building, encountering no one. We began to fear that the whole congregation had been taken away. At last we entered the dining hall, and here we found the women and children, huddled about the great stove.

I will hasten to assure you that all are well and rejoicing in the Lord, though in much concern over the state of their husbands, fathers, and sons. The king's men had made every effort to find money that they are sure is hidden among us. They seized all the food in the kitchens, the grain in the barns, and the roots in the cellars. But the secret food stores are safe, so the Lord has provided and none go hungry.

On the second day following your apprehension, some children of tender years took some cattle and goats up into the forests on the mountainside to secure them, and not too soon, for the soldiers came that day and led the remaining beasts away. Several women go each day to milk the cows, so there is milk for the little ones. Brother Guttenhann has undertaken to bring in wood enough to keep us warm. You may rest assured that the Lord is providing.

The food stores will not last long. I am encouraging the sisters to go to Moravia and seek refuge with bruderhofs there. But they are reluctant to leave while you are still in the castle. They pray daily for your deliverance.

The wife of Brother Joosen has given birth to a son.

Sister Boewen has gone several times to the castle kitchen disguised as a beggar. It is through her that we received your letters. She fears that some of the servants are becoming suspicious, and she dare not appear too often.

This missive is sent to you by the hand of the peddler, Patlo. He graciously offered to deliver it safely into the hands of Sister Agathe at the castle by some means. God speed him.

Now, to come to the affair of the brethren who have not yet received the rite of baptism. It pleases me much that they are accepted as one with us, on their confession of faith. They have made their calling sure and are willing to suffer for His sake. I will prepare letters to this effect and send them to the churches by the hand of our friend Patlo. We praise the Lord for using him as a vessel and plead before the throne for the salvation of his soul.

I myself plan to remain here to assist Brother Guttenhann in caring for these helpless ones until the Lord directs otherwise.

We will try to devise a plan for your escape, but at present the cares of daily sustenance fall heavily upon us.

May the God of all comfort keep your hearts and minds through Christ Jesus. Encourage one another in the faith, and give yourselves to prayer and fasting that ye may withstand the fiery darts of the wicked one.

Your humble servant,
Peter Riedemann.

The paper rustled in the hush that followed the reading of the letter. Tears of joy and thanksgiving fell freely.

At Peter's side, Casper's deep sigh showed his relief at hearing his father was safe.

Michel Blauer cleared his throat. "Let us pray."

XII

Soldiers or Slaves?

After several days of uncertainty concerning their status, the men who had been taken from the cell for questioning were welcomed back with relief and rejoicing.

While the men surged around them, Peter edged his way through the throng towards Big Peter.

His father's crushing handclasp reassured him that all was well, and he stepped back momentarily while others greeted and questioned the men.

"Where have you been?"

"What did they want?"

"How have you fared?"

After the first flurry of greetings, and the returned brethren were informed briefly of the letter from Brother Riedemann, the men asked for silence so they could tell their story.

"We were conducted to a small room in one of the towers," began Big Peter. "The room had a table and four chairs. You can be sure we made good use of those chairs."

"What a luxury," thought Peter, "to sit in a chair again."

"We were not tortured, but all we were given to eat was black bread with water—and not much of that."

There were exclamations of sympathy. The men nearest the

door hastily checked the food vessel still standing there from their last meal, but as usual, it had been wiped clean by hungry fingers.

"Does anyone have food?" Mathes Legeder questioned the group.

While they all shook their heads, Big Peter demurred with a wave of his hand, "Never mind; we were expecting much worse treatment. Our Lord fasted for forty days, so this was as nothing.

"We were questioned and lectured by the four officials. They had the same theme as the marshal.

"Where was our money hidden? Would we enlist in the king's army? And why will we not support the Holy Church? They used much the same tactics—persuasion, bribery, and then threats.

"They had papers they wished us to sign, confessing that we had sinned against the church by refusing Communion, and that we were guilty of conspiring against the king."

"I can't understand why they are so sure we are wealthy," a brother from among the listeners said.

"It is because we have well-built homes and food to eat—something that not all the common people of Austria enjoy."

"That is not the only reason," an elderly Philippite supplied. "They are afraid that all the Anabaptists are united in planning a major revolt against the authorities. They expected to find not only money but also caches of arms in your possession. Often, our brethren in Moravia were arrested on false charges of securing weapons and plotting rebellion. They think our nonresistance is a cloak for our true intentions."

"What were the results of your questioning?" Michel Kramer asked the six. "Did they give any hint of what they intend to do with us?"

"Yes," Big Peter answered. "They offered us our freedom." He swept his eyes over his fellow prisoners to note their reaction to his announcement. Hope flared in the listless eyes before him, but it was quickly quenched as he added, "If."

"If, what?" a dozen voices clamoured.

"They said that we would all be released immediately if we would promise to scatter."

"Scatter?"

"Yes. If we will separate ourselves into groups of not more than eight adults and settle not closer than twenty miles from each other, they will allow us to go free."

The cell buzzed with conversation.

Peter's thoughts turned somersaults over one another. It was almost too good to be true. Maybe he would be out of here before long. He turned excitedly to Caspar. "Hear that? Free! And they aren't even asking us to give up our faith!"

Caspar was slow to answer.

"Come on!" Peter thumped his cousin's shoulder. "Aren't you excited? Where's George?" He craned his neck and stood on tip-toe to look over heads.

"Aren't they?" Caspar finally asked in a dull voice.

"Aren't they what?" Peter came down onto his heels again and gave Caspar an annoyed look.

"Asking us to give up our faith?"

"Why, no. All we have to do is break up into smaller units."

"What will that do to our faith?"

Peter's exuberance melted. "I don't know," he admitted.

All the men were discussing the same issue.

"Can we comply with that stipulation?" That was the question.

"Groups of eight or less would mean as few as one or two families," one pointed out.

"Twenty miles apart would severely limit our fellowship," another said.

"We would need to dissolve our common treasury and function as individual families."

"The Swiss Brethren do that," someone argued.

Several brethren agreed that it would be possible to continue on in the faith without operating in a community context, but it would not be as convenient or satisfying.

"I don't see why we couldn't accept those conditions," Leonhardt Blöcher argued. "We would still practise the faith as families."

"The early church had all things common," reminded a voice.

"But they were scattered by persecution also."

"We need one another in these trying times."

"We can soon win our neighbours to the Lord, and then we will have fellowship."

"Don't believe the authorities won't break up any new groups we form."

And so the debate continued. Some felt that the offer was reasonable and that they could comply without endangering their faith. Others were certain that the suggestion was only another method of weakening their resolve and destroying their conviction.

"Suppose we don't accept these terms for our release?" Mathes Legeder finally thought to ask. "Did they give any indication what the alternative might be?"

"Yes, indeed."

The voices hushed as they all listened to the verdict they would have to accept if they refused the officer's leniency.

"They said we would be sent to the galleys."

"Galleys!"

"Slaves!"

"To row!" Distressed exclamations swirled through the air.

"Galleys? What does that mean?" a younger boy beside Peter asked.

Brother Joseph was nearby, and Peter listened to his explanation.

"We will be placed in ships to sit in the hold and row. It is a miserable life. Galley slaves are treated harshly, worked past their limit, and usually do not last long. Only the worst political prisoners and basest offenders are sent to the galleys."

As the realization of the severity of this sentence swept over the men, the arguments continued afresh.

"We would die on the ships. Better to go free and then try to escape into Hungary."

"We would be under suspicion and so closely watched, I'm afraid escape would be impossible," Big Peter said.

"We could meet together in a field, or woods, even though we'd have to travel long distances," one suggested.

"Our fellowship would be very limited, and we would be often without an ordained brother to minister to us," an older man cautioned.

"Couldn't each father just conduct worship in his own home?" Leonhardt Blöcher asked.

"Yes, that could be done," it was agreed.

"There is a practical aspect we have to consider as well," a young harness maker ventured. "As a group, we can help one another and supply our material needs. As individual believers, we will be ostracized anywhere we settle, and no one will do business with us. How could I, knowing nothing of farming, provide for my family if no one will come to me to have harnesses made or mended?"

"The Lord would provide," someone answered.

Heads nodded. To be sure, the Lord would provide, but it was a point to be considered in making a final decision.

"We are to give our answer tomorrow morning," the men said.

Michel Blauer held up his hand to stop the discussion. "Until then, let us pray and consider the matter. Let each one be honest with himself before God, and we will take a vote tomorrow morning. Weigh the alternatives carefully. Either we accept their terms, that we promise to part company and settle as individual families wherever they place us, or we face the sentence of serving as galley slaves on the king's ships."

For the rest of that day, the matter was discussed up, down, and around. Peter listened to arguments for both sides until his head spun. Circulating from one group to another, it seemed that the majority felt that to accept this restricted freedom would put their souls in jeopardy. On the other hand, no one relished the idea of wearing out his life at the end of an oar. Here too their faith could easily be lost, the proponents of accepting the offer pointed out. How could they fellowship chained to a post in the hold of a ship? And what good would they be to their families if they were taken away? Would their families not be left in a worse situation with no fathers or brothers to support them materially or spiritually?

Since Peter was now an acknowledged member of the congregation, he would be expected to vote with the rest, so he was glad when evening came and he could talk with his father.

"Wouldn't it be better to be together as a family, even if we were poor and couldn't meet with the other believers, than to let the women fend for themselves?"

"If you look at it from that angle, yes," Father agreed.

"We could do more for the Lord if left free than as slaves in a ship."

"How do you know that?"

Peter had no answer.

"It is up to God how He will use our lives to bring glory to Himself. If He chooses to place us among slaves, we can be sure He has a purpose for us there."

"But the choice is ours," protested Peter.

"Yes." Father nodded thoughtfully.

"How will you vote?" Caspar, who regarded his uncle as a father in the absence of his own, now asked.

Big Peter did not answer directly. Gazing at the wall, he spoke slowly, as though thinking aloud. "Some of the brethren feel it would be wrong to dissipate our community. I personally don't feel that it would be un-Scriptural. Certainly it is preferable to live together, blending our skills for mutual sustenance and encouraging one another in the faith; but many believers have not had this advantage, yet the Lord blessed them also and gave them a good testimony even unto death.

"However," the big man went on, "I like to look ahead when making decisions such as this. I see our acceptance of their offer as a compromise. If we allow them to situate us where they will, you can be sure they will also want to dictate how we shall live. One demand they will make will be that we must attend mass in our new locality. This we must refuse to do, and we will soon be back in bonds—along with our families. We would only be buying time. Christ warned that His followers would suffer persecution, and if we do not take up our cross and follow Him, we cannot be His disciples. There will always be enmity between the Christian and the world until Jesus returns and Satan is finally defeated."

"Some of the men were saying that the galleys would be warships. By helping to row them, we would be engaging in the war against the Turks," Caspar said.

"So the king will have succeeded in involving us in the war after all," Big Peter said with a smile. "Yes, even the merchant vessels have been pressed into service and are likely armed with guns or carrying war supplies."

"Could we conscientiously row then?" asked Peter.

"No. If we knew that our ship was used to take men's lives, we would have to refuse."

"What would happen to us then?"

"I expect they would speedily dispense with us. I have heard that sick or weak galley slaves are unceremoniously thrown overboard and replaced with others."

Peter swallowed. A knot of fear tightened in his stomach. Why could he not face the thought of death with more fortitude? He shrank from it.

Sensing his discomfort, Big Peter quoted, " 'For I am persuaded, that neither death, nor life, nor angels, nor principalities, nor powers, nor things present, nor things to come, nor height, nor depth, nor any other creature, shall be able to separate us from the love of God, which is in Christ Jesus our Lord.'[42] Remember, they can kill the body but cannot destroy the soul. And to die and be with Christ is far greater than anything this life has to offer. Meditate on the promises of God."

"He has promised that He will not allow us to be tempted above what we can bear," Caspar added.

"His grace is sufficient for any circumstance," Big Peter stated with quiet confidence. "And don't forget"—Peter could hear the smile that was hidden by the darkness—"the day of miracles is not over. It is not wrong to pray for release. The Lord may be planning a greater deliverance for us than this. Let us wait on Him."

When the vote was taken the next morning, the decision was almost unanimous that they reject the officials' offer and trust in the Lord to deliver them if and when He chose. Garth led two men from the cell to relay their answer to the officials.

The clouds had settled in again, and the dampness in the atmosphere pressed on their spirits as well as their bodies. Although he felt at peace with the decision, Peter shrank from the thought of more long days of sour soup; damp, smelly clothing; and hours of monotony.

According to the notches on the door, they had been here now

for two weeks—two weeks that seemed like two years. Peter felt
that he had grown up in those two weeks. His grandiose dreams
of travelling and being a popular evangelist seemed so childish
now. He was learning to live one day at a time—to trust the Lord
for strength to fight the boredom, despair, and hopelessness that
threatened to wash over him as he sat or paced on the dirty straw.
How thankful he was that he was not alone! That would have
been a sore trial to bear!

He studied the men around him. Shaggy, matted hair tumbled over grey foreheads. Cheekbones were prominent, and
untrimmed beards and moustaches hid the lower part of their
faces. The overcoats, for which they were very grateful, were wrinkled and dirty. Bits of straw decorated the coats and trousers of
nearly everyone. How good it would feel to have a bath and a clean
change of clothing. Peter shook himself. Might as well not dwell
on impossibilities.

The two men were soon back in the cell. Their report was not
encouraging. "The officials were very angry, of course. They called
us fools and worse names.

"They let us know that the king was not through with us yet.
'If you won't listen to military men or officers of the court, maybe
the priests can reason with you!' they said. We understood that
they will be sending some learned churchmen to try to win us
back to the state church."

"We should appreciate the warning," Mathes Legeder remarked
wryly.

"Yes." Michel Blauer was more serious. "We can spend our
time preparing ourselves for questioning and strengthening
our resolves. Our older men can draw on their previous experience to show us what to expect, and our young men should
devote themselves to memorizing Scriptures with which to
answer them. There is no better way to defeat falsehood than

with the Sword of the Word."

Although the decision had been made, the situation continued to be the most popular topic of conversation. The boys discussed it after their memorization session.

"Surely the Lord wouldn't want us to row warships," Martin
contended, who, with his father, had voted to accept the release.

"He is able to deliver us," Andreas assured him.

"Father says we should ask the Lord to deliver us in His own
time and way," Peter said.

"Maybe through that door?" Caspar made an attempt at
humour.

The other door in the wall had intrigued the boys. The first
few days they had spent hours fantasizing about what lay on the
other side of it. They had let their imaginations soar. Lukas hoped
it led to some underground stables where they could mount horses
and ride through a hidden exit to freedom. Caspar envisioned a
well-stocked root cellar where he could fill up the empty cavity
within him. George wished it contained an ancient library of old
manuscripts where he could read to his heart's content. Peter
would have been happy if it only led to a place of light; pure, fresh
air; and cleanliness.

"Seriously, though," Peter said, coming back to the subject,
"Brother Michel seems to think that we will be delivered. I heard
him say so again last night. He said he just has a premonition
that we won't be here very long."

The other boys' eyes lit up, for they cherished this hope as well.
They had given their word that they were prepared to die for their
faith; nevertheless, they were healthy young men, and the desire
for life flowed strong in their veins.

"I know I won't be here very long." George spoke quietly and
calmly.

"You, too? Did you have a vision?" Martin asked eagerly.

"No vision." George coughed slightly. "I just know I won't be here long."

The others were quiet. Peter blinked back sudden tears. He knew what George meant. In the past, the boys had always been quick to tell their frail friend that he would feel better when the weather grew warmer, or that he would outgrow his cough. Now they did not have the heart to continue voicing false assurances.

"I wish I were as good a man as you are." Peter impulsively put his arm around George's shoulders.

George turned large, surprised eyes to him. "But you are. We are all sinners saved by grace."

"But you seem to be able to accept everything so calmly and be content."

The other boys drifted uneasily away.

George smiled ruefully. "For as long as I can remember, there were things I couldn't do. I couldn't climb mountains with the rest of you, or play vigourous games. I always had to sit by and keep score. Remember? I've learned to accept my limitations and be content with the small pleasures that come my way. I knew my life would never be as full as a normal person's. Maybe it is easier to give it up when there is less to give up. You have so much to hope for. It is harder to lay it on the altar."

The long speech set George coughing again. Peter offered his own soiled handkerchief and watched helplessly as his friend spat blood. He helped George to a sitting position and waited for his laboured breathing to quiet.

"You may get better, yet," Peter soothed. "God still works miracles."

But George shook his head. He winced as he drew one leg over the other.

"Do you have pain?" Peter had never noticed before how drawn George's face grew and how his lips tightened when he moved.

"It's not so bad," the sick lad answered.

"Where?"

"My back hurts sometimes, but it will soon be better." His face lit up with an unearthly glow.

"You mean . . . ?"

George nodded. "I'll soon be where there is no pain or sorrow or persecution. I only hope," he whispered, "that my life hasn't been in vain. I regret that I must meet the Saviour empty-handed."

"Oh, but you dare not feel that way," Peter protested. "You have been a great help to me. Many times when I wanted to give up, I have looked at you, and your calm acceptance and faith in God has given me the urge to go on—especially during these days in prison. I've been ashamed of myself when I saw how, sick as you are, you could love our enemies and find something to sing about when all was dark."

"Thank you." George smiled a weak smile. "I'm glad if I could be used to help someone."

"I'm sure many others would say the same," Peter defended loyally. He resolved to spend more time with his friend, making his last days pleasant and relieving his discomfort as best he could.

"Here," he said suddenly, "take my coat." He hurriedly undid the buttons and slipped his coat over George's own.

"No, no!" George shrugged in protest. "You keep it. You need to keep your strength. The Lord has other work for you. My time is nearly over, and I won't need your coat."

"But I am warm enough. I can exercise, and I have more layers of fat than I need," Peter insisted, although he had to admit to himself that some of those layers were fast disappearing on this prison diet.

In the end they compromised. George agreed to wear Peter's warm shirt if Peter would keep his coat.

Later that afternoon, Peter was again helping Brother Jacob tend the sick men. "We should have more clean straw," the old doctor sighed wearily, trying to kick some dry bedding under an invalid while Peter lifted the man.

"We'll have to get Sister Agathe to do some more 'bossing,' " Peter suggested. He stood and glanced at the four slits in the wall. "Speaking of Sister Agathe, she hasn't been here yet today."

"No," Jacob mumbled. "Just one more swallow," he urged as he tried to convince one patient to swallow the bitter medicine he offered to him. "It is time for Garth to come with food. Maybe in all the confusion of having these officers here, he forgot to bring her earlier."

But Garth came with their supper and without Sister Agathe. "Where is the lady?" someone asked as he poured the watery soup into smaller bowls.

"Eh? What lady?" Garth peered absent-mindedly at the speaker while he continued to pour.

"The lady who comes to help with the sick."

"Eh, heh! All locked up. All locked up. Enough of ladies." He set the large cauldron on the floor and, placing his hands on his hips, he glared triumphantly at them. "All locked up. Yes, sir. All locked up. Enough of ladies. No more ladies getting in my way. No more boss, boss; no more chitter chatter. All locked up."

"You mean they are back in the tower?"

But Garth quickly turned and refused to answer as he gathered his utensils and pushed his helpers towards the door.

"We need more straw," pleaded Brother Jacob, threading his way towards the jailor.

Garth sent him an offended glance and mumbled, "No more ladies . . ." before hastily withdrawing and slamming the door.

Jacob stared at the closed door. Turning to face his companions, he declared, "That also means no more messages, brethren."

Waiting for sleep to come that night, Peter felt a great wave of homesickness sweep over him. How wonderful it would be to lie on his corner bunk at home, with a warm quilt tucked around him, watching rosy lights from the fireplace dance on the walls, and listening to mother's voice as she hummed a quiet lullaby to his baby brother.

He saw them all so clearly, the way they had looked that last evening at home. Mother on the rocker, pressing the baby against her shoulder as tears fell on his soft head for the other little one she had lost. Ursula, her round, rosy, dimpled face bending earnestly over her knitting as she tried to turn a heel as neatly as mother. Did Ursula still have dimples? he wondered. Or had she forgotten how to smile?

And Maria. How he missed her singsong little girl voice and the playtimes they had together for her enjoyment. He could see her as she was that last night, peering impishly over Father's arm, saying, "I told you so," after Father had assured her that the Bible did not say that if someone pulls your hair you should tell him to pull it again. How he longed to toss her in the air again or to have her come dancing into the shop on a bright spring afternoon and lay a crumpled bunch of wildflowers and weeds on his dusty knee. He was so glad Maria was not here in this dingy place. He hoped she was happy and had enough to eat.

Another day dragged by. The temperature had dropped, and it was harder to keep warm. Exercise periods took up a good part of the day as the men attempted to generate their own heat.

Garth surprised them by appearing in the middle of the afternoon, alone. Without deigning to waste words on them, and ignoring their questioning glances, he shuffled across the room, the crowd parting to let him pass. At the mysterious wooden door, he stopped. Peter sidled along the wall to see.

Garth fumbled with the ring of keys in his hand. Finally, he found the one he was looking for. "Clean straw, dry straw, more blankets," he muttered. "Maybe this will suit ye better." He used both hands to turn the old key in the rusty lock. With a jerk, he yanked the door open, then stood back to let the men peer into the darkness beyond.

"Go on in," he chortled, enjoying their curiosity.

The first men hesitated, but as those behind clamoured to see too, they stepped over the threshold. Peter followed the rest through the door. Once inside he looked around him. No library, no stables, no food stores, no escape tunnel; it was just another dungeon like the one they were in. Although this room had the same musty, ancient odour, the floor was bare dirt. The room was almost as large as their tower dungeon, only it was square. Three large stone arches supported the roof. There was no exit other than the door he had just entered.

Caspar, right behind him, shrugged his shoulders. "Oh, well, it was fun to speculate."

"At least we will be able to spread out a bit." Peter tried to cover his disappointment by pointing out some advantages.

"There will be more air to go around," agreed Caspar, stepping aside to let others pass.

"Now we have a choice. Shall we sleep on rotten straw or damp ground?" Lukas joined them.

Making their way back to George in the other cell, the boys learned that Garth had taken several men with him to fetch clean straw.

"Maybe Sister Agathe is still bossing Garth from her tower," Caspar surmised.

Andreas's friend, Johan, was among those chosen to carry straw. He told the boys later, "Not all the women are 'all locked up': I saw one young sister carrying a big pail of potato peelings past the stables. She smiled at me."

"What did she look like?" Andreas asked eagerly.

"Let me see." Johan tried to think. "I hardly know. She just glanced in our direction once, and then she was out of our view. I think she had blonde hair. She was quite short. That's about all I know." He threw out his hands sympathetically.

"It was Bridgit!" Andreas's voice was tense with excitement. "I wish I could have gone. Instead I was looking for treasure in that second dungeon. If I would have been there, I'd have dropped my fork and gone to her."

"Maybe it's as well you weren't," Johan chided him. "Garth kept his eyes on us and barked if we so much as looked at a stableboy. And Bridgit might have been locked up, or worse, for her involvement."

The fresh straw was spread in the newly opened cavern, and Peter helped move the sick men into it. The room seemed a bit warmer than the original cell—probably because it was under the main part of the castle and not in an outside tower.

It was a little easier to move around now, without colliding with someone. Peter felt like he could spread his wings. Living in such close proximity left no room for privacy, and he had felt at times as though even his thought life was in danger of invasion. Thoughts usually translate themselves into actions sooner or later, and there had been very few actions in the last two weeks that had gone unnoticed by someone.

Nothing else had improved, Peter reflected gloomily at mealtime as he dipped his bowl into the common kettle of thin soup. Ah, he had two hunks of cabbage in his dish tonight. He tried to be thankful for small blessings.

"What?" Cornelius, who was dipping out his portion, stared in puzzlement at his bowl.

While the others watched curiously, he swirled his fingers in his soup. Something hard clattered against the wooden bowl.

Then, to their amazement, he held up a flat, circular object dripping with grease.

"A watch!" they gasped in unison.

"Why is a watch in my soup?" Cornelius still held the strange "vegetable" aloft over his soup bowl, looking utterly confused as he stared incredulously at it.

Men from other groups were crowding around, exclaiming over the find.

"Could I see the watch?" The men parted to allow one of the chief watchmakers to reach Cornelius.

The man took the watch and carefully wiped the broth from the face and silver back. He turned it over, examining it studiously. "It is one we made," he declared. He looked over the crowd. "If I had a pick, I could open it."

"Will my knife do?"

With the versatile knife, the watchmaker pried at the back of the watch.

"Why open it?" Peter wondered.

He soon saw. The watchmaker held up the watch, and they could all see that instead of the usual arrangement of tiny screws and wheels, a tightly folded piece of paper lay inside the two covers.

"A note!"

The precious missive was passed to Brother Kramer, who read it aloud to the eager men.

Dear Brethren in the Faith,

Greetings of love. The Lord provides. Trust all are well. Patlo is with us still. He had learned from servants in which tower you are held. Brother Guttenhann and myself plan to begin working at the outside wall of your cell this night. It will take us a long time, we fear, as the walls are thick. If you should hear us, sing loudly to drown the noise of our picks. We will only be able to rescue some of you to avoid suspicion. But you will hear from us further. God bless you and keep you faithful.

Your servant,
Peter Riedemann

A plan of rescue! Hope was born anew. Excited talk filled the dungeon.

Reality soon asserted itself, and the clamour faded. They all realised that it would take a long time for two men to carve their way through the stone wall. They might be discovered in the act. In the meantime, the priests from Vienna might arrive and condemn them all to slavery or death. Even if the men did succeed in making a large enough hole to squeeze a body through, only a portion of them would dare escape—and then only a few at a time. It would be next to impossible for one hundred twenty men to stage an exodus from the valley unobserved.

And so this latest communication brought hope mingled with doubt to the prisoners of the Falkenstein castle.

XIII

Dark Winter Days

"Do you know what day this is?" Lukas held his cupped hands in front of his mouth and blew in an effort to warm them.

Caspar was busy flinging his arms across his chest to slap his shoulders, so it was Peter who had the obvious answer, "Sunday."

"But what date?" Lukas asked between puffs.

"Twenty, twenty-one, twenty-two," Martin counted the notches on the doorpost near him. "Why, it's December 22."

"Feels like it too," Caspar stated, stamping his cold feet.

The Lord's Day sermons were brief that day because of the cold that penetrated even their heavy coats. It was necessary to keep moving to stay warm. They sang a great deal, swinging their arms and occasionally marching in time to the music. The brethren took turns rubbing warmth into the limbs of those that were sick.

That night was one of the most miserable they had spent yet. The portions of soup had been meager and barely lukewarm. The cold grew more intense. The men curled up against each other and dozed fitfully; then they stumbled groggily to their feet to stamp circulation back into their limbs. They listened in vain for the tapping that would mean Brother Riedemann and Guttenhann were chipping at their prison wall. Likely it was too cold outside to work. Spirits were low as all of them thought of their families and contemplated a Christmas season in their dismal surroundings.

While the boys were still swallowing their porridge the next morning, Mathes Legeder clapped his hands for silence.

"Even though we are in a dungeon, let us honour Christ's birth in our usual way. Remember, God's Son lay on straw too, so He can feel with us in our extremities." He went on to outline a programme of activities that would last most of the day.

Involvement in listening to sermons, singing, prayer, exercising, testimonies, recitation of Bible verses, and relating of previous Christmas experiences kept their minds from dwelling on the cold and on their empty stomachs.

Each man and boy told what Christ meant to him personally. That consumed several hours of the afternoon and left their hearts warm with appreciation for God's gift to humanity. Most of these men had lost friends, homes, possessions, professions, or families; yet they felt rich in the love of Christ and looked forward to sharing His riches in glory.

On Christmas Eve, Peter, Andreas, Caspar, Lukas, and Martin were standing in a circle in the inner cell, stamping their feet. Their hands were in their pockets and their collars were pulled up around their ears as they took turns by verses to recite Luke 2.

" 'And she . . . wrapped him in swaddling clothes, and laid him in a manger,' " droned Martin.

"Wonder if it was cold in Bethlehem that night," interrupted Caspar, rubbing his right ear.

"Likely not as cold as this," guessed Andreas. "Now where were we? Your turn Peter. Hey, Peter," he said, nudging him, "your turn. We're ready for, 'And there were in the same country.' What are you looking at?"

Peter was staring fixedly through the doorway into the other room. "The men out there have all stopped talking," he answered, starting in that direction. The others followed at his heels.

In the open doorway, they stopped.

In the cleared space just before the door to the corridor stood three priests.

One was slight and dark-skinned. His voluminous brown robe hung loosely from his shoulders and was gathered about his waist with a knotted rope. His fingers fidgeted with the simple wooden cross hanging from a string about his neck. With his tongue he licked his lips nervously while his eyes darted restlessly from the men before him to the stone walls and back again.

Behind and slightly to one side of him stood a short, very stout, black-robed priest. His shaved head glistened in the light from the lanterns held by the two soldiers who guarded the door. His jowls moved up and down rhythmically as he coolly surveyed the sorry-looking group of prisoners. His pudgy hands were folded piously over his protruding stomach.

The third priest was tall and dignified in appearance. He wore a square headdress signifying his higher station. A jeweled crucifix hung prominently from a heavy gold chain about his neck. His habit hung in precise folds from his broad shoulders. His hands, clasped before him, were hidden in the full cuffs of his embroidered sleeves. Hard eyes shot arrows of disapproval, and the cynical smile on his arrogant face sent shivers up Peter's back.

This priest moved slowly forward, his robes seeming to flow with him. The men had fallen silent and, in the stillness, his voice was smooth and controlled. "I have been sent, by the leniency of our king, God bless his soul, to convert you from your false and evil beliefs and bring you back to the faith of your fathers and the protection of our gracious King Ferdinand. These two worthy brethren will assist me. We have been given authority to use any means at our disposal to dissuade you from the error you have fallen into and"—his voice became hard—"I intend to succeed in my mission.

"Where are your leaders?"

The three deacons stepped forward and stood before the priests.

"Are you not ashamed to have led so many innocent victims to sell their souls to the devil?" he demanded coldly.

Michel Blauer replied, "In fact, Christ has bought our souls from eternal damnation with His own blood."

"You claim the blood of Christ?" the priest snapped. "Why do you then refuse to drink that blood as He commanded us?"

"We do observe Communion among the redeemed saints," Michel said quietly.

"Are we, your spiritual fathers, not then redeemed?"

"Christ told Nicodemus, a Pharisee and a ruler of the Jews, 'Ye must be born again.' Only those who are born of the Spirit of God are Christ's."

"Those who are baptised with holy water by the priest are Christ's," the priest contradicted.

"Nowhere does the Scripture say that baptism saves a person," Michel pointed out.

"Now you speak of baptism. If baptism does not save, then why do you relentlessly baptise again those who have already been sprinkled with the water of baptism?"

Peter and the other boys followed closely as the priests debated with the deacons. Although they had been schooled to answer for themselves in just such a situation, it was the first time they had witnessed an actual inquisition. They were thankful for the opportunity to observe the manner in which the brethren defended their faith.

It was obvious that the Anabaptists had a better command of the Scriptures than the church officials. They often answered with direct quotations from the Bible, which the priests could not contest. At last the priests ceased their questioning and ordered the men to be quiet and listen to them.

For an hour the priests spoke persuasively, trying to turn them from their faith. To anyone less knowledgeable in the Scriptures, their appeal might have sounded convincing; but to these sincere believers, their words were empty and vain, carrying only partial truth and much reasoning of men.

The nervous priest began to fidget. He turned his crucifix first one way and then another; he shifted his feet, cleared his throat, and twitched his shoulders. Finally, he tugged at the sleeves of his elegant colleague and whispered something to him. The other, annoyed at the interruption, shrugged him off and prepared to continue his lecture. But after the corpulent priest muttered to him, he said, "I see that you do not wish to accept our charitable attempts to save your souls. Perhaps if you had opportunity, each of you alone would see reason and give up this blasphemous heresy. Starting tomorrow, we will deal with you separately. Good night."

Gesturing to the soldiers to hold their lanterns high, he gathered his robes about him and glided noiselessly through the doorway, followed by his companions. The heavy priest stumbled and nearly fell over the half-empty water bucket. With a curse, he kicked it against the wall. Then they were gone.

"Who is willing to be the first to go when one is summoned for questioning in the morning?"

"I will."

"I will."

"I'm willing." All the mature men were ready to face this trial of faith.

"Let me be the first," pleaded Brother Joseph. "I was once a priest myself, and I understand their tactics. Perhaps if they fail with me, they will become discouraged and forego interrogating the rest of you."

They agreed to follow this plan, and several others prepared to accompany Joseph. It was possible the priests might remain in the castle until they had questioned each prisoner.

Peter lay between Caspar and Big Peter, wondering how he would answer the priests should his turn come. He was determined that he would not renounce his faith nor deny his Lord, but just how to answer their subtle questions . . . He hoped he could remember the appropriate Scriptures at the right time.

Christ had promised that when His children were delivered up before governors and kings for His sake, the Spirit would give them in that hour what they should speak.

He tried to console himself with this thought, yet, when he recalled again the glib words the priest had spoken that afternoon, he felt uneasy and very ignorant.

He wondered if Peter Riedemann and Uncle Guttenhann were working outside the castle tonight. Maybe. Oh, let it be, that they would succeed in rescuing them before the priests were able to question all the prisoners.

The next morning after Garth, muttering and grumbling about "priests and soldiers; fetch carry," had delivered their breakfast, he said, "Three of you, come with me." Turning, without waiting to see who would follow, he stepped into the corridor, shaking his head and mumbling, "Up and down, up and down these steps it will be. Oh, my aching bones."

Brother Joseph and two older men stepped quietly into the corridor to the accompaniment of a chorus of "God bless you" from the cell.

"One advantage of having extra visitors in the castle is that the dogs and prisoners are better fed," Caspar remarked. There were bits of egg and meat thrown in with their porridge that morning. "We get a Christmas breakfast." He licked his lips and sighed with satisfaction.

"I wonder what the women at home are having today?" Peter reflected. "Their food must be almost gone."

"The hidden food stores held only enough provisions for about two weeks," Caspar recalled.

"Of course there are no men there to help eat them," Peter pointed out, wiping his mouth on his coat sleeve.

"Brother Riedemann said he was encouraging them to go to Moravia. I wonder if any have gone yet." Peter did not like to think of his mother and little brother and sister starving, but he hoped they had not gone just yet. Even though he could not see them, the knowledge that they were only a short distance away was comforting. And he still nursed a secret hope that they might be miraculously freed soon. He would be very disappointed to find his home disintegrated if that day should suddenly come.

"It's too cold to travel now," Lukas said, shivering and drawing his coat closely about him. "Surely they can hold out until spring."

Peter brushed his hands on his coat. "Let's go see George."

The boys all filed after him into the inner room where George lay on a pile of dry straw, covered with his own and Andreas's coat. His brother bent over him solicitously.

"How is he?" Peter knelt by Andreas.

"Worse," Andreas whispered. "He couldn't eat anything this morning."

The still figure on the straw coughed weakly. Andreas stooped and lifted his head until the spell had passed. "Could you help me turn him? He has such pain in his spine that we must do it gently."

Peter, Caspar, and Lukas bent and, between them, slowly shifted their friend onto his other side.

"Poor George." Lukas shook his head sadly.

"Maybe he is better off than the rest of us," Andreas said. "He suffers now, but he is looking forward to heaven. What will we have to face?" He sounded discouraged.

" 'My grace is sufficient for thee.' "[44] Even in his agony, George's faith reached out to his friends. His eyes remained closed, and they almost thought they had imagined that he spoke, but the slight smile on his pale lips assured them otherwise.

Each boy felt ashamed of his weakness and determined anew to trust the Lord for strength for the day.

The brethren gathered to pray especially for Brother Joseph and his companions.

An attempt was made to carry on the memorization programme, but with their minds elsewhere, the young men fumbled over their verses so badly they gave it up.

Towards evening, while the men were singing together, the door burst open and the three men, each supported by soldiers, were half-carried into the dungeon and deposited on the floor. Each lay in a limp heap as though dead. Brother Jacob and several others immediately knelt by them.

"They live," the physician reported to the relief of all.

He carefully ran his fingers over the arms and legs of the oldest man. He pressed his ribs and turned his head gently from side to side.

"No bones broken," he reported. "It appears that he has been racked. Let's make them comfortable."

Racked! Peter felt the blood drain from his face. His legs felt trembly. So they were to be tortured. "Lord help us," he cried.

The men were made as comfortable as possible, and soon they were able to talk. They had been stretched on the rack, they said, because they refused to accept a communion wafer from the hand of the priest. They had not been questioned extensively, but the priests' mission was to win them back to the mother church.

In the days that followed, more brethren were removed from the cell for questioning. Some were stretched on the rack; others were beaten with cudgels by the soldiers for refusing to take Communion from the priests or to kneel before them and confess their sins. Some were returned without having been tortured.

Brother Joseph and the deacons drilled the young men in preparation for their inevitable confrontation with the priests. They were advised to remain silent unless forced to answer. "The priests are subtle and will deceive you if they can embroil you in useless argument," explained Brother Kramer.

"Do not debate with them. Do as our Lord and answer nothing, or else reply with a Scripture that the Holy Spirit lays on your heart."

Peter had asked Brother Joseph about his experience on the rack. But the teacher only replied, "I thought of my Lord, stretched between heaven and earth, suffering for me, and that sustained me." About the pain he would say nothing.

These were dark days. Intense cold continued to torment them. Although the food had improved with the coming of the priests from Vienna, there was never enough to satisfy. There had been no word from the women since the watch in the soup over a week ago, and Garth refused to be an accomplice in carrying messages for them. The questioning continued relentlessly, and the turn of the young men drew daily nearer.

And then came a day when Brother Jacob gently drew a coat over an invalid's face. It was the first death. The first martyr had gone to his reward. It served to emphasize for Peter and all of them, that their faith was being tried to the death. One had already passed through the valley of the shadow. How many would follow?

Garth allowed two men to carry the body of their uncle

upstairs, and he promised to see that it was delivered to the village. A message of consolation to the widow and encouragement to all the lonely wives and mothers was secreted on the dead man's body before it left the dungeon.

Peter was squatting against the far wall of the inner room, tracing aimless designs with his finger in the dirt at his feet, when he sensed a shadow fall over him. He looked up to see his father gazing down at him. Big Peter lowered his large frame. "What are you doing?" He smiled, searching in vain for some meaning in the scrawled lines on the floor.

"Nothing," Peter replied dully, brushing his fingers on his trouser leg.

"Is Brother Friedel's death bothering you?"

Peter shrugged. "Yes and no. He is better off than we are. Sometimes I wish I could die too. This"—he swept an arm at the mouldy stone walls and the clusters of dishevelled-looking men—"is so discouraging."

"The desire to be with the Lord is commendable," his Father assured him. "But we want to be in the Lord's will. If it is not the Lord's will to take you home just now, you must be content to let your light shine where you are. Remember Grandfather Boewen's advice to cultivate the fruit of the Spirit and to grow in the inward man through this prison experience."

"I'm trying," Peter said softly.

"I know you are, son." His father squeezed his shoulder. "You have been a good lad," he went on huskily. "If anything should happen to me . . ."

Peter looked up sharply. "Wha—What?"

"Oh, don't be alarmed," Big Peter hastened to assure him. "I am not ill, but that death today made me realise that none of us has a promise of tomorrow. And I just wanted to take the opportunity to say some things to you that I might never have said under normal circumstances."

Big Peter cleared his throat. "Peter, you have been a good son. You have always been conscientious and trustworthy. As all parents do, your mother and I had high hopes for you. I was looking forward to establishing you as a partner in my trade. Your mother pictured you marrying and blessing her with grandchildren. I must confess"—his voice lowered—"that your absorption in maps and interest in travel alarmed me. You talked sometimes of becoming an evangelist. I am ashamed to say that I resisted that desire."

"I didn't know you even knew about it."

"Boys might be surprised how much their fathers know about them."

Peter was silent, waiting for his father to go on.

"The Lord has been teaching me through this trial too. I realise that I was selfish in not wanting to think of your becoming an evangelist. I knew that the brethren who are sent out usually do not return. I did not want to lose you. I had not given you to the Lord as I should have. And now . . . now we are both here, for His sake.

"If we ever get out of this dungeon, and several of the brethren feel that we will, I want to be ready to support you in whatever the Lord leads you to do."

"Thank you, Father," Peter murmured, his throat tight.

"And I started to say," Big Peter added, "that if anything should happen to me, I want you to take care of Mother and your brother and sisters if it is within your power. Provide for them physically, but most of all, see that they each make their peace with God. Watch for their souls.

"You are given to discouragement," his father chided, "and you must learn to live victoriously. Joy is not dependent on our outward circumstances. Have faith that the Saviour is with you and will guide you through the valleys. Look for the sunshine tomorrow. Seek to help some struggling soul, and think on the Lord's mercies to you when the clouds threaten.

"Yet, you are steadfast, Peter. I am confident that under test you would not yield and deny your Lord. Faith is the victory, and your faith has grown mightily in these last weeks, has it not?"

Peter took a deep breath and drew his shoulders up straighter. "I know that Jesus lives, and I trust Him to keep me day by day, by His power. I will try to live up to your expectations."

The next day the sun shone. Their dungeons felt warmer. The two latest groups of men to be questioned had not been tortured. They reported that the priests seemed to be tiring of the endless questioning and had let them off very easily.

To the delight of his brother, father, and friends, George felt much better. Andreas and Peter helped him out into the original dungeon so that he could better hear the Lord's Day services, which were being conducted by the deacons.

By the time Garth came with their evening meal, George was able to walk shakily and feed himself. His recovery was almost miraculous, and it raised the spirits of the boys tremendously. It was so good to have George back in their midst. They each fished in their bowls for tidbits of meat and potato to offer to him until he protested, "No, no, I'm not that hungry. Next you'll have me sick with an upset stomach."

That evening, the men distinctly heard the tap-tapping of hammers on stone. The men were working at the wall! For many hours, the prisoners of Falkenstein sang heartily to drown the sounds of activity outside their tower. Was their deliverance near?

But the next morning, Garth was in an ugly mood. He snarled at his helpers, and when they worked too slowly, he grabbed for one soup caldron himself. "Here! Take all day!" He snatched the proffered bowls, splashed them into the kettle of runny porridge, and thrust them back into the men's hands, spilling much of the precious food on the straw. "Hurry! Hurry!" he muttered. "Bring up more hams. Fetch the ladies! Run up and down. I should have eight legs. Get that bucket filled!" He kicked at the water bucket.

"Six of you can come get straw," he said, tossing the empty caldron to an assistant and fumbling with his keys. "If I had my choice, I'd just leave this door open, and you could all get out of my sight. Up and down. Up and down. Well," he demanded impatiently, "who's coming?"

"Why don't you just leave the door open?" one man boldly ventured.

Garth glared at him and hesitated a moment. Peter, along with everyone else, held his breath. Would he really do it?

The jailor looked at his keys, then at the door, then at the men, and then back to the door. But then he shook his head. "Ha! And lose my job?"

Lukas was one of those chosen to fetch straw. Mathes Legeder had tried to grant the privilege to different ones each time. Before Lukas reached the door, however, he spied Andreas among the men nearby. "You go instead." He beckoned to Andreas and stepped aside.

Andreas started forward. "But I already had a turn," he said, hesitating.

Lukas gave him a shove. "Go on. You might see Bridgit."

That was all Andreas needed to send him scurrying after the others.

Lukas was growing too, Peter decided. He knew how much his friend liked horses and how he would have enjoyed getting into the stables, aside from the pleasure of a momentary release from the confines of prison. But he had given up the privilege for another's sake.

The last day of the year 1539 was dragging to a close when

the boys received their summons to appear before the priests. The churchmen had sent word that they specifically wished to interrogate some young men.

So this was it. Now that the time had come, Peter felt almost relieved. The suspense of waiting his turn for the inevitable trial and wondering how or what he would answer and whether he could endure possible torture was over. As he made his way to the door, where Garth stood jingling his key ring impatiently, he heard Michel Blauer's hurried advice: "Answer not unless the Spirit gives you the words." And a chorus of "Stand steadfast. We are praying for you" came from his fellow prisoners.

Along with Caspar, Lukas, Martin, and one younger boy, he stepped, for the first time in four weeks, outside his prison cell. At the last minute before Garth closed the door, George slipped through the opening too. Peter turned and whispered, "Are you strong enough?"

"I wanted to come," George returned.

Peter was glad for his presence. He hoped the ordeal would not cause a relapse of his illness.

Down the dark corridor they filed and up the thirty-five steps. At each step Peter breathed a prayer: "Father, strengthen me," "Give me courage," "Show me the words to speak," "Help me to love my enemies," . . . until he reached the top. In front of him, Caspar stooped through the low archway into the hallway that Peter remembered from having entered that way a long month ago—though then he was travelling the opposite direction.

In a few seconds they were in the open courtyard. Peter blinked and then squeezed his eyelids shut in the unexpected brightness. Although the sun was setting, his eyes had so long been accustomed to semidarkness that even this diffused light caused tears to course down his cheeks. He hastily brushed them away and, by squinting, was able to see two armed soldiers, who led the way across the courtyard.

Through the tears that continued to stream from his eyes, Peter looked up at the grey sky. How open and free it looked. If he were a bird . . .

"Get along there." The broadside of a sword whacked against his thigh, and he stumbled against Caspar.

He managed to draw only a few breaths of fresh air before the soldiers hurried them through another doorway, into a small chamber.

The five boys stood in a tight huddle before a wooden table behind which sat the three priests. Two tall candles in brass holders threw flickering shadows over the table on which also rested a large wooden bowl of fruit.

Peter felt his eyes drawn involuntarily to the juicy grapes and plump figs in the bowl. The prisoners had not yet been given their meagre supper, and his system craved the almost-forgotten savor of fresh fruit.

As if to tantalize the young men further, the stout priest selected a large bunch of grapes, surveyed them appreciatively, and rolled one slowly between his pudgy fingers before popping it into his mouth.

The well-dressed priest with the square headdress sat between his two comrades. "Form a line before the table," he ordered in a cold voice.

The boys rearranged themselves into the required formation. The stout priest continued to devour the grapes, smacking his lips loudly over each mouthful. The dark-skinned priest, on the other side of his superior, toyed with his wooden crucifix and eyed the five young men with piercing, critical eyes.

The stout priest reached for a fig. Seeing the hungry eyes of the boys resting on the bowl of fruit, the centre priest suddenly asked in an artificially kind tone, "Would you like some fruit?" He pushed the bowl across the table towards them. "Help yourselves," he offered generously. "The grapes are delicious. Imported from southern Italy." He helped himself to a plump bunch, to demonstrate.

None of the boys moved.

The priest studied them thoughtfully as he chewed slowly. "Come now," he urged suavely, "you poor lambs have been deceived by your own fathers. They have led you into grave error. You see what this new heresy has earned you—a dungeon. We know that you do not really believe in this new doctrine. We will make it easy for you to return to the benevolent protection of the Holy Church. All you need to do is kiss the cross." The dark-skinned priest held up his wooden crucifix. "And we will not even ask if you have been rebaptised. All will be forgiven. You have been led astray against your wishes. Come, now," he remonstrated. "Surely you can perform such a simple act."

The priest rose; stepped around the table; and, standing directly before him, held the wooden cross almost against George's pale lips. George turned his head deliberately. With an angry motion, the priest thrust the cross before the face of each boy in turn. When Lukas, the last in line, refused, as the others, to comply, he gave an angry snort and butted the end of the crucifix against Lukas's mouth. Peter watched the blood ooze from Lukas's battered lips, but not a word was spoken. He prayed silently.

"So you will be stubborn then?" The inquisitor's voice was icy. "Do you not know that we are your spiritual fathers, ordained of God to save your souls? By refusing to obey us, you are disobeying God and will be punished in hellfire." He looked from one to the other, waiting for a response. There was none.

"Why will you not listen to us and confess your sins to us? Come, now. Has the devil stolen your tongues too, as well as your minds? I demand an answer," he shouted suddenly and banged his fist on the table, making the candles dance.

" 'For there is one God, and one mediator between God and men, the man Christ Jesus,' "[45] Caspar answered for all of them.

"And we are Christ's representatives on earth," snapped the priest, tapping his cross on the table top. "We have the authority to forgive sins and mete out penances."

"In the Book of Revelation we read that He has made us kings and priests unto our God," Caspar answered.

Peter wanted to point out that nowhere in Scripture had God granted to any man the right to forgive sins, but remembering the advice to refrain from debate, he kept silent.

"I see that you have been grossly deluded," the middle priest said, not refuting Caspar's reply. The obese priest clicked his tongue, "Tut-tut," before reaching for more fruit.

"Do you know what happens to Anabaptists?" The priest's eyes narrowed to slits. "I'll tell you how we treat such heretics in Vienna. First, they are led through the streets and flogged. We have some very persuasive whips made of tough camel skin with nine tails, with bits of sharp metal on the ends. Very persuasive. The good people of Vienna line the streets to see that the executioners do their duty to these enemies of the church.

"Then, if there is anything left of the poor sinners"—here he smiled cynically and exchanged glances with his stout colleague— "sometimes we pull out their tongues, or we might brand them with hot irons."

Peter heard Martin, beside him, draw in a sharp breath and shift his weight from one foot to the other. "Lord, help Martin not to yield," he prayed desperately, knowing the boy's weakness.

"Have you ever seen anyone burned?" The priest leaned forward slightly and flung the unexpected question at them. Peter felt the blood drain from his face. That horrible scene rose before his eyes. Yes, he certainly had.

"It isn't a pretty sight," the cruel voice went on. "The flames work slowly. First they devour the feet, then the legs. Sometimes it takes many hours before the prisoner is reduced to ashes."

"And such screams," the stout one added dolefully, reaching again for the dish.

"But that need not be your fate," the first priest declared. "You could leave this room as free men. We will put money in your pocket, give you new clothes, feed you a good meal, and send you on your way to Vienna on a fine steed to join the battle against the heathen Turks. Do you not agree that we Christians must unite to stop these hordes of infidels from invading our land?"

No one ventured a response.

He motioned to the dark-skinned priest at his side. "The wafers."

The priest drew some small pieces of communion bread from the folds of his tunic and spread them on his palm. He held them towards the young men and chanted a phrase in Latin.

"The body of Christ has been blessed. Accept these wafers, and we will let you go free." The priest looked from one to the other.

None of the boys showed any sign of relenting.

"Enough!" said the priest. "If you are determined to destroy yourselves, we will not prevent you."

"The torture?" the stout one asked between bites, arching his brows at his superior.

"Not now," replied the priest. "They will feel that when they get to Vienna."

"Get to Vienna?" thought Peter as he followed his friends from the room. "Are we going to Vienna?"

They indulged in the luxury of a few gulps of fresh air as they crossed the courtyard, and then they were again descending the stairs to their dungeon.

To be in prison with the saints was far more satisfying than to be free in the company of unbelievers.

The cell buzzed with the latest news brought by the straw carriers while the boys were away. The stable hands had apparently been engaged in frenzied preparations for the arrival of more visitors. Dozens of stalls were being bedded with clean straw.

"They must be expecting a good-sized regiment very shortly," reported Andreas to his friends.

This, along with the priests' allusion to Vienna, set the men to wondering what the new year would bring into their experience.

"Did you see Bridgit?" Peter suddenly thought to ask Andreas.

"No."

XIV

Farewell to Falkenstein

The early days of the new year brought no new changes to the routine of prison life. The captives moved within the confines of the same stone walls. They swallowed the same watery gruel. They lay on the same damp straw and watched the same four blocks of sunlight creep slowly along the wall to mark the hours of the passing days.

The questioning by the priests had stopped. No one but Garth and his helpers had visited their cell for several days. No new communication had arrived from the village, but each night the men took turns singing to drown the muffled taps of hammers on rock. They all wondered what success the men outside were having at breaking through the formidable wall.

George had suffered a relapse. He lay on the straw, his legs drawn up in pain. Violent coughing spells left him breathless; and his skin, stretched over his slight frame, seemed chalky against his dark clothing. Peter spent many hours, along with Andreas and Brother Kramer, at George's side, trying to ease his discomfort.

"There will be no pain or suffering over there." The sick lad's thoughts were often on heaven. "A mansion is awaiting me. Soon I will go. Meet me there, Peter."

"Wait for me. I will come soon," Peter choked.

"God has work for you here yet," George whispered.

"I wonder what, and how."

"Just serve faithfully where you are," George's father encouraged Peter.

"Over there, the Lamb is the light." George brought the conversation back to heaven.

"Jesus is the Light here too," Andreas pointed out. "We don't have much natural light to cheer us, but we can still experience peace and joy."

"Yes, Jesus truly is the Light of the world," reflected Peter. What would he or any of them have done in the last few weeks without the indwelling presence of the Holy Spirit? The love of Christ had constrained them from criticizing and hating one another, and instead had bound them together and strengthened them in the faith. The fact that Christ had also suffered as a man gave them courage to endure their own trials. Truly God had prepared a wondrous plan for man's salvation.

On the morning of January 5, the congregation arranged themselves in rows in preparation for the Lord's Day services.

"I wish Garth would come," Caspar complained to Peter, lowering himself gingerly to the floor. "If he doesn't arrive soon, we'll have to wait until after the service to eat."

"That would be bad, wouldn't it?" Peter teased.

"Rather."

They had waited in vain for their supper the evening before. And now Garth had not appeared with breakfast either. What could it mean?

"Maybe he fell down those stairs he's so tired of going up and down," Lukas suggested from his place on the other side of Caspar.

"We don't know whether the priests have left or not. It could be they've decided to starve us into submission," Peter suggested.

"I think burning would be easier to endure than starvation," declared Caspar, rubbing his empty stomach.

" 'We praise Thee, O Lord . . .' " Someone led out in a song, and the boys abandoned their conjectures to join in.

Brother Kramer chose Psalm 102 for an opening devotion. Peter appreciated how these faithful brethren were able to recall Scriptures that fit their circumstances so well. With the occasional prompting from others of the congregation, he recited David's cry of distress: " 'Hide not thy face from me in the day when I am in trouble; incline thine ear unto me: in the day when I call answer me speedily. . . . My heart is smitten, and withered like grass. . . . Mine enemies reproach me all the day; and they that are mad against me are sworn against me . . .' "[46]

Even King David had had his moments of despair. He had been hounded by enemies and had lain in dark caves also. At times he felt that the Lord had deserted him. But, as in many of his prayers of affliction, he returned to the mercy of the Lord.

" 'But thou, O LORD, shalt endure for ever; and thy remembrance unto all generations. Thou shalt arise, and have mercy upon Zion: for the time to favour her, yea, the set time, is come. . . . He will regard the prayer of the destitute, and not despise their prayer. This shall be written for the generation to come: and the people which shall be created shall praise the LORD. For he hath looked down from the height of his sanctuary; from heaven did the LORD behold the earth; to hear the groaning of the prisoner; to loose those that are appointed to death. . . .' "[47]

Peter sat up straight, hanging on every word. Why, it was amazing that these words penned so many centuries ago could describe so accurately their condition! God was looking down from heaven and listening to the groanings of the prisoners.

" 'I said, O my God, take me not away in the midst of my days. . . .' "[48]

Peter blinked. The sweet singer had prayed for God to extend his days. Then it would not be wrong for him, Peter, to pray that God would not cut him off before his life had scarcely begun. Yes, he had said he was ready to die for the faith; but really, deep inside, he wanted to live. He wanted to live for many years, serving the Lord and experiencing the fullness of joy that comes from a life of service.

"O Lord," he prayed silently, "take me not away in the midst of my days. Deliver us from this dungeon and give me years of service. Nevertheless, not my will but Thine . . ."

Mathes Legeder was speaking now. "The recent deprivation of two meals has prompted me to speak on fasting. Our Lord fasted often. Sometimes for short periods, but at least once he fasted forty days."

Lukas cleared his throat and glanced significantly at Caspar. "I know that many of you spent the night just past in prayer." There was a scuffing at the door.

"In our present circumstances, it behooves us to pray often, and perhaps we should have been more faithful in this matter of fasting."

The door swung open, and Garth could be heard muttering, "Up and down, take this, take that. Here's an end to the business."

Here and there, a curious man turned to look at the jailor. Mathes continued to speak. Peter made an heroic effort not to turn his head in the direction of the door, but when Garth repeated in a loud voice, "Here's an end to it, I say. No more, up and down. An end!" Even the deacon stopped in midsentence to stare at him.

Garth waved his arms. "Come on. Up with ye. All of ye. Get up! Up the stairs with you."

The men continued to stare at him, stupefied.

"What's the matter. You want to stay here? I'd have thought

ye'd be glad to get out of here. Up now. Get moving." He continued to wave his arms impatiently as if to sweep them through
the doorway.

"You mean we are to come upstairs with you?" asked Mathes.

"That's right. Up you go. No more up and down for me."

"All of us?"

"Every man o' ye. Come now. Carry those sick ones."

Peter could not believe it. Just like that. All of them. Out of
this cell. He scrambled to his feet. Some men were already filing
through the door. He joggled Caspar's arm. "Hey, we're leaving."
His voice was tense with excitement.

"Sounds too like we're not coming back." Lukas exulted.

"We aren't free yet." Caspar was not so jubilant.

"No, but at least we can say good-bye to these walls." Peter
turned to peer into the inner room. "I wonder if they need help
to carry the sick men."

But others had already made chairs out of their entwined arms
and were bearing their ill companions from the cell, so the boys
followed the crowd into the corridor.

What would happen to them now? Would they be released?
Peter hardly dared to hope. But he felt that the Lord had, that
morning, miraculously reached down through time and spoken
to their need through His inspired servant. And now He had
answered their pleas and delivered them from their prison. He
is a prayer-answering God!

Again, the sudden brightness was dazzling as they stepped
into the sunlit courtyard. Just as a newly freed, caged bird hud-
dles on the ground, ruffles its feathers, and waits for the sun's
warmth to penetrate before it cautiously spreads its wings for a
first tentative flight, so the released men stumbled about awkwardly as though in a daze. Peter drew in great gulps of fresh air.
He swung his arms slowly back and forth. He stretched his legs

and stepped forward without colliding with anyone. All about him men were stretching, opening their coats to feel the sun on their chests, lifting their faces to the infinite sky, and breathing deeply.

They were a pathetic-looking company. Long, matted hair and bushy, ragged beards framed gaunt, colorless faces. Wrinkled garments, matted with straw and dirt, hung on their undernourished bodies. And yet, Peter noted with satisfaction, there was a calmness and joy shining through the grime on their faces; and the eyes, sunken in their sockets, sparkled with life. How good to be alive under God's heaven. Prayers of thanksgiving rose from every heart.

Stone walls still ringed them about however, and two massive gates lay between them and freedom.

"Look at those soldiers. They look foreign." Caspar pointed towards one of the towers.

Peter's eyes followed his pointing finger. "They certainly aren't Austrian soldiers," he agreed.

Seven guards leaned against the wall, watching the prisoners with ill-concealed amusement. By their gestures, the boys could understand that they were mocking the unkempt beards and heads.

"They're almost all dark-skinned," Peter observed.

"Maybe they are Italians," Lukas suggested.

Caspar soon lost interest in the strange soldiers. "We still haven't had anything to eat," he complained.

Andreas, who had been settling George in a place in the sun, hurried over to join them. "Do any of you know in which tower the girls are kept?" he asked eagerly.

"No." They all shook their heads. They looked in turn at each of the four towers in the corners of the court. Small oblong openings placed at intervals high in the stone walls offered no clues as to the occupants of each tower.

"I wish we could see them!" Andreas was almost desperate. "I have a notion to call out. Maybe they could hear us."

"What good would that do?" Caspar tried to reason with him. "They likely couldn't get out by themselves anyway."

"No, I suppose not." But Andreas still kept his eyes on the towers, looking first at one and then another.

"Look, there are more soldiers here now," Lukas said.

Moving away from the crowd, Peter could see about a dozen more dark-complexioned men in foreign armour, moving along the wall to the right of the huge gate. Turning, he saw several more emerge from the archway leading into the square keep, the central defense structure that contained the principal living quarters of the castle.

While he watched, a man, obviously an officer of superior rank, appeared in the archway. The sun glinted from his silver helmet, and the colourful ribbons on his epaulets waved in the breeze. He raised his arm. The soldiers immediately advanced on the prisoners from all sides. They began herding the men into the keep.

Peering eagerly over the heads of the throng, Peter was propelled through the archway, down three, wide, polished steps and into a large chamber. Lukas was right at his heels. "This must be the great hall," he breathed.

The walls of the vast hall were hung with decorative shields and picturesque tapestries. Between the shields and tapestries, ornamental bronze candlesticks held flickering tapers.

As moths to a candle, the ever-chilled men were drawn instinctively towards one of the great fireplaces that radiated waves of heat from both ends of the great room. Underfoot were fresh, clean-smelling rushes. Along the far wall, six arched windows framed glimpses of snow-clad forests and pale blue sky.

The prisoners huddled gratefully about the fire, with the

soldiers forming an armed semicircle about them. The officer strode to the far end of the hall, where two houseboys were busily removing dishes from a long wooden table. Under the table, three dogs growled and fought over some bones. The officer waited until the boys had disappeared through a side door. Then he lifted a roll of parchment from the table and solemnly approached the waiting men.

Sensing the portent of their impending fate, the men hushed their whispers and every eye followed the officer as he mounted the three steps, deliberately unrolled the missive, cleared his throat, and surveyed his audience thoughtfully.

He read:

> Ferdinand, King of the Romans, semper Augustus; Archduke of Austria; Duke of Burgundy, Brabant, Styria, Carintha, Carniola, and Luxemburg; Count of Hapsburg, Flanders, and Tyrol; Count of Swabia; to his loyal servant Baron Fünfkirchen, Lord of Falkenstein and Steinborn, concerning the heretics held in Falkenstein Castle. I, Ferdinand, King by the grace of God, having made all attempts to convert said heretics and said heretics having refused my offers of leniency, now command that said heretics be delivered into the hand of General Carlos of the Spanish Regiment to be conducted in chains to the Adriatic Sea and given into the service of Admiral Doria for use as galley slaves on his warships in the Mediterranean.

In the stunned silence, the paper rustled noisily as the officer rolled up the fateful parchment. He straightened his shoulders and saluted smartly. "I," he announced shortly, "am General Carlos."

Peter could not believe it. It must be a dream. Surely there was some mistake. They could not just take a whole village of men and send them into slavery. Why didn't somebody wake him up?

Agitated voices buzzed about his ears.

"Chains? Did he say chains?"

"Lord, preserve us."

"The Adriatic. How will we get there?"

"Slaves! Galley slaves!"

Slaves! Slaves! The word pounded in Peter's ears. Slaves in a warship. Endless hours of gruelling labour. Chained to a post, at the end of an oar. A slave!

The soldiers were hustling the men from the hall. From a distance, he heard the general's voice. "Leave the sick here."

The sick? George! George would have to stay behind. He'd never see him again. Peter froze on the bottom step. Someone stumbled against him. He turned and frantically tried to elbow his way back. He had to say good-bye to George. He struggled against the current, and then he felt strong arms about him, turning him. "I have to see George," he gasped, twisting desperately.

"Easy now, son." It was his father.

Peter stopped struggling. "But I have to say good-bye to George. I may never see him again."

Big Peter gently but firmly propelled him up the steps. "Don't resist. Leave George in God's hands. You will meet again, someday."

Peter stumbled blindly into the courtyard. The melodious strains of a familiar hymn floated faintly over the heads of the distraught men. Peter lifted his eyes. Just ahead of him, Andreas stood, his head flung back, staring in despair at one of the towers. He looked frantically about him, as though seeking a way to reach the source of the music. Peter paused beside him, thinking of the sister with whom he had shared so many childhood adventures. "Oh, Ursula, keep the faith. We will meet again." Tears stung his eyes, but he blinked them back manfully. The crowd milled confusedly about the courtyard. Other men had stopped to gaze longingly at the tower where their daughters were incarcerated.

"Move along." The general urged his soldiers to keep the men moving.

"Come, Andreas." Peter clutched the older youth's arm. "Leave her in the Lord's hands. You will meet again; if not here, then in a better land."

"Yes." Andreas allowed himself to be led towards the gate.

They followed the same route around the central fortification and past the stables to the spacious area just inside the main gate, which now stood wide open.

For so long we have prayed for release from Falkenstein, Peter thought as the men stood waiting uneasily for further orders. Now it has come. But what a release! A slave! The indignity of it stung his pride.

Beyond the cluster of prisoners, there was a bustle of activity. Shouts of stableboys and the neighing of horses bounced from the stone walls. Peering between arms and over shoulders, Peter could see several dozen fine horses tossing their manes and stamping their hooves as they were outfitted with saddles and bridles. Were they to ride? For the first time, Peter began to wonder how this overland journey to the sea was to be made? It was January. How could they travel four hundred miles in the winter?

A soldier roughly shouldered Peter to one side. "Over there!" he ordered in broken German, indicating that an elderly prisoner who had been standing near Peter was to go stand by the outer wall next to the gate. Peter followed the man with his eyes and saw him join several other old men and young boys who were already standing uncertainly by themselves.

The soldier next singled out Grandfather Boewen, who had

gallantly stumbled along with the brethren. "You, old man. Over there."

Grandfather's cane remained planted firmly. "Why?" he asked politely.

"Too old. Need strong men," the soldier answered. "Go."

"I can walk," Grandfather insisted. "I wish to go along."

The soldier looked helplessly about for aid. "Come here." He beckoned to a comrade who had just sent two fourteen-year-old boys away from the crowd. Between the two of them, they hustled the unwilling elderly saint away.

"Old man," the second soldier grunted. "Can't walk. Can't row. Only strong men on ships."

Peter was glad that the younger boys would escape the horrible fate that awaited the rest of them, but what would become of them? Maybe they would be sent back to the dungeon. He was not sure which was worse.

"Start working on the chains." The commander had mounted a handsome chestnut steed. He directed some soldiers to lead several men across the yard beyond the gate. Peter heard, above the clamour of the stableboys, the ring of metal on metal. Chains!

"We're to be chained," groaned a voice beside him.

Just then there was a commotion near the gate. Soldiers began shouting and running in that direction. The prisoners stood on tiptoe and peered around each other to see.

"Beggars," muttered a castle guard as he hurried past the men.

But it was not beggars. After a hurried scuffle and much shouting, a group of women and small children surged through the great portal towards the prisoners. Glad shouts rang in the frosty air as the men recognized their wives, mothers, and little ones.

Before Peter could come to his senses, he was in his mother's arms. And then Big Peter was there too, trying to clasp his whole family to him at once.

"How? Where?" Big Peter stammered, holding his wife at arm's length and gazing through tears into the face of his infant son. Maria clung to his leg, laughing and crying at the same time. Her father scooped her into his arms while his wife answered breathlessly.

"Someone left a message on the dining hall door that you were to be taken away this morning. We felt we just had to see you. Oh, Peter, where will they take you?"

Father briefly told her what he knew of their destination. "Don't grieve," he soothed as his wife's tears flowed. "We knew, when we committed our lives to the Lord, that we faced hardship and tribulation in this life. But remember the joy that is set before us."

"Yes," Mother replied, nodding through her tears, "but it is so hard."

" 'Cast thy burden upon the LORD, and he shall sustain thee.' "[49]

The familiar words reminded Mother of something. Handing the baby to Peter, she fumbled in her apron pocket. "Here, I brought . . ." and glancing furtively about, she slipped a parcel into Father's pocket. "You may have need of this." She had one for Peter too. As he quickly secreted it in an inside pocket, he could feel that it was a notebook. "I sent your maps along, Peter," she said.

His maps! Of what use were maps to a slave? Well, he would keep them, regardless.

She also gave each of them a pouch full of coins. "They may be taken from you, but then, they may be useful some day."

The general was riding around the crowd of reunited families, calling to his soldiers to take the women away.

Big Peter hastily pled with his wife, "Take good care of the little ones. Bring them up in the ways of the Lord. Teach them to love the truth and be faithful until death. We may never meet again on this earth," he said brokenly, "but my prayer is that we may meet someday in glory, where we will be forever with the Lord. Maria"—he crushed the wondering child against his shoulder—"obey your mother, and always do what is right."

"Brethren," Michel Kramer called for attention. "The general has granted us the privilege of praying together one last time. Let us come before the throne of mercy."

The entire congregation sank to their knees, and there on the frozen ground, the voice of the saintly deacon committed each one to the Saviour's care. Even the watching soldiers and guards fell silent, and the words of the final benediction ascended to heaven unhindered.

"And now the Lord watch between us while we are absent one from another. And if it be according to Thy will, bring us again to our place.

" 'But the God of all grace, who hath called us unto his eternal glory by Christ Jesus, after that ye have suffered a while, make you perfect, stablish, strengthen, settle you. To him be glory and dominion for ever and ever. Amen' "[50]

As Peter stumbled to his feet, he was startled to see one of the swarthy soldiers near him brush a hand furtively across his eyes. Did even these hardened soldiers have hearts?

With much lamentation, the women and children were parted from their loved ones and driven towards the gate. Peter gave his little sister a hug. "Take care of Mother," he whispered into her ear, "and don't forget me."

"Why don't you come home with us now, Peter?" The innocent brown eyes were big with puzzlement.

"I can't." He returned Maria to her mother's side and gazed long and sorrowfully into the face of the baby brother he would never really learn to know.

"Good-bye, good-bye." The brethren stood helplessly by as the soldiers hustled their families out onto the drawbridge. Most heartbreaking were the confused looks on the faces of the children who did not comprehend the finality of the parting, and were mystified and frightened by the depth of the adults' emotions.

The soldiers returned to their task of leading the men to the forge, where a blacksmith waited beside an untidy pile of chains and iron rings.

Peter and Big Peter attempted to stay together, but they were led in two different directions. When an iron band was bolted securely around his left wrist, Peter felt that all hope was lost. From the band dangled a three-foot chain.

"Got another his size?" The burly blacksmith scanned the men before him. "You there." Lukas was pushed forward to have his right wrist banded and fastened to the other end of Peter's chain.

The boys stared unbelievingly at the chain that swung between them. Finally Lukas cleared his throat. "Looks like we'll be inseparable friends now."

Peter did not answer. He wished it were Caspar at the other end of the chain. But then, the thought came to him, maybe the Lord had a purpose for linking him with Lukas. He managed a weak smile. "Yes, you won't be able to keep any secrets from me now."

"Did your mother give you some money?"

Peter looked sharply at Lukas. How did he know? "Why?"

"Mine did," the other boy confessed.

"Yes, she did."

"Better hide it. They may search us."

Lukas was proving to be a blessing already. Peter had not

thought of that. Where would he hide it? The man who had managed to hang on to his knife during the first search had concealed it in his boot. With his eyes on the nearby soldiers, Peter carefully felt for the pouch of money in his pocket. He could feel the shape of the coins inside. Twisting his fingers, he squeezed several through the neck of the bag and closed his hand around them.

"Watch out," Lukas hissed. "That sentry."

Peter quickly withdrew his hand, several large coins clutched in his fist. The soldier was watching him suspiciously. On impulse he raised the hand and faked a sneeze. *"Ker-choo!"* Then he fumbled again in the pocket for a handkerchief. The soldier turned away.

Watching his chance, Peter bent down and, on pretense of scratching his leg, dropped the coins into his shoe top. They would work their way down as he walked, he hoped. Straightening up, he caught Lukas's approving glance.

The chaining took several hours. During this time, the men did very little talking. They withdrew into private thoughts of their helpless wives and little ones, and in contemplation of the uncertain future. Many stood with bowed heads, seeking help and strength from the Source of all power.

Finally the chaining was completed. The Spanish soldiers mounted the horses that had been led from the stable area. Peter counted forty mounted men in addition to General Carlos. The king must be very concerned that his prisoners not escape. With more chains, the blacksmith now moved among the men. The central link of the chain joining each pair was larger than the rest. A long chain was passed through this centre link on five pairs of men. Each end of this main line was locked onto the pommel of a horse's saddle. So they were forced into a double line, with mounted soldiers at regular intervals on either side of the column. Peter and Lukas were gratified to see that Caspar and Andreas were directly behind them.

After seemingly endless inspections and rearrangements of the horsemen, General Carlos took his place at the head of the line. "Forward!" The order was given, and the line moved slowly through the gates of Falkenstein.

The long march to the sea had begun.

On the March

Scrunch! Scrunch! Scrunch!

Peter placed one boot in front of the other in the snow-packed road that led to Vienna.

Scrunch! Scrunch! Scrunch! Each step took him farther away from all that was familiar. Back there in the valley was home and Mother and Maria and the baby. Back there were the memories of school days and pleasant hours in the cabinet shop. Back there were the fields where he had stooked wheat, the slopes where he had played, and the rock where he had shared confidences with Caspar.

Scrunch. Scrunch. Scrunch. Behind him, somewhere within the ramparts of the Falkenstein castle, were his sister Ursula, and his friend George. Would he ever see them again? He plodded on, his eyes fixed on the boots of the man before him. With every step he felt more lonely, more forsaken. Although he had often longed to see what lay over the crest of the mountain, now the finality of this departure frightened him. And, of course, he had never envisioned himself leaving in this shameful fashion.

He twisted his wrist irritably. The heavy iron band chafed his skin. With his free hand, he worked some of his coat sleeve under the band. There, that felt better. But it was still heavy. If he held his arm straight down, the chain binding him to Lukas nearly dragged on the ground. He could not move his left arm very far without jerking his friend's arm painfully. Chained! A slave! The reality of the status pierced sharply into Peter's thinking.

He had to remind himself that he was suffering for righteousness' sake. "For what glory is it, if, when ye be buffeted for your faults, ye shall take it patiently? but if, when ye do well, and suffer for it, ye take it patiently, this is acceptable with God. For even hereunto were ye called: because Christ also suffered for us, leaving us an example, that ye should follow his steps: who did no sin, neither was guile found in his mouth: who, when he was reviled, reviled not again; when he suffered, he threatened not; but committed himself to him that judgeth righteously."[51]

Peter tramped forward resolutely. His Master had walked this way before. Jesus, who was the perfect Son of God, had allowed Himself to be led out, bound to an ignoble death. Because of His sacrifice, he, Peter, could have his sins forgiven and anticipate a glorious eternity with the Lord.

Ahead of him, the long double line of chained prisoners snaked upwards and disappeared over the next hilltop. Beside, and a little in front of Peter, a soldier rode astride a black horse, the end of a mainline chain attached to his saddle. The other end of the chain, locking Peter and Lukas to four other pairs of men, was secured to the saddle of a second soldier riding at the left of the column.

They were almost at the crest of the hill; soon they would be out of this valley and out of sight of Steinborn and the castle. Peter turned for a last longing look at his home.

"Heh!" Peter jerked around as a searing pain shot from his elbow to the tips of his fingers. He turned to see the soldier watching him with a contemptuous sneer on his narrow, dark face. The soldier yelled at him again, and Peter stumbled forward.

"Are you all right?" Lukas whispered.

Peter nodded although his whole arm still tingled from the blow. That soldier was anything but gentle. Peter studied the straight, armoured back of the figure on the horse. Who were these soldiers? For the first time, Peter thought of them as individuals. Each one of them must have dreams, fears, likes, and dislikes. From where had they come, and where were they going? Peter prayed that God would give him a love for this one who had lashed out at him. He had an eternal soul too. Maybe, just maybe, he could help this soldier to a saving knowledge of Christ.

In all their weeks of imprisonment, Peter had experienced difficulty understanding why God would so incapacitate such a large number of Christians. There had been no opportunity to share the Gospel with anyone in prison. But perhaps He had been preparing the hearts of these foreign soldiers, who were accompanying them to the sea, to be touched by the Gospel of love.

The road twisted downward into a valley. Here the forest-clad slopes and snow-covered fields looked much like those at home. Nestled against one mountainside was a small cluster of houses. Slowly the procession descended into the valley and passed silently within shouting distance of the village. Smoke curling from the chimneys and the barking of dogs were the only signs of life. Within those neat houses, women were likely stirring pots of soup or rocking babies before cozy fires while their men sat together whittling wooden figurines or mending harnesses.

A wave of homesickness again swept over Peter. Why must the godly suffer so? Why should he be here, forced, in the middle of winter, to leave all the comforts of home, when the unredeemed enjoyed comfort and security?

"Even the psalmist asked himself such questions," the Spirit reminded Peter. "But as for me, my feet were almost gone; my steps had well nigh slipped. For I was envious at the foolish, when

I saw the prosperity of the wicked. For there are no bands in their death: but their strength is firm. They are not in trouble as other men; neither are they plagued like other men."[52]

Peter knew that this psalm was no doubt copied in the notebook his mother had given him, but he did not dare risk taking it from his pocket. The men had not been searched before leaving Falkenstein, and he knew that most of them had been given notebooks, money, knives, and other useful or valuable items by their mothers or wives.

Now what was the rest of that passage? It had seemed to the psalmist as though God was blessing the wicked while the righteous suffered. "For all the day long have I been plagued, and chastened every morning."[53]

But then he had come to his senses. "Then understood I their end. . . . How are they brought into desolation, as in a moment! they are utterly consumed with terrors."[54]

Peter had grown up in an Anabaptist home. He knew nothing of the slavery of serving the state church. But he had heard his parents and others speak of the fear and restlessness that had accompanied them before they embraced the true faith. They told of having to do penance and say endless prayers and pay money to the priest to pray for them. They called on Mary and the saints for protection from evil, and yet they lived in terror. They were never sure that all these activities were going to keep them from hellfire. There had often been scarcely enough money earned for food in some families, yet the church dues and offerings to get their dead forefathers out of purgatory had to be paid first.

"Thou shalt guide me with thy counsel, and afterward receive me to glory. Whom have I in heaven but thee? and there is none upon earth that I desire beside thee. My flesh and my heart faileth: but God is the strength of my heart, and my portion for ever."[55]

Peter had a foreboding that his heart and flesh would often

fail in the uncertain days ahead. But God was the strength of his life. He had no abiding city here, but looked for that eternal city whose builder and maker is God.

Lukas stepped closer until their shoulders almost touched. "I feel like Joseph," he confided in a low voice.

"Joseph?"

"Joseph in the Bible. He was marched away as a slave to a strange land. He didn't know where he was going either."

"And he was all alone," Peter added.

"At least we have each other."

"I'm not sure what I would do if I had to face something like this alone," Peter admitted.

"Me either. I don't know if I could stand."

"If our faith is strong, it will withstand any trial, even if all other props are pulled out from under us. If we can know that our sins are taken away by the blood, and the Lord is on our side, nothing can separate us from the love of God which is in Christ Jesus."

Just in time, Peter saw the soldier beside him turn his head, and he closed his mouth quickly. The dark eyes glared at the two boys, and the mouth twisted into a haughty sneer. The soldier's hand rested on the hilt of his sword, but after a moment he raised his horse's reins and urged the animal forward.

Apparently they were not allowed to talk.

Yes, Joseph had been abruptly cut off from a comfortable and even coddled life and led away into slavery. His fate must have been even harder to accept, knowing that his own brethren had betrayed him. Yet, look how God had planned Joseph's life. He had raised him from a dungeon to a throne. Peter did not really expect that God had a throne waiting for him. But who knew what purposes God was unfolding in this circumstance.

"For my thoughts are not your thoughts, neither are your ways

my ways, saith the LORD. For as the heavens are higher than the
earth, so are my ways higher than your ways, and my thoughts
than your thoughts."[56]

Peter noticed that the line seemed to be moving slower. His
own legs felt wobbly. His stomach was empty. None of the brethren
had eaten since the morning of the previous day.

Although a march of ten miles was not unusual for these sturdy
farmers, now, in their weakened condition, the few hours' trek
had exhausted them.

They were climbing again, and the soldiers cracked whips over
the heads of the flagging men. The soldier beside Peter seemed
to delight in flicking his whip between the pairs of men, so close
to their faces that they could feel the wind whistle as the rawhide
barely missed their noses. When the men jerked their heads back-
wards, the soldier would laugh mockingly, say something in Spanish, and snap his whip at them again. Was it only his imagination,
or did this man really pick on Lukas and him more than on the
other men in their unit? It was going to take a large dose of divine
grace to love this one, Peter felt.

It was growing colder. Peter shivered. His feet felt numb. He
buried his hands in his pockets and hunched his ears down into
his coat collar. He wondered where they would spend the night?
Surely not out on the snowy mountainside.

As darkness spread over the countryside, the weary line of
men stumbled forward, urged on by the whips and shouts of the
soldiers. When Peter felt he could go no farther, the order was
given to halt. Peering ahead, past the crowd, he could see several
faint lights ahead. Must be another small village.

After what seemed an interminable wait in the cold, the two
soldiers uncoupled their charges from the mainline and led them
through a low doorway into a dimly lit building. Peter's nose told
him they were in a stable. The tired men sank gratefully onto the

straw. A few weeks ago he might have felt indignant about sleeping on straw in a stable, Peter reflected; but tonight, it felt like
luxury. After all, he'd slept on straw every night for the past five
weeks. At least this was clean and he could breathe fresh air here.

The soldiers came with some thin soup that helped to warm
the men and take the edge off their hunger. Then, still joined by
their chains, the two boys followed the example of others; and
burrowing into the straw, they fell asleep almost instantly.

What seemed like only moments later, the boys were wakened
by harsh shouts. Peter squirmed in the straw and attempted to
roll over. Something jerked at his left arm. He stared bewilderedly
at the iron ring circling his wrist. Slowly it all came back to him—
the release from prison, the sentence, the chaining, the tearful
parting, the weary march. Now they were on their way south to
the sea to serve as galley slaves. He determinedly pushed the
thought of their ultimate destination from his mind. He would
rather not think about that.

Before it was fully light, the ninety Anabaptist prisoners—for
that was the number that remained after the young, the sick, and
elderly had been culled out—were on the march again.

The clouds hung low over the mountains, and the air was
damp. It penetrated their coats and forced the men into a fast
pace to keep themselves warm.

There was more talking today. In the conversation of the two
men in front of them, Peter thought he heard the word Vienna.
Were they going to Vienna then? He stepped closer; and Lukas,
necessarily, did also.

"Vienna, where the king is," they were saying.

"Are we going to Vienna?" he asked politely.

The speaker turned his head with a smile. "Yes, some of the
men were speaking to General Carlos last evening. He is the commander of this regiment, you know," he contributed by way of

explanation. "He seems to be rather lenient in his attitude towards us. The deacons asked if we were not to be given a trial."

"Trial?" Lukas questioned.

"Yes. Prisoners are not normally condemned without a trial, even though religious trials are often a farce," the man explained. "The general said he had orders only to conduct us to Trieste, on the Mediterranean, but that the route lies through Vienna; and if we want to appeal to the king for a trial, he will see whether he can arrange it."

"You mean we might be freed and never reach the sea?" Lukas asked eagerly.

The older man shook his head. "Don't count on it. Even if we were given a trial, the priests and inquisitors would have their way. However, the sentence might be altered. We must not put our confidence in princes," he cautioned, "but in the Lord. Remember, they can do to us only what He allows."

The two lads fell back again.

"If the general is kindly towards us, he surely isn't." Lukas pointed his chin at the soldier riding, straight backed, just ahead of Peter. That morning, the soldier had taken pains to make things miserable for them. He had deliberately spilled some of their gruel onto their laps when handing them their bowls; and later he had tripped Peter, laughing raucously when he sprawled, face first, into the snow.

"I don't think he's very old," Peter replied. "I wonder what drives him to be so cruel?"

"His name is Alfonso," Lukas supplied. "I heard one of the others calling him that."

They were approaching a small town. As they passed the first houses, several dogs ran out, barking and snapping at the invaders. Attracted by the noise, women came to stand in doorways, staring at the pathetic procession.

In the square, the soldiers paused to let their horses drink from the fountain. A crowd of curious townspeople gathered to stare and point and jeer at the dirty, untidy prisoners.

"I feel like a freak animal at a fair," Lukas whispered to Peter.

"It is unpleasant to be the object of ridicule," Peter agreed.

The men of the town had been talking with the general. They pointed and gesticulated at the chained men. Their actions became more and more agitated. Suddenly, one young man picked up a handful of snow and, packing it into a hard ball, hurled it at the nearest prisoner. "Heretic!" he shouted. Soon others followed suit, and the air was thick with flying snowballs accompanied by insults.

The general quickly commanded his men to fall into line, and they made a hasty exit from the square. The crowd followed them, enjoying the sport. Peter had often engaged in harmless snowball fights, so the shower of cold snowballs breaking on his head and falling down his neck was no new sensation, but the ferocity with which they were hurled astonished him.

The snowballs soon changed to hunks of frozen ground. The men were forced to run past the last houses, the angered crowd in pursuit. A hard clod caught Peter on the side of his face and made him see stars. He held his hand to his face and ran on, chains clanking. Beside him, Alfonso, the soldier, laughed coarsely at his discomfort.

At last the villagers tired of the sport, and the column slowed to a walk.

"See; they drive you off like dogs," Alfonso jeered at the boys.

Peter had a good look at him. He did appear to be young in spite of his proud bearing.

"And to think I wanted to be a soldier." Lukas shook his head.

Peter looked at him sharply. "You? Wanted to be a soldier?"

"When I was younger."

"That's correct. Your family only joined the brethren a few years ago, didn't they?"

Lukas nodded.

"But your father was a blacksmith. Why did you want to be a soldier?"

Lukas did not answer the question directly.

"Our family was quite well-off," he reminisced. "My grandfather, a tailor, had a prosperous business sewing for rich lords. I used to love to dress up in the garments he sewed and to pretend I was a count or an earl. I had two brothers, but they both died in an epidemic; so I was the only child, and my parents and grandparents bought me whatever I wished for. I had playthings and books. But what I wanted most was a horse."

Peter smiled. He knew of Lukas's passion for horses.

"I had an uncle who had run away from home and become a soldier," Lukas went on. "He would come home occasionally and entertain us with tales of faraway places and exciting battles. I wanted to be a soldier and ride a fine horse." Lukas again shook his head sorrowfully at Alfonso's back. "I'm so glad my parents came to the true faith."

"But you still like horses," Peter reminded Lukas.

"Oh, yes. I do. And even after I had received Jesus as my Lord and Saviour, I still hankered after fine things."

Peter was silent, sensing his friend's need to talk.

"I sometimes schemed how I could be a Christian and still ride a fine horse and wear expensive clothing. I thought maybe I could be a merchant, selling the wares the brethren produced. I could take goods to distant towns, dine in good inns, deal with wealthy customers. I thought I could witness to these nobles and inspire them with my honesty."

Peter stared at him in astonishment. He had not known all about Lukas. He really did not know Lukas very well at all, he realised. For the last number of years, the boy who was now joined so firmly to him had been a casual friend. He and Caspar had been inseparable for almost as long as Peter could remember. He had known George well too, but Lukas was rather quiet. He was agreeable and willing to pitch in when there was work to be done or a game to be played. When George and Peter joined the instruction class for baptism, Lukas came too. But he had never been close enough to any of the others to share freely with them. Now Peter chided himself for not having made a greater effort to be friends with Lukas. The other boy must have gone through some spiritual struggles during those weeks in the castle. It was no coincidence that he had been chained to Lukas rather than, as he would have preferred, to Caspar.

"I was trying to serve two masters," Lukas confessed. "When the deacons asked us there in the dungeon whether we were ready to cast our lot with the believers, I did some serious thinking. I had sincerely wanted to follow Christ and be baptised before, but those weeks of imprisonment forced me to see that following Christ meant giving up everything. I was accustomed to following the crowd; but I knew that, even though we were together there, it might not always be so. I realised that I might have to face persecution by myself someday. And my picture of a prosperous Christian merchant disintegrated."

"I'm glad you won the victory through Christ," Peter rejoiced.

Lukas nodded. "But the flesh dies hard," he sighed. "I can hardly bear to go about in such filthy rags." He glanced distastefully at his rumpled coat.

"Think of the white robes you can wear in heaven," suggested Peter.

At noon the men were allowed to sit under some overhanging evergreens while the soldiers handed out dry bread. Soon after they had started walking again, it began to snow. The men were still weary from the unaccustomed exercise of the day before; and the wet snow, which settled soggily on their unprotected heads, added to their discomfort. The flakes swirled about them thickly, obscuring the scenery. The prisoners plodded on, alone in a silent world of whiteness.

General Carlos called a halt early that evening. There was no village nearby, so the company prepared to spend the night on the mountainside. Grumbling, some of the soldiers extricated axes from the supply bundles on the pack horses, which brought up the rear of the column, and went to chop wood for fires.

The men were ordered to break off evergreen branches and fashion crude shelters. Working in pairs was awkward, but eventually they were huddled around smoky fires, the branches affording enough protection to keep most of the snow off them.

Peter and Lukas hunched as close to the fire as they dared. The smoke made their eyes smart, but it had been so long since they had been really warm, that they gladly suffered that irritation. Two of their chain group had been ordered to make soup, and the men now consumed this with gusto. Alfonso and his fellow soldier crouched across the fire from their prisoners, enjoying their own meal of soup, bread, and cheese.

"Did you hear about Martin?" Caspar asked between sips.

"No; where is he?" Peter asked. "I haven't seen him, but then I haven't seen anyone else very closely either."

"He's not with us."

Peter and Lukas lowered their bowls.

"You mean?"

Caspar nodded soberly. "Andreas's father told him that Leonhardt Blöcher and his nephew, Johan, went to the general while we were being chained, and accepted the conditions we had been offered earlier."

"You mean to scatter and live by themselves, apart from other Anabaptists?"

Caspar nodded.

Peter looked to Andreas for confirmation of this disclosure.

"It's true," Andreas said. "Someone overheard him, and when we left the castle, Leonhardt, Johan, and Martin were standing near the old men and sick ones who were left behind."

"Oh, no!" Peter felt sick. Poor Martin. What chance had he with such a weak father?

"What will become of them?" Lukas asked.

"No one knows," Andreas replied. "But we can be sure that they won't receive any favours. In the end, their fate will be worse than ours."

" 'But whosoever shall deny me before men, him will I also deny before my Father which is in heaven,' "[57] quoted an older man.

Peter shuddered. His own future was uncertain, but even though they could kill his body, he felt his soul was secure. What of Martin and his relatives? If they compromised with the enemies of the truth, could they expect to remain faithful?

"There is some good news," Philip, a harness maker whose back Peter had stared at for two days, volunteered.

They all watched him expectantly.

"While we were waiting in the courtyard before entering the great hall, some of the men spoke with Garth about his soul's need. He just shook his head and muttered, 'Ye're all good men, good men. Shouldn't do this to good men.' They urged him to be a 'good man' too and to trust in Jesus to save his soul, but he only shook his head. Then later, when we were leaving, some of the brethren saw him in the shadows by the gate. He was weeping, and he said, 'Pray for my soul.' "

"He is not far from the kingdom," Philip's partner said. "Let us be faithful in remembering him in our prayers."

So all those days in prison were not wasted. Peter gazed drowsily into the flickering flames. If Garth would become a Christian, it would make those dreary days worthwhile.

Philip suggested that they pray together before sleeping. He reached inside his coat, hesitated, looked at the two soldiers on the far side of the fire, and then deliberately withdrew a worn notebook. Alfonso scowled and made as if to stand up, but he looked first at his older companion. The man had clearly seen Philip's notebook, but he continued to gaze impassively into the fire. Encouraged, Philip read one precious passage after the other. Around other fires, the brethren all rejoiced in the privilege of praying together and hearing the Word.

Even though they were out in the cold on a desolate mountainside, the men felt warmer, inside and out, than they had felt for many days.

The next morning, the sun shone weakly from a pale winter sky. Although their path took them up and down, Peter noticed that the hills were lower and less rugged now. On the lower slopes, snow-covered stone walls encircled small fields and a few vineyards. Here and there across the snowy landscape, clusters of buildings indicated a denser population than was found in the higher mountains to the north.

Several miles before they reached it, Peter knew they were approaching a large town. The narrow, rutted mountain trail they had followed thus far had led them onto a broader, well-travelled highway. At intervals, other travellers joined them. Most rode in high-sided farm carts that trundled noisily past the chained men, their occupants casting curious glances in their direction. They passed one small boy who was trying valiantly to keep two lively goats from leaping over the low stone wall beside the road. All of the country people kept their distance from the strange, dishevelled-looking prisoners and the imperious soldiers who rode beside them.

"Do you think they'll drive us out like they did in that other town?" Lukas asked anxiously.

"I don't know." Peter hoped they would not. He dreaded having to go where there were people. "Give me a love for those who would revile us," he prayed.

Soon the roofs and church steeples of the town appeared in the distance. The traffic had increased, and the soldiers forced the men to plod through the deep snow in the ditch, while they rode on the roadway.

Just outside the open gates of the town stood a scaffold. Such a device was common to any town; but now the Anabaptists, especially the younger ones, viewed it with apprehension. Someday soon, their bodies might swing from just such a scaffold outside some strange town.

In the crowded confusion of the narrow streets, the soldiers had difficulty keeping their chained units together. The prisoners were jostled against bundle-laden donkeys, bleating sheep, and women carrying baskets of eggs and fresh buns. It was market day.

In the square, hawkers cried their wares; and the squawks of chickens mingled with the neighs of horses. Progress was slow. The soldiers stopped to buy food supplies and to water their horses.

Peter and Lukas found themselves standing beside a man with a wagonload of wood to sell.

"Wish this man had cheese or eggs instead of wood," complained Lukas.

"Come." Their chain jerked as Alfonso yanked them back into formation. In his left hand he held a sweet bun. He held it out to tantalize them and then took a huge bite, chewing it with exaggerated enjoyment.

They made their way slowly through the throng, the soldiers laying about with their whips, when necessary, to clear the way.

Peter became aware that a man had been stepping along beside Philip, who was directly in front of him. While keeping his eyes forward and pretending to be concentrating on the bundle slung over his shoulder, this man addressed Philip in low tones.

"What crime have you committed, my friend?"

"The crime of believing that Jesus Christ died for my sins," Philip quickly replied, without seeming to pay any attention to his fellow traveller.

"But is that not the truth?"

"Yes, it is true, according to the Scriptures."

"But do not the priests need to forgive your sins?"

"No man has power to forgive sins, save one, the Son of God."

"Do you read the Scriptures?"

"Yes."

"But this is forbidden."

"Therein lie the words of life."

"Where could I get a copy of the Scriptures?"

"Go to the print shop of Handler in Vienna. Tell them you wish to purchase some fish."

"Thank you, and God go with you." The man moved away.

Who would have thought they would have an opportunity to witness while bound so closely?

"Do you think he was an informer?" Lukas asked.

"I doubt it."

"If he was, the Vienna printing shop might be closed."

"The brethren always run that risk," Peter reminded Lukas. "We should be cautious and not betray our fellow Christian, but we must always be ready to help sincere seekers after the truth."

Peter pondered on the marvelous designs of God in using prisoners to point the way to a seeking soul.

"Whist, Peter." Peter turned his head slightly and felt Caspar press something into his free hand. It was a hunk of cheese!

"Where?" he said out of the corner of his mouth.

"One of the men was able to buy some back at the market. Take a bite and pass it on."

The mellow goodness melted in his mouth. What a treat after a tasteless diet of soup and dry bread.

He wondered where his father was. He could not spot him in the line ahead, so he must be behind. He hoped he would be able to talk with him sometime.

They must be close to Vienna by now. What awaited them there? Oh, how often he had longed to visit the capital of this country, and now he was almost there—but under much different circumstances than he had ever imagined!

XVI

Trial in Vienna

Towards evening of that third day on the road, General Carlos rode back along the line of prisoners, pausing to speak briefly with several of his men. At the next small town, five of the units of ten chained men were led off to the side while the remainder plodded on.

Finally, Peter, Lukas, Caspar, Andreas, Philip, and the other five of their group were led into a small inn yard along with thirty other brethren.

The mules and horses of several other travellers already occupied the courtyard, which was surrounded on two sides by stables; while on the third side, doors opened into the inn itself. As more travellers arrived with their beasts and servants, the Anabaptists were crowded rudely back against the walls.

Peter crouched wearily against the stable wall while the heterogeneous shouting and braying swirled around him. Occasionally a scurrying stableboy tripped over a prisoner and retaliated by uttering a loud oath or by kicking the unfortunate individual who had placed his legs in his path.

Eventually, all of the animals had been unloaded, curried, watered from the well in the courtyard, and stabled for the night.

"Looks like the animals get to sleep inside and we don't,"

remarked Caspar, flexing his arms, making his chain rattle.

"At least these walls afford some protection," Andreas replied, trying to be grateful for small comforts.

The soldiers had lit a fire on the cobbles, and they indicated that their charges could come and sit near it.

Peter and Lukas, following the example of others, removed their shoes. They rubbed their aching feet while the flames sent waves of warmth over them.

Peter had a painful blister on one heel. He wished he could ask Jacob for some of his healing ointment, but his physician friend must have been sent to another inn, for he was not here. But Big Peter was. Maybe later he would have a chance to talk with his father. Oh, here were the coins he had dropped into his shoe back at the castle. They were rather uncomfortable to walk on. He wondered if he dared return them to the pouch along with the rest of the money?

A shadow loomed over him. He looked up into the cynical face of Alfonso. It was too late. He had seen the coins.

"I—buy food?" Alfonso asked shortly in heavily accented German.

Peter hesitated. Did he mean he would buy food for them? But what if he just kept the money? Peter looked to Lukas for help.

"Buy food—for you." Alfonso stood over him, holding out his hand deprecatingly.

"He's seen the money now," Lukas pointed out. "Might as well give it to him. It may be we'll get something good to eat."

Above him Alfonso was becoming impatient. "No food?" He shrugged his shoulders carelessly and withdrew his hand.

"Here." Peter quickly held up two coins. "Meat, milk, bread," he pronounced distinctly.

Without a word, Alfonso took the money and disappeared into the inn.

"Wonder if that's the last we'll see of the money." Peter was uneasy.

But to their surprise and delight, a few minutes later, Alfonso emerged from the building, a large jug in one hand and a laden platter in the other. He handed the jug to Peter, and then he deliberately tipped the platter and spilled its contents onto the ground in front of the boys. He roared with laughter at their dismayed gasps and then left them to retrieve their meal.

"He would," Lukas sputtered.

"Never mind," Peter soothed. "Look; it's a real roast of mutton—and it's warm. Finger manners only." He gaily extricated a hunk of the juicy meat before passing the piece to Casper. After the dirt had been brushed from the soft, fresh bread, it was shared out as well, and the whole washed down with foaming warm milk. What a meal!

They all ate well that night, for other men had purchased food with their secreted coinage.

The boys were sucking the marrow from the bones of their roast when Big Peter and his partner, Mathes Legeder the deacon, made their way around the fire to them.

"How are you faring?" asked his father.

"Quite well, now that my stomach is full," Peter replied cheerfully.

"Tomorrow we get to Vienna."

"Really? And what will happen there?"

"We aren't sure," Mathes answered. "But the general sent a messenger on ahead tonight, requesting a trial for us."

"Can we hope for anything from such a trial?" Andreas asked.

"Not really. The Viennese courts specialize in executing religious offenders. But there is always the chance that some of the councillors or judges will be lenient. However, even if our sentence remains unchanged, we will have given our testimony, and it may be the means of salvation for some who sit in judgment on us."

"When the brethren are put on trial," explained another man, "they have an opportunity to preach to audiences who would otherwise never deign to listen."

"That is why we are requesting a trial," Big Peter added. "Not that we hope to be acquitted, although that would be a welcome consequence, but so the Gospel can go forth."

"Will we all go on trial?" someone asked.

"Not likely. We will send some of the older and wiser men to represent the whole group," Mathes answered. "But then, we never know. They may insist on trying all of us, or they may pick on you younger men, thinking you are easy prey."

Peter hoped not.

"Or they may refuse to hear us at all," Big Peter reminded them.

"It's going to be a cold night again," someone said.

The statement brought them all back to their present extremities—weary limbs, chafed wrists, ragged clothing, unremitting cold. When they allowed their minds to dwell on these things, they soon became despondent.

" 'Save me, O God; for the waters are come in unto my soul.' " One brother had withdrawn his notebook; and holding it close to the fire, he read prayerfully, " 'I sink in deep mire, where there is no standing: I am come into deep waters, where the floods overflow me. . . . They that would destroy me, being mine enemies wrongfully, are mighty. . . . For thy sake I have borne reproach; shame hath covered my face. . . . Deliver me out of the mire, and let me not sink: let me be delivered from them that hate me, and out of the deep waters. . . . Hide not thy face from thy servant; for I am in trouble: hear me speedily. . . . I will praise the name of God with a song, and will magnify him with thanksgiving. . . . For the

LORD heareth the poor, and despiseth not his prisoners. . . .' "58

Then these faithful prisoners of the Lord lifted up their voices in prayer, remembering their loved ones at home, the coming trial in Vienna, their persecutors, and the soldiers who escorted them, and giving thanks for the blessings of shared fellowship in their privations.

Towards noon of the next day, the company broke out of the fir forest through which they had been travelling, and paused on the crest of a hill from which they could see a broad, frozen river winding away to the east. On the far side of this waterway spread the city of Vienna, enclosed by high stone walls.

The size of the metropolis astonished Peter. The graceful Gothic spire of St. Stephen's Cathedral soared above the elaborate domed roofs of the Rathaus and the university that flanked it. He picked out the oblong parapeted roof of the Hapsburg palace, chief residence of the king. Surrounding these prominent buildings were the snow-clad gables and roofs of countless lesser structures. Many smaller shops and houses nestled up against the massive walls, spilling over onto the wide bridge that spanned the great river.

The Danube. In his mind's eye, Peter could see the heavy dark line on his map, snaking westward to the great European centres and wandering eastward through Turkish territory to the Black Sea. In the time of the Romans, the Danube had formed the northern line of defense against the Celtic barbarians. Even then, the river had been the major trade route to the spices and riches of the Orient. From Vienna the traveller could go east, west, or south on well-travelled highways to the great trade centres of the world. Even though he was entering as a lowly prisoner, Peter's heart thrilled as they descended towards this historic and colourful city.

Marching along beside neatly terraced vineyards, Peter and

Lukas shared their knowledge of the area.

"Ten years ago the Turks floated up that river on barges and swarmed over the wall."

"But they were driven back."

"I guess they aren't very far away though. That is why the king is so eager for us to become soldiers."

"I've often wondered if a person could convert the Turks," Peter ventured.

Lukas grinned. "You too?"

"Why?" Peter asked in surprise. "Don't tell me you wanted to be a missionary to the Turks. I thought you were going to be a rich merchant."

"Oh, I had visions of travelling with my wares to Far Eastern cities, converting the Turks as I went."

They laughed heartily at their separate ambitions, which had been so similar. But they soon became sober as they realised that their opportunity for preaching to the Turks, or anyone for that matter, might never come now.

Peter flinched inwardly at the curious stares of onlookers as they passed through the gates of Vienna. Would he ever become hardened to the pointed fingers, the jeers, the yapping dogs, and rowdy children who ran along beside them? It was a relief to be led into an enclosed yard, away from the taunting throng.

They were again accommodated in separate inns, so there was no way of discovering whether there would be a trial, or who it would involve. Peter spent a restless night. A disturbing picture of himself sitting in a dark box, his feet chained to the floor, pulling endlessly on a huge oar, flitted in and out of his dreams. Once a vision of himself being tossed into the sea scared him awake, and he was relieved to find himself lying on the straw, chained only to Lukas, while the stars twinkled overhead. "Thy will be done," he mumbled valiantly.

In the long day that followed, the men whiled away the hours by washing some of their clothing and themselves. It was invigourating to be reasonably clean again. A tailor among them helped them to patch their torn garments. All the while their thoughts were on the trial. One of the most frustrating hardships about being a prisoner was lack of knowledge, Peter decided. He had been accustomed to being informed of future developments. In the bruderhof, a man planned his next day's activities; he knew when there was to be a service or when the next meal would be eaten; he knew that in spring he would plant, and in fall he would harvest. At least, if the Lord willed, all these things came to pass. But now, they did not know where they were going, where or whether the next meal would be, how they would spend the night, what they could expect of the next day or week or month. It was an exercise in faith, this walking in the dark.

The simple phrases of the Lord's Prayer[59] could now be uttered with more fervent sincerity. "Thy kingdom come." How Peter longed to see Christ returning to claim the saints and put an end to this dreadful nightmare that had engulfed them all.

"Thy will be done." It was a constant battle to submit to the Lord's will, when his whole being longed for freedom and he remembered the joys of home and family.

"Give us this day our daily bread" was an earnest plea for necessary sustenance. The forced march in such cold weather drained their energies, and their bodies cried out for food. Some days, as today, they enjoyed a solid meal, but often their rations were weak soup and crusts of bread.

"Lead us not into temptation." Depression and discouragement constantly threatened to gain the upper hand. At times it was hard for faith to assert that all was well and that God was still in His heaven.

"But deliver us from evil." Especially today, when the brethren were defending themselves against principalities and powers, was this prayer vital.

"For thine is the kingdom . . . for ever." Oh, help us to cling to this victorious verity.

The next morning Peter and his companions were breathing clouds into the frosty air and flinging their arms across their chests in an effort to warm up, when General Carlos with several of his men arrived in the courtyard.

"Your immediate presence is requested in the courthouse," he announced.

The courthouse! Then they were to be put on trial after all. Peter's heart thumped. Would he have to speak for himself in front of the officials? His mind went back to that other questioning before the three priests at Falkenstein. The Lord had been a very present help in trouble at that time, and He would be again.

They hurriedly gulped down the breakfast that had been brought for them; and lifting their chains above the cobbles, they followed the general into the street. There were few people about at this early hour, and they were spared the searching stares that followed them whenever they appeared in public.

When they reached the courthouse, they found the rest of the brethren already standing in the large room. Soldiers guarded the exits; and except for two very ordinary-looking men seated on a bench to the side of the judge's desk, there were no other councilmen or churchmen present. Those two individuals did not look at all formidable to Peter.

It did not take him long to find his father in the crowd.

"What happened yesterday?" he asked eagerly.

"I wasn't here," Big Peter answered. "Apparently they only tried ten men, all of whom were billeted at a different inn from ours."

Lukas's father and his chain partner had also joined them.

"Let's go find out what went on," he suggested.

Brother Joseph, the schoolmaster, was relating his experience in one corner. "We are charged on three different points," he said. "First, our stand on baptism was challenged. On this point, our crime is twofold, according to them. By refusing to have our infants baptised, we are disobeying the laws of the land and defying the authority of the church. Then, our practise of rebaptism is considered a work of the devil. Yesterday we tried to answer their charges by quoting Scriptures to support our beliefs. Secondly, we are accused of refusing to accept Communion at the hands of the priests. Again, we pointed out what the Bible teaches on this subject. Now, today, we must answer for our refusal to join the king's army and fight for our country."

"How did they accept your explanation of baptism?" someone asked.

"We showed them that the Bible teaches that only those who believe in the atonement should be baptised, and after baptism they must follow a life of discipleship. Infants are incapable of repenting of sins, not having committed any, and of believing in the atonement and dedicating their lives to God's service. We explained that we believe in a pure church composed of sincere believers rather than one that embraces all manner of sin. Several of the council members, those two included"—he indicated the two seated at the table—"nodded agreement when we spoke of a pure church of regenerated believers. But the bishop who represented the church pointed out that such a church was only an unrealistic ideal and impossible to practise."

The men shook their heads in disagreement. They knew that it worked. They were a part of just such a living body, where each member sustained a personal relationship with Jesus Christ and where discipline was exercised to keep the church pure.

"We challenged them to show us a place in the New Testament where an infant was baptised," Brother Joseph went on. "The bishop answered that since Christianity was a new thing in those days, of necessity the first converts were adults. But thereafter, as children were born into their homes, they were undoubtedly baptised immediately to assure the growth of the church. He couldn't find a Scripture to substantiate his argument, of course."

During this time several other council members had arrived in the courtroom as well as three priests.

Brother Joseph hurried on, "When the discussion turned to our practise of baptism, they began accusing us of witchcraft. They claim that our ministers are not ordained of God. They are not ordained by the recognised church; therefore their authority must emanate from the devil." There were sober countenances now. Accusations of dabbling in the dark arts were common, they knew, and the consequences were very serious. A totally uninvolved and innocent person could be unexpectedly charged with casting spells and causing illnesses, and there was little one could do to disprove it. The victim often faced burning or drowning.

"One council member said he had heard that we carry a secret potion with us, and when we preach, we use this evil compound to cast spells over our audiences, and that is why so many have been deluded into following after our faith."

There were a few smiles at this far-fetched notion, but most faces remained grave. If they were suspected of sorcery, there would be little leniency shown on the part of the judge.

"Did they give any indication yesterday of what their final decision concerning us would be?" Lukas's father asked.

"No, but I think we should expect the worst. Although they could not disprove our arguments, it is quite apparent that the churchmen and the judge have already concluded that we are heretics. Our only hope is that our testimony will touch the hearts of some of the councillors and be the means of pointing them to the Light."

He was interrupted by the insistent pounding of a gavel on wood. Turning, Peter saw a bewigged judge seated at the desk. The chairs behind the council table were filled as well. There were a few benches close to the front of the room, but no one invited the prisoners to be seated.

"Who is going to represent this group?" the judge now asked. The three deacons along with their chained partners stepped forward.

The court clerk read the charge in a high nasal tone: "You are hereby charged with refusing to bear arms according to the order of your king, and also with refusing to contribute funds to the war effort against the Turks."

"You have heard the charges," the judge said sternly. "Do you wish to answer them?"

Brother Michel Blauer spoke. "Your honour, we plead not guilty to the second part of the charge. I am not aware that such monetary support was ever requested, and may I respectfully point out that our homes were searched thoroughly after our arrest and everything of value was removed from them."

A councilman rose. "According to the records, the value of the goods confiscated was negligible. Under repeated questioning, these prisoners refused to divulge the whereabouts of their main treasuries."

There it was again. The assumption that the brethren had great hidden stores of wealth.

Another councilman jumped to his feet. "It is common knowledge," he said irritably, "that these Anabaptists use piety as a cloak to hide their true subversive activities."

"Subversive activities? This is really absurd," Peter thought in amazement. Surely no one would believe such nonsense. But to his surprise and consternation, the rest of the council members, except for two or three, were nodding their heads in agreement.

More evidence was given along the same vein. The monstrosity of the lies staggered Peter. They were accused of having huge caches of weapons, along with fellow conspirators in Moravia. And they reportedly were planning a major invasion of Austria because of having secret alliances with the Turks, which is why they refused to fight against them. The council members grew more and more excited as they hurled indictments at the prisoners. If it had not been a matter of life or death, the false accusations would have been humourous. The spokesmen for the brethren were given no opportunity to refute these claims, and their attempts to deny the charges were largely ignored.

When the judge returned the discussion to the matter of armed service, however, he required an answer.

"Our Lord taught that we should love our neighbour—furthermore, that we should love our enemies. In the Sermon on the Mount, He said, 'Resist not evil,' " Michel Kramer defended.

"Have you not been taught to obey them that have the rule over you?" interjected the bishop. "Has not God given authority to kings and rulers to keep peace in the land?"

"Yes," Michel answered. "We believe that God has ordained the sword to punish the wicked and protect the good. But this office is to be conducted by worldly governments and not by the church. God never intended the church to mete out justice. The mission of the church is to win souls for the kingdom of God through preaching and prayer, with love and compassion."

"Did you not just tell us yesterday that you teach that the church should discipline disobedient members? Now you are saying that the church does not have the right to punish," one priest charged, trying to trap the brethren.

"We believe that discipline, as exercised by the true church, should be redemptive and not destructive. We discipline the erring by banning them from our Communion table, and we strive by prayer and exhortation to return them to the fold. Even if, as you say, the church had the authority to mete out justice, killing with the sword—whether it be a Turk or a heretic—does not save that man's soul."

The two council members who had appeared sympathetic, were nodding their heads. They were following the proceedings with interest. Peter remembered that Brother Joseph had tried to explain to them this matter of the separation of church and state authority. For centuries, the law of the land had been inextricably woven with the functioning of the church. All babies born within the borders of a given territory became citizens of that country; and by the rite of baptism, they also became members of the church of that country. To be an Austrian was to be a Roman Catholic. As far as the common people understood, it had always been so. The people of Austria therefore were all Christians, whereas the Turks—being unbaptised and not coming from a "Christian" country—were not. Therefore, these bold radicals who refused to baptise their children and instead practised the strange rite of adult baptism must, necessarily, be heretics akin to the Turks.

But it had not always been so. According to the New Testament, the apostolic church had consisted only of regenerate believers who maintained a life of purity through a personal relationship with Jesus Christ. It had operated independently from the governments of that day. The amalgamation of church and state authority, along with the accompanying practise of mandatory baptism, had been introduced much later. As the brethren attempted to explain this to the council, the frowns and dark looks on most of their faces deepened.

They do not want to know the truth, Peter realised helplessly.

This trial was not a fair trial. He was certain that the verdict had been decided before the men ever walked into court. What was the use of making a defense at all?

But then his attention was drawn to the eager faces of the two men who had been in the room before he entered. They were leaning forward, hanging on every word the brethren uttered. Silently Peter breathed a prayer that the seed sown here would bring forth fruit regardless of the outcome of the trial, that God's true church would triumph no matter what this earthly court would decide.

As the churchmen continued to twist Scripture and accuse the brethren of rebellion and spying for the enemy, Peter had to think of Jesus. He too had stood before judges and borne the false accusation of sinful men. Yet He had answered not a word in His own defense. And they had led Him out and crucified Him.

When he saw the hatred in the eyes of the priest and councilmen, Peter began to wonder if they would all be burned right here in Vienna. He could almost feel the flames licking at his legs already. It would not be impossible. The Viennese churchmen were the instigators of the cruel campaigns against heretics, and many religious fires had burned outside the walls of the beautiful city. He heard again the agonizing screams of the victims he had seen at Nikolsburg one time. The faces contorted with pain, the writhing bodies . . . His father had explained that those men were not Christians and that God gave faithful Christians grace to bear the severest trials. He shifted restlessly on his aching feet. By God's grace he would be faithful to the end.

Finally the judge banged his gavel on the desktop. "I think we have heard enough evidence. Remove the prisoners," he ordered the soldiers. "We will notify you of the verdict later."

So the men were led again through the streets of Vienna. Much as he had longed to visit this city and see its famous buildings with their elaborate architecture, Peter found that now he had little interest in such things.

The men spent the remainder of the day and that evening in prayer, Scripture reading, and encouraging one another. The suspense weighed heavily on their minds. Would their sentence be altered? Would the morrow find them tied to a stake outside Vienna, or being flogged through the streets, or trudging the road to the south? Or maybe, hope against hope, on the way home? Peter did not let himself dwell on that last possibility, for the dashing of hopes would be too great a disappointment.

" 'Take therefore no thought for the morrow: for the morrow shall take thought for the things of itself. Sufficient unto the day is the evil thereof,' "[60] Caspar quoted, knowing that they were all thinking the same thoughts.

"Each day certainly has sufficient evil in it just now," Lukas sighed.

Early the next morning, before the first streaks of dawn had crept across the sky, Alfonso jerked roughly on Peter and Lukas's chain. "Get up! Today we go!"

The young men sat up, rubbing sleep from their eyes. Go? Where? They did not know, but by the light of lanterns, they could see that the pack horses were being loaded and that other prisoners were moving about.

As Alfonso coupled his unit together and fastened the main chain to his pommel, he informed Peter dourly, "In Spain, all heretics—*whffft.*" Then he ran his index finger across his throat meaningfully. Peter had heard of the Inquisition in Spain. Thousands of enemies of the state church had fallen under the ruthless campaign to purge the church. Apparently Alfonso felt that the Viennese authorities were being too easy on them.

"Looks like we're on the march again," Lukas concluded.

"But where to?" Caspar asked.

Nobody could answer.

Through the silent city they trooped, the rest of the brethren joining them. At the city wall, they had to wait for the guards to open the gate for the day. The rising sun on their left told them they were heading south.

News travelled along the line from prisoner to prisoner that their destination remained unchanged. They were still headed for Admiral Doria's warships on the Mediterranean. So the trial had been a waste of time. Peter had feared as much. It was too much to hope that the authorities would deal justly with the believers. He felt that one more door had closed between him and the carefree years of his youth.

From his map study, Peter knew that many long and treacherous miles lay ahead of them. How many of them would survive the journey? And more important, how many of them would keep the faith through the tedious days and miles?

Up ahead, someone started a song. Others joined in. Soon they were stepping briskly along, in time to the music of the hymns that had lifted their faith in years past.

The soldiers sat stiffly on their mounts, not seeming to hear the songs of praise that floated around them. Peter stared at Alfonso's armoured back. He took such pleasure in taking out his frustrations on his charges. What had soured his disposition so? Peter determined to watch for opportunities to show kindness towards him, although in his position as a slave, it would be difficult.

At their first rest stop, Philip, the harness maker, passed several small papers to each of the other men in his unit. "The Christian printer in Vienna managed to hand one of our men a bundle of printed tracts," he explained. "If you have opportunity, pass them to fellow travellers, stableboys, or to whomever you contact. We may be passing through parts where none of our evangelists have ever gone."

Peter glanced at one paper. It was portions from the Gospel of John.

"Even as chained slaves, we are not free from the Great Commission," Philip reminded them.

XVII

Letter From Home

The company of future galley slaves was two days out of Vienna when the letter came. The news sizzled like lightning along the line of chained men.

"A letter."

"A letter has come."

"A letter? From whom?"

"From home!"

A letter from home! How thirsty they all were for news from home.

"How did it get here?" Peter asked over his shoulder as his feet kept tramping along.

Caspar, who had relayed the good news, answered, "A courier on one of those fast horses that passed us a few hours ago, tossed it to one of the brethren while the soldiers weren't looking."

The weary marchers quickened their pace as though by moving faster they could speed the passing of the hours.

Peter could hardly wait. Would the letter tell what had become of the sick ones left behind? or of the girls in the tower? Had the women left for Moravia? Was Brother Riedemann still safe with them? He was bursting to discuss the possibilities with Lukas, but he did not want to risk it for fear that the soldiers

237

would discover the letter before it had been read.

Peter was relieved when someone started a chorus. If the soldiers noticed that the singing was more exuberant than usual, they did not show it. Accustomed to contending with rebellious and surly prisoners, General Carlos's troops were already beginning to realise that these religious offenders were much more amiable and cooperative than most criminals. If they wanted to sing, well and good. It kept them in good spirits and helped to set a faster pace.

Late that night in an inn yard, the precious dispatch made its rounds from one small group to the next. At last Peter saw Cornelius slide something along the floor to Philip, the harness maker. Philip had been reading to them from his notebook, as usual, and now he quickly slipped the letter into the open pages and continued to read in the same tone of voice.

His audience leaned forward and listened with bated breath.

Dearly beloved Brethren in the Faith,

Greetings to you in the Name of the One who loved us and gave Himself for us.

Know this that our thoughts and prayers are ever with you in your bonds. We bear you continually before the throne of grace. He is able to deliver, as you will see shortly, while I relate to you the events which have transpired here.

The same evening of your departure with General Carlos, the young women were released from the castle. They found their way in the darkness back to Steinborn, where they were received with great joy and thanksgiving.

Two days later, Lord Fünfkirchen himself arrived at the castle. As we had suspected, he was not pleased with the manner in which the marshal had treated his villagers, but he was powerless to interfere.

The elderly and sick men and youths who had remained at the

castle had been locked in a tower; and with the return of Lord Fünfkirchen, their rations were increased and they were given extra
blankets for warmth.

The day following, they were led from their tower into the courtyard where, for the benefit of the several imperial soldiers who
remained there, Lord Fünfkirchen addressed them sternly. He indicated that he was displeased with their lack of loyalty to the king and
their suspected subversive activities. He complained of the added
expense in feeding so many extra prisoners and finished by announcing that he had decided they must work for their keep. He planned,
he said, to send them out, starting that day, to cut wood for the needs
of the castle.

The brethren protested in behalf of the sick ones, some of whom
were scarcely able to walk, but the lord was adamant. He insisted
that everyone must go, and so those who were stronger supported
the weak, and they prepared to face a cold day on the mountainside. Six of Fünfkirchen's private soldiers were sent along as guards.

The soldiers led them far up the mountain into the forest, away
from the castle. When at last they permitted the already exhausted
men to stop, the soldiers told them, 'You are free. Go home. Do not
return to the castle.'

Needless to say, the men could scarcely grasp the wonder of it,
but the soldiers assured them that they had had their orders from
Lord Fünfkirchen.

Grandfather Boewen expressed concern for the welfare of the
soldiers who would, for the sake of the king's men still at Falkenstein,
have to be punished for their carelessness in letting the prisoners
escape. But the soldiers said they had had orders not to return to the
castle, but to travel to a country house in the north and await further
instructions.

And so, the Lord brought about a marvelous deliverance
through our benefactor in this valley. May he see his need to make

his calling and election sure before a holy God.

Because of the possibility that the escaped men might be sought here, we thought it best to send them away immediately. Several wagons have left for Moravia already, and we are making plans to evacuate the village. Our food is almost gone; and without men to make wood, we find it difficult to carry on.

As the weather permits, we will make our way to Nikolsburg and, from there, to bruderhofs in the east where there is, at this time, relative safety. Brother Riedemann has gone before to prepare refuge for us.

If God, in His mercy, sees fit to deliver you from your bonds—and we pray fervently to that end—make your way to Nikolsburg and inquire at the Inn of the Golden Sheaf for Calius Woolner. He will be able to direct you further and reunite you with your loved ones.

We have had some sickness among us. Janus, little son of Brother Joseph, died two days ago. Several more children are suffering from fever. The Lord giveth, and the Lord taketh away. Comfort our brother in his loss.

Greetings of love to my son, Caspar. Stand steadfast in the faith.

Just a word of the fate of Brother Blöcher. As you know, he, his nephew, and his son agreed to accept the conditional freedom offered by the king's officer. They were not seen again after your departure. The soldiers who released the brethren were certain that they had been given into the service of some baron or lord—the usual procedure with recanting heretics. Remember them in prayer that they may see their error before it is too late.

And now, 'the God of all grace, who hath called us unto his eternal glory by Christ Jesus, after that ye have suffered a while, make you perfect, stablish, strengthen, settle you. To him be glory and dominion for ever and ever.'[61]

By the hand of your brother Guttenhann Hans at Steinborn.

Sleep eluded them that night. Curled up together in their corner, the four young men rehearsed the contents of the letter.

"How do you think we could escape?" Andreas longed to find his way back to his fiancée. He had resigned himself to never seeing her again, but now hope flared anew.

"If you go, I go too." Caspar rattled their chain.

"Has Andreas's affliction rubbed off on you since you are in such close contact with him?" Peter felt almost carefree tonight after hearing such encouraging news from home.

"He didn't catch it from Andreas. He had it before." Lukas gave a grunt, "Ooof," as Caspar jabbed him in the ribs. But Peter noticed that his cousin did not deny their teasing remarks.

There had been something more between Caspar and Hulda Reimer than simple friendship; Peter was sure of it now. Somewhere a young lady was longing for Caspar's return. It almost made Peter feel left out. Oh, sure, he had Mother to go home to, but that was not quite the same.

"Calius Woolner. The Inn of the Golden Sheaf," Andreas repeated. "We must remember that name."

"You sound as though you intend to get there," said Lukas.

Andreas sighed heavily. "Oh, I hope so. I don't know how, but . . ."

"Look how George and the others were unexpectedly released," Peter reminded them. "We may be too."

"Speaking of George, I wonder how he is?" Caspar asked.

"The letter didn't mention him, so I presume he's still living," Andreas answered. "But I don't really expect to see him this side of heaven."

"Nor I." Peter felt certain that George's sufferings would soon be over. They were quiet for a few moments, contemplating the brevity of life.

"Brother Michel still thinks that we will be miraculously

delivered." Andreas came back to the theme that engrossed him.

"How?" Lukas's voice held a touch of bitterness. "If we did escape from the soldiers, we couldn't go far in these chains without being caught."

No one had an answer for that. The restricting chains were a constant and painful reminder of their helplessness. With every move, the iron rings chafed their wrists, and the harsh rattle of the links grated on their nerves. Whenever their partners stepped sideways, they had to follow; Peter could not roll over at night without waking Lukas to inform him of his intentions; Caspar could not bend to tie his shoe without forcing Andreas's head down. If they walked too fast, they collided with the men in front; if they limped because of a pebble in their shoe, those behind were soon treading on their heels. If they could only be rid of those chains! Peter felt that they had grown fast to him.

"Maybe we won't get away," Lukas said gloomily. "Maybe we'll walk all the way to the sea and get put onto the ships."

"Then we could jump overboard and swim to freedom," Caspar suggested.

"With these chains?"

"Can you swim?" Peter demanded.

"No."

"Brother Joseph had a picture in one of his books," Peter said slowly, "of galley slaves on a ship. It wasn't a pretty picture." He stopped.

"Go on," Caspar urged.

"There were three men chained to a low bench, holding one long stick about as thick as my arm. A cruel-looking foreman stood over them with a whip. The men on the bench looked the ultimate in despair."

"Let's not think of that." Andreas assumed responsibility as the oldest. "We are forgetting that there is a God in heaven who sees and cares. It is foolish for us to imagine what might happen. We'll keep praying that His will be done and that our lives would glorify Him."

"Did you catch what the letter said about Brother Joseph's little boy?"

"Yes." Peter pitied the schoolmaster from the bottom of his heart. Brother Joseph had married later than most men, having been a priest bound by laws of celibacy, and his little family had been a great delight to him. Janus, the child who had passed away, had been such a bright-eyed, inquisitive little fellow, following his father about with endless questions. Now he was gone. There it was again. Separation. Severing of earthly ties for the cause of Christ. Had the men been home, they could have provided better care for the sick ones.

"I wish the Lord would come and take us all home, right now," Peter blurted suddenly.

"That would solve all our problems," Lukas agreed.

"I too long for that," Andreas added. "But the longer He waits to return, the more souls will be won for the kingdom. Just think of all the people who don't know that they can have the joy of sins forgiven."

"Maybe we'll be able to hand out some of those papers from the printer in Vienna," Caspar suggested.

"Wouldn't it be wonderful if someone would believe after reading a tract we distributed," Peter reflected.

"It would make this all worthwhile," Andreas agreed.

The boys were quiet for a time. In the inn yard, the fires burned low. From the shadows came snores and a few muffled voices.

Peter rolled tighter against Lukas. "Poor Martin."

"Yeah," Lukas grunted sleepily.

"He's probably a slave too."

"Yeah."

"We're slaves, but at least we're free in the spirit. He and his father are bound by a guilty conscience too. If we deny Him, He will also deny us."

Lukas did not answer. He was asleep.

For three days an icy wind hurled pellets of hard snow into the faces of the marching men. With relief they descended into the valleys, where the trees offered some protection from the biting wind; but then they must stumble upwards to face it again on the mountain ridges.

Peter trudged along through the deepening snow, in the scant shelter of the men in front. His throat felt raw; his eyes burned; he shivered uncontrollably in his damp coat. He was afraid he was sick. Last night two men suffering from coughs and fever had been left behind in an inn with instructions that they were to follow when and if they recovered. Peter did not want to be left behind. If only this wind and snow would let up, he was sure he would feel better.

He had ceased to think of escaping, of reaching home, of Brother Joseph's loss, or of being a galley slave. It took concentration just to place one foot in front of the other. It seemed as though he had been damp and cold as long as he could remember.

His eyes. They smarted so. He closed them and stumbled on, propelled by the chains that bound him to his fellow prisoners. He was unaware that the column had halted, until he stumbled against Philip and then swayed dizzily, blinking to clear his fuzzy vision.

"You're sick." Lukas steadied him.

Peter shook his head. "I'll be all right." His voice did not want to come out right.

He was dimly conscious of his father's solicitous voice, and then he was lying on something soft. Firm hands rubbed a greasy substance on his throat and chest, and soon a pleasant warmth began to spread through him.

Peter was not the only one who was sick. General Carlos decided to rest for a day or two to give the men and his own soldiers a chance to recover and wait for more clement weather.

Because of Peter's illness, Peter and Lukas shared a straw tick on the floor inside the inn. By the afternoon of the second day, Peter's temperature had dropped and his natural good health asserted itself. His throat still felt scratchy, but he was ready to sit up on a bench and eat the soup that Alfonso brought to him.

"Tomorrow we go," the irascible soldier grunted as he sprawled in a nearby chair, waiting for the men to finish eating.

Without his cumbersome armour, Alfonso looked even younger and slightly more approachable.

Peter ventured, "Has the snow stopped?"

Alfonso gave him a disgruntled look. "No," he said shortly. His dark eyebrows drew together. "Snow, snow, snow. This is cold country." His tone implied that he did not appreciate the cold. He shifted irritably in his chair. "In Spain, warm sun. Nice." His features softened into a thin smile.

Peter took the cue. "Is your home in Spain?"

"Yah! Spain. On the sea."

"Is it always warm there?"

"Yah. Nice. Warm sun. Blue sky. Blue sea. Green grass. Nice." Alfonso's eyes held a faraway look. "But here"—he pushed himself to his feet and snorted—"snow, cold. Bad country." Snatching the empty bowls from Peter and Lukas, he tramped off noisily.

"Wonder why he ever left Spain if it is so nice," Lukas said.

"And why he stays here if he thinks it's such a bad place,"

added Peter reflectively. "We'll have to see if we can make him talk some more about his homeland. It may be the way to his heart."

XVIII

Evangelists in Chains

Billows of dazzling white snow rolled over the land under a deep blue sky. After their eyes adjusted to the brilliance, the prisoners and their escorts stepped along briskly in the track broken by the lead horses. Within a few hours, they found themselves beneath the walls of a substantial town.

Other travellers all but crowded the chained men off the road as they milled about confusedly before the gates. Horsemen shouted and cracked whips to clear their path. A pig dodged, squealing, around the skirts of women with huge market baskets over their arms, and between the wheels of farm carts.

A flock of sheep, woolly in their winter coats, baaed plaintively, and darted impulsively through every available opening. Two shepherds and a dog tried unsuccessfully to keep them together. The sheep plunged through the indignant crowd towards the edge of the roadway and were brought up short by the solid line of prisoners who spread their arms and braced their feet to stop them. The grateful shepherds were soon able to gain control of their flock, and Peter saw someone pass each of them a folded leaflet before they moved ahead.

"What's the delay?" Lukas asked.

"Don't know." Caspar stood on tiptoe to look over the heads of the throng towards the town gate. "Can't see anything."

Peter did not care. He was still weak from his illness, and his legs felt wobbly after the march of a few hours. He was glad to stand still for a while. He wished he could sit.

"Where are we?" Andreas asked.

The long-legged Caspar again used his superior height to search for a signboard. "Neustadt," he announced shortly, coming down on his heels again.

"Neustadt," Peter echoed. Neustadt. He knew that name was on his maps somewhere, and there was something about it . . .

"They must be stopping everyone to pay tolls or something," Caspar reported. "The people are moving through the gate very slowly. I see General Carlos up there near the gate."

Alfonso too, from his seat on his horse, had been peering ahead restlessly. Hearing Caspar's diagnosis of the problem, he looked at them and stated, "Sit here long time." He settled sullenly into the saddle, prepared to wait awhile. His eyes closed.

Peter put his hand inside his overcoat and drew out the bundle of maps his mother had given him. Replacing the rest, he carefully unfolded one far enough that he could see the area he was searching for.

"Vienna . . . Neustadt," he mumbled, tracing a line with his forefinger. "Here it is."

Lukas held one edge of the map. Caspar and Andreas peered over their shoulders.

"See," Peter indicated, "Neustadt is a dividing place. From here, there are two major trade routes going south. The one cuts through the mountains and heads east, almost to the borders of Hungary, before turning south. The mountain route leads over the Semmering Pass, here, down through Schöttwein and Bruck and follows the Mur River to the south."

"Wonder which one we'll take," Lukas commented.

"The eastern route leads more directly to the Adriatic," Andreas pointed out. "See; it ends at Trieste. I'm not sure if Trieste is our destination, but there is a harbour if I remember correctly."

Peter nodded agreement. "That road would be the easiest to travel at this time of year. Not so many high mountains to cross."

"Do you think they'd take us so close to the Hungarian border just now with the Turks so near?" Lukas asked.

"I hadn't thought of that," admitted Peter. "But is the road over the pass open in the winter? I'd think the snow would get deep up there."

"We'll just have to wait and see," Andreas said. "They didn't ask us to help plan the itinerary."

"Ask him," Caspar said, pointing at Alfonso, dozing on his horse.

"I'd rather wait until he's awake." Peter folded the map and replaced it in his inner pocket. "Will we stand here all day?"

Caspar craned his neck. "Looks like a few more people have moved through the gate."

"Say." Lukas pointed. "Doesn't that man over there remind you of old Patlo?"

A short, stooped man was plodding along beside an ancient mule piled high with lumpy bundles.

"No purple coat," Andreas said.

"Maybe he got a new one," Lukas replied.

"Then he wouldn't be Patlo," declared Andreas. "Besides, Patlo wouldn't be here. Last we knew, he was heading from Steinborn, carrying messages to our people in Moravia."

"It wouldn't surprise me to see that fellow anywhere," Peter laughed. "According to his own testimony, he gets around."

"I'm sure he's been up and down these routes more than once," Caspar agreed.

After a wait of several hours, most of the travellers had passed through the gate and the general could be seen negotiating with the officials.

Having gained clearance, he led his troops through the city by way of narrow back alleys and refuse-strewn streets. There was another delay at the gates on the other side of Neustadt, so it was late afternoon before they were again moving southward.

"Looks like it's to be the pass," Lukas confirmed.

"Hope the weather holds." Peter cleared his still-scratchy throat and looked anxiously to the west. The sky remained cloudless.

They sheltered that night behind the crumbling stone walls of an ancient Roman fortification. In one corner, a few leaning beams supported the remnants of a roof. The men huddled together under its protection while a large bonfire glowed at the open end of the triangle.

The soldiers relaxed their guard and retired behind the remains of a blockhouse at the far side of the ruin. They took turns keeping a wary eye on the prisoners from a jagged hole in the wall.

The men were able to hold their first worship service as a group. It was one of thanksgiving for the mercies God had shown to them thus far on this unplanned journey.

Peter was unable to keep his eyes open, and before the prayers were ended, he was sound asleep. He did not feel Lukas roll him onto the ground and curl up beside him.

Several hours later, Peter woke suddenly. Where was he? Above him was a dark jumble of beams and supports. Around him soft snores and deep breathing told him that the other men were still asleep. He rolled slowly onto his side so as not to wake Lukas and closed his eyes again. Through the sleep sounds he heard the murmur of voices. Who was talking? The soldiers? No. They were too far away. Groggily he raised himself on one elbow and looked about. There. Over at the edge of the carpet of sleeping bodies were a dozen men, sitting up.

Must be they can't sleep. Drowsily Peter settled down again, but something would not let him relax. What was it? There was something strange about those seated figures. He lifted his head again and studied the shadowy shapes against the wall.

Hats! That was it. Hats! Three of those men were wearing headgear. None of the men from Steinborn had left the meeting house with hats on the night of their arrest. They had missed their caps sorely, especially in the recent cold weather. But there were three men sitting in their midst now with hats—one was a proper broad-brimmed dress hat. The other two were fur caps.

Who were they? Peter lay on his back wondering. Where had they come from? What did they want? He asked Big Peter the next morning in the few moments he had with his father before Alfonso chained him to the rest of his unit.

Peter could hardly wait to get on the road so he could tell the other boys what he had learned. He waited until the singing was in full volume before blurting the news.

"Did you know three men from Neustadt came last night to inquire about our faith?"

"Really?"

"When?"

Peter told about waking in the darkness and seeing the three strangers in hats. "One was one of those shepherds who were having trouble with their sheep outside the gate yesterday."

"I saw the men passing papers to people in the crowd," Andreas broke in.

"He read his paper and shared it with a friend," Peter went on. "It was John chapter 3—on the new birth. They had never heard of the new birth, and when they read how Nicodemus came at night to seek answers to his questions, they took it as a sign that they should come at night also. The Lord planned it so that we were not heavily guarded last night, and our men were able to talk with them for most of the night."

"You said there were three men," Caspar reminded Peter.

"Yes. The third was a merchant from Neustadt. He has a shop near the gates, and he had seen us pass by. His curiosity was aroused, and he made inquiries with the officials at the gate as to our identity. He marvelled that so many able-bodied men would let themselves be led into slavery rather than deny their faith. Such a deep commitment moved him to find out what kind of a faith was worth suffering such degradation for."

"What was the outcome of their visit?"

"All three wished to be born again. Our men said they were so thirsty for Bible knowledge; they knew practically nothing of the Scriptures. Their priests say mass in Latin, and religion, to them, was a system of rituals that left their souls barren."

Andreas shook his head in wonder. "Who would have believed that we could lead souls to the Lord while bound in chains? Those men might never have heard the Gospel had we not been led through Neustadt."

"Peter, looks like your dream has come true." Caspar's tone was lighthearted.

Peter turned to stare at him. "My dream? What dream?"

"You always wanted to be a travelling evangelist, didn't you?"

"Well . . ." Peter was rather embarrassed to have his private goals publicized.

"Well—you're travelling now, and it looks as though we'll all be evangelists on this trip."

"Travelling evangelists," Lukas repeated.

"Evangelists in chains," Andreas corrected.

So they began to think of themselves as evangelists in chains. Forced from their comfortable homes into an arduous overland journey, they dedicated themselves to use every opportunity to share their faith as they went.

"'My thoughts are not your thoughts, neither are your ways my ways, saith the Lord. For as the heavens are higher than the earth, so are my ways higher than your ways, and my thoughts than your thoughts.' "[62] Andreas quoted.

"Isaiah 55." Caspar withdrew his notebook and flipped the well-worn pages. "'For as the rain cometh down, and the snow from heaven, and returneth not thither, but watereth the earth, and maketh it bring forth and bud, that it may give seed to the sower, and bread to the eater: so shall my word be that goeth forth out of my mouth: it shall not return unto me void, but it shall accomplish that which I please, and it shall prosper in the thing whereto I sent it,' "[63] he read.

"Sure is something, the way God planned this evangelistic effort, isn't it?" marvelled Lukas. "Here we are, visiting many foreign cities, able to pass out literature, sing, and even teach those who are seeking—and all expenses are paid."

"Well . . ." Caspar sighed. "If we were travelling under our own volition, we might have more ample rations and better beds."

"I'm glad you said 'might,' " Andreas reminded him. "Because I'm not sure our travelling evangelist brethren always enjoy comfortable bed and board. Another benefit we have in this arrangement is the protection of an armed escort. Just think. Most of our missionaries have to dodge the authorities wherever they go. They must preach secretly, travel at night, and most often they are arrested, thrown in dungeons, or even put to death. No one can bother us now—we are already in chains."

"You are forgetting where we will end up," Lukas said.

"We don't know that either. Let's leave that in God's hands."

"Doesn't the first part of that chapter you read speak about strange nations or foreigners believing on God?" Peter asked.

Caspar ran his eyes over the fine script. "Verse 5 says, 'Behold, thou shalt call a nation that thou knowest not, and nations that knew not thee shall run unto thee because of the LORD thy God, and for the Holy One of Israel; for he hath glorified thee.' "[64]

" 'A nation that thou knewest not . . .' " Peter mused.

The boys fell into silent meditation, and Peter found himself praying that nations that knew not God would follow after them— not because of *them* (for they were certainly not attractive in their state of slavery) but because of *their God.*

They had reached the Semmering Pass—a vast wilderness of gleaming white glaciers and rippling ice fields. The air was bitingly cold, but the panorama of jagged mountain peaks marching into the blue sky awed the travellers. The view from the top was far more splendid than that from the valley, Peter thought. He had always loved the mountains, but one only began to comprehend their vastness and complexity from a high vantage point. Surely the God who carved out these ranges could be trusted to mold his life into perfection according to His own design.

They were not allowed to linger long on the pass. The general was impatient to leave this area of prevailing blizzards. More than a few lives had been lost on this mountain route.

Peter felt all bones that night as he lay on the uneven board floor of a low loft above a country inn. Directly below, the soldiers were celebrating their successful crossing of the pass. Raucous laughter and loud, boisterous talking were punctuated by shouts for more beer.

Peter shivered. It was cold in the loft. The scraping of bowls and clinking of cutlery from below reminded him that supper had been scanty. What would it be like to be able to eat all he desired again? He wiggled. His legs and elbows ground against the rough floor. Even straw was better than this. Those soldiers down there, though ungodly men, had full stomachs and would be able to fall into soft beds.

Crash! Bang! It sounded like a table falling over. Angry shouts and more smashing noises rose from below him. It was a fight. Cheering and scuffling. What a life! Slaves to their passions. Drunkenness and brawling were too high a price to pay for soft beds and good food, Peter decided. He would rather be chained to his Christian brethren than bound by the devil to depravity such as that.

They were a long time getting started the next morning. The soldiers were groggy and ill-tempered after their night of debauchery. Alfonso was even more irritable than usual. His hands shook as he linked his charges together, and twice he dropped the chain. He swore in a thick voice, and kicked Peter for good measure. While the prisoners looked on compassionately, he leaned against his horse and retched violently. After stumbling clumsily into the saddle, he fumbled for the reins, which had fallen to the ground. Peter bent and handed them to him.

Slowly the procession wound down the mountainside into a valley.

By noon, Alfonso was steadier on his feet; but he slumped, exhausted, against a stone and refused the food that his companion offered. "Too much beer," he muttered sheepishly, seeing Peter and Lukas watching him. "Not good." He shook his head as if in disapproval of his actions. "You not drink beer?"

The boys shook their heads.

"Ah—good time," he said, smiling at the memory of last night's antics. "But, now," he groaned, his hand on his stomach, "not so good."

This was a different Alfonso. Peter felt he ought to say something meaningful, but he did not know what to say.

"Now"—the young soldier withdrew a small pewter crucifix from under his tunic—"I say prayers." He held the cross in front of his face. "Ten prayers—maybe fifty prayers." He sighed heavily and replaced the crucifix. "Next town. I see priest. Confess." He gave a short laugh. "All better then."

"Will you never get drunk again?" Lukas asked.

Alfonso looked startled. "Never drink?" he laughed. "Oh, yes. Drink again—good time."

"But then you'll be sick again," Peter reminded him.

Alfonso shrugged.

"Then you'll have to go to the priest again and confess again," Peter pressed.

Alfonso shrugged again. He grinned and patted the invisible crucifix. "More prayers."

"You don't have to get drunk and then go to the priest, get drunk and then go to the priest. Jesus died on the cross so that we could be forgiven once, and then we don't need to sin any more." Peter felt keenly the language barrier. Alfonso had never been so open before. Brother Joseph could speak Spanish. He must ask him to explain the plan of salvation to this soldier.

"Never sin?" Alfonso's expression was doubtful.

"Jesus forgives our sin. We don't need to confess to the priest. The priest can't forgive your sins. Only God can do that."

His listener looked confused. These were new concepts.

It was time to go. Peter prayed that the seed of truth would swell and sprout in Alfonso's heart.

Peter sat, chin in hands, on the wide stone steps of the courthouse of Schöttwein, studying the scene before him.

An ornate stone fountain in the centre of the large open square boasted four rearing horses with water trickling from their open mouths. How such a small town came by such an elaborate fountain, Peter could not imagine. Perhaps the town had produced a sculptor who bestowed some of his talent on his birthplace. Or possibly it had been the gift of a wealthy benefactor. The focal point of most Austrian towns was a large clock decorated with intricate woodcarving and surrounded by banks of flowers in summer. Fountains belonged in warm climates. The water splashing into the circular pond below the horses steamed slightly in the crisp winter air. This area was noted for its warm mineral springs. Several soldiers sat on the stone rim of the pond, flipping coins onto the ground and passing winnings back and forth.

Beside the fountain, three shoemakers were tapping industriously at improvised anvils.

Two days ago General Carlos had inquired among the prisoners for shoemakers, harness makers, and blacksmiths. It was time to stop for repairs. The prisoners had been allowed to sleep, in great discomfort, on the porches and steps of the public buildings surrounding the square in Schöttwein.

Yesterday the required artisans had been temporarily unchained and set to work mending the boots of the soldiers and repairing harnesses. Several horses had been led away to be reshod.

Towards evening, the general had circulated among the brethren, offering that they could have their shoes mended also. That was why Peter now sat in stocking feet on the steps of the courthouse.

The other eighty-odd prisoners lounged around the square— some beside Peter, some on the steps of the guildhalls, some near the fountains, while those with shoes strolled about in pairs, conversing with each other or the villagers.

Yesterday the townspeople had gathered, warily at first, to stare at this strange expedition camping in their streets. By evening, a few had been bold enough to address the brethren and satisfy their curiosity. Now, here and there about the square, groups of citizens were engaged in earnest conversation with the chained pairs of brethren. Peter knew, without listening, the main topic of discussion. He had seen some pamphlets change hands last evening under cover of twilight. The truth always planted conviction in the souls of its hearers and drove them to seek answers to their questions.

"Look," Caspar interrupted Peter's reverie. "Brother Mathes is reading from his notebook."

Brother Mathes Legeder had daringly pulled out his notebook and was reading aloud to half a dozen men. Four more villagers drifted over to hear. Some women, who had come to fetch water, stopped to listen. Very shortly, he was surrounded by a silent group who strained to catch his words. Seeing the size of his audience, Mathes paused in his reading and looked about him cautiously. No one contested his activity, so after quick consultation with Big Peter, his partner, the two strode purposefully across the square and mounted the steps of the weavers' guildhall. The crowd followed. The soldiers on duty made no move to interfere.

Mathes voice carried across the open space to where the boys sat on the courthouse steps.

" 'Verily I say unto you, Whosoever shall not receive the kingdom of God as a little child shall in no wise enter therein. And a certain ruler asked him, saying, Good Master, what shall I do to inherit eternal life? And Jesus said unto him, Why callest thou me good? none is good, save one, that is, God."[65]

More villagers drifted to the edge of the growing crowd. Even the soldiers, though they did not deign to turn in his direction, could not help but hear Mathes's words.

" 'Yet lackest thou one thing: sell all that thou hast, and distribute unto the poor, and thou shalt have treasure in heaven: and come, follow me."[66]

Peter marvelled at the hungry looks on the faces of those who crowded around the deacon. They listened breathlessly. No one left while he read on and on. It was hard for Peter, who had heard the Scriptures read to him from his childhood, to fathom what it would be like to hear them for the first time. Here were people who mouthed the name of Jesus, Mary, and the disciples, but whose religion was a dead form. They had never experienced Jesus as a living person who loved and sorrowed, laughed and cried, ate and slept—just as they did. To them, God was a stern, unapproachable being who had to be appeased with endless offerings and prayers.

"They don't know that God is love and that we love Him because He first loved us, and gave Himself for us." Peter tucked his feet under him. He hoped his shoes would soon be mended. His heel had come off on the pass and he had hobbled awkwardly ever since, so he was glad that would be fixed. But right now his feet were cold.

Brother Mathes had stepped down, and now another older man took his place. The reading went on. After reading a passage, the brother would stop to explain it. A cumbersome chain dangled from the hand that held the notebook, and the speaker's companion stood silently by, bound to the other end of the chain.

"Evangelists in chains." Peter repeated the fitting appellation.

"Oh, oh. I see trouble." Lukas pointed to the church.

A priest, his hands tucked inside the wide sleeves of his robe, stood scowling in the open doorway.

"He doesn't look too pleased," Peter agreed.

"Think we should warn the speakers?" Caspar asked.

"I think not," Andreas said slowly. "The people are so engrossed that the priest may not be able to do anything."

The disgruntled churchman soon disappeared, and the preaching went on. The sun passed overhead and began to drop towards the west. A few people left, but most stayed on, forgetting their noon meal to hear the words of life.

But the priest had not given up so easily. Some time later an official in a gold-embroidered scarlet cloak rode into the square. He spoke briefly with the soldiers and then departed the way he had come.

He soon returned, in company with General Carlos and more soldiers. The general rode to the edge of the crowd and, after listening for a few moments, called to the speaker: "The mayor requests that this public meeting be disbanded immediately."

Brother Kramer, who had been preaching, lowered his book and looked over the crowd. The audience tore their eyes from the speaker reluctantly. Some cast annoyed glances in the direction of the mayor. One bold voice rang out, "But this is a peaceful assembly."

"Read on," another called to the brethren.

Brother Kramer looked at the general for confirmation. The general, in turn, looked at the official. Other voices clamoured for the meeting to go on. But the mayor shook his head resolutely. He pointed meaningfully to the church and spoke sternly to the crowd.

The brethren, not wishing to cause trouble, stepped down from the steps. The crowd, muttering angrily, began to disperse.

The general rode about, issuing orders to his men. The mended and unmended shoes were quickly distributed. Horses were brought and hastily loaded. Reluctant townspeople stood about, questioning the prisoners.

Wishing to be part of the action, Peter quickly laced his shoes—with heels intact—and pulled Lukas with him into the commotion. They were able to hand out several printed Gospel portions before Alfonso, out of sorts at his interrupted holiday, caught up with them and chained them into line.

The evangelists in chains, escorted by the truth-seeking crowd, marched from Schöttwein, preaching as they went.

XIX

The Gospel Goes Forth

Peter and Lukas pressed their backs harder against the wall of a warehouse as a group of small schoolboys stopped to stare openly at the motley line of chained prisoners. They pointed and made rude remarks about their long beards and dirty, ragged clothing. Peter wished he could melt into the wall. He knew Lukas, whose appearance had always been impeccable, felt the same. At last the boys moved on across the cobbles, holding their noses meaningfully as they passed the men.

Lukas looked after them. "I suppose we do smell."

" 'But if, when ye do well, and suffer for it, ye take it patiently, this is acceptable with God,' "[67] Philip, the harness maker, reminded the two young men.

They were in Bruck-on-Mur this warm Monday morning in January. Water dripped from the tile roofs of the buildings, and some—Peter squirmed uncomfortably—was running down his neck.

They had arrived here in the government seat of the province of Styria in time for the soldiers to attend afternoon mass in the cathedral. Peter supposed that Alfonso had received absolution for his night of revelling and was all primed to enjoy another round of drinking and gambling at the next opportunity. He seemed to be in reasonably good spirits this morning, at any rate. The men were not sure just why they were standing here in the marketplace instead of moving along through the town. As usual, they had not been informed of the plans.

"Let's get away from this dripping roof," Lukas complained. "My back is getting wetter and wetter."

"Just be thankful for the warm weather," Caspar chided. "Enjoy it while it lasts. Winter isn't over yet."

Several vendors had entered the square and were busy setting up their tables.

"Don't those rolls look luscious?" Caspar fairly drooled.

They watched a woman unpacking eggs and rounds of hard cheese from her basket. Beside her, her back to the men, stood a small girl in a bright red cloak and knitted cap. From under her cap dangled two thick brown braids. Peter's heart jumped. If he did not know better, he would think that was Maria. Just then the child turned. Catching sight of the row of chained men leaning up against the walls, she stared with open curiosity. She stepped timidly in their direction. Just then her mother turned and, quick as a flash, reached out her arm and jerked the little girl back. Speaking harshly and shaking her head, she hustled her daughter behind the table, where she could not see the nasty men.

"No, she is not Maria," Peter sighed. They were not even fit for a child to look on.

Alfonso dismounted and wrapped his horse's reins around a nearby hitching post. Turning to the men, he asked, "Have money? I buy food." He waved his arm at the rapidly filling market tables.

Caspar was the first to delve into his pocket for coins. Their precious funds were dwindling, but this was what they were for. They had to keep up their strength if they were to walk several hundred miles yet. While they watched the soldiers bargaining for food, they were able to ignore the rude stares and pointed fingers of the local folk.

Having to eat on the march did not reduce their enjoyment of the good cheese, bread, and sausages their money had bought. Alfonso was so amiable that he even tossed pieces of molasses candy to the four young men. The warm weather loosened his tongue.

"Ah, warm sun. Like Spain," he remarked expansively from above their heads.

"Your mother and father, they live in Spain?" Peter thought he had better talk while Alfonso was in a talking mood.

Alfonso's face darkened. "Yah," he said shortly. "In Spain."

Apparently his parents were not a pleasant topic of conversation. Peter racked his brain for another. "Do they have horses in Spain?"

Alfonso's countenance brightened. "Yah. Nice horses. Not like this." He slapped his stocky mount's neck depreciatingly.

Lukas was all ears. "What kind of horses?" he asked eagerly.

"Small. Not heavy. Fast horses."

"Did you have a horse in Spain?"

"No." Alfonso shook his head. "But boys catch horses of rich man. Ride over moor. Go fast. Races." His eyes sparkled at the memory.

"How do you say *horse* in Spanish?" Peter knew, but he wanted to keep the soldier talking.

Alfonso gave him a searching look. Then he said, *"Caballo."*

"What about *river?*" Peter pointed at the frozen Mur along which they were walking.

"Rio."

"Mountain?"

"Montaña."

The young brethren kept their escort supplying Spanish words and phrases for some time. Their faulty pronunciations amused Alfonso mightily.

"His German isn't so perfect either," Lukas said under his breath to Peter.

"That's all right. Let him laugh."

"Why you want learn Spanish?" Alfonso asked suddenly. "You row Spanish oars on ship maybe?" He roared at his own joke.

Andreas shrugged. "It gives us something to do while we walk."

They camped that night in a grove of wild plum trees beside the river.

Peter had been sleeping for a number of hours when he was startled awake by a hand shaking his shoulder. Thinking it was Caspar, or Lukas, he mumbled sleepily, "Whadya want?"

"Sh-sh-sh," a voice hissed in his ear, and in the moonlight, he saw a strange face bending over his. Suddenly he was wide awake. He started to sit up, but the hand on his shoulder restrained him. "Sh-sh-sh; don't be afraid. I will not harm you. I have come for help. Tell me, do you worship God in spirit and in truth?"

Peter blinked dazedly. He was too astonished to answer at first. "Wha-wha-at?" he stammered.

The voice pleaded again, urgently, "Are you Anabaptists? Are you true followers of Jesus Christ?"

This time Peter managed to answer, "Yes; who are you?"

"My name is Henry. I have longed to speak with someone who is an Anabaptist. As you passed by my uncle's shop today, I heard someone remark, 'There goes a bunch of Anabaptist prisoners.' I followed you from town. I would like to know of your faith. Can you help me?"

"Yes, indeed." Peter thought rapidly. "Would you mind if I call my father?"

"Will the soldiers stop us?"

Peter raised his head and looked around cautiously. "Not if we are careful." He knew where his father lay, not ten feet away, for they had been together during the evening devotions and prayers.

While Henry crept around the sleeping men to awaken Big Peter, Peter roused Lukas, Andreas and Caspar, Philip and his partner.

Big Peter and Mathes Legeder crawled over on their bellies, and they all lay with their heads together while the new arrival told his astounding story.

"I am an orphan," he began. "I live with my uncle and aunt and am an apprentice in my uncle's cabinet shop."

"Interesting," thought Peter. "Another young man who works with wood."

"My parents died eleven years ago, when I was only five. My uncle and aunt have told me that they died in a plague, but I know differently. They think I do not remember, but I do. My parents were Anabaptists."

Gasps of surprise met this announcement. The brethren had not known of believers in this area.

"I do not remember," the speaker went on, "but I think they were not Anabaptists very long. I do not know how they learned of this faith, nor do I know much about it. I only know that one night some soldiers came and took my father away. The next day my mother took me on her knee and spoke very seriously to me. She said that she was going away too and that I must go to live with my aunt and uncle. She said I must obey them.

"Then she told me to remember that my parents were Anabaptists. 'Do not forget that word,' she said. She made me repeat it over and over. 'Your uncle and aunt will not want you to say that word, but keep it in your heart,' she told me. 'Promise me that when you are grown, you will search for those who worship God in spirit and in truth. They are called Anabaptists.'

"Then she wept and held me close for a long time. I cried too because I didn't want her to go away. But that same day she took me to my aunt's house, and I never saw her again.

"I was not treated kindly by my aunt and uncle. They had a large family, and they begrudged the food I ate. I always wore old clothes and shoes that were too shabby for their children. My baby brother died soon after my parents went away, and I was all alone. I often cried myself to sleep. I wanted my mother badly; but whenever I mentioned her, my aunt would become very angry. 'Your mother was a fool,' she said once. So I learned not to speak of her, but I would repeat that word *Anabaptist* over and over to myself. I felt that somehow, if I could find someone who knew about Anabaptists, I would find my mother.

"I know now that my parents were drowned because they were Anabaptists. Eight other men and two women perished at the same time. If there were any other believers in Bruck, they moved on or recanted. I have been apprenticed to my uncle these years, but I planned that, when I was free, I would go and search until I found the people who hold the faith my parents died for.

"Since I learned that they believed something worth more to them then their lives, I have felt a great emptiness in the religion of my aunt and uncle. My uncle cheats his customers and beats his helpers. Yet he is considered a good Christian. My aunt chases beggars from her door, but she regularly sends a basket of baked cakes to the priest, who lives in a fine house and doesn't need them. To me, this is not right, and I have a feeling my parents would not have acted so.

"When I heard the name 'Anabaptist' today, it was like a spark lighting the dry straw in my soul. I knew I must follow and speak with you. Are you truly the people called Anabaptists who worship God in spirit and in truth?"

"Praise the Lord," Big Peter whispered. "God has preserved the seed of the faithful. He has led us together according to His

divine plan. We can indeed show you the way of life, and when
your journey on earth is ended, you can be reunited with your
courageous parents in glory."

"Tell me quickly," the young man begged.

"Do you believe that you are a sinner, under the power of Satan,
and are unable of yourself to do any good thing?"

"Yes," he answered promptly. "I have hatred in my heart
towards my uncle and aunt, and although I have confessed this
and done penance, I still hate them. This is not right."

"Do you find yourself guilty before God?"

"Oh, yes," the young man confirmed. "I have known that I do
not know God as I should, and I have lived in fear that I would
die before I found those who knew the truth, as my mother said."

"The Scripture says that all have sinned, and come short of
the glory of God,"[68] Mathes explained. " 'There is none righteous,
no, not one.' "[69]

"But God has made a provision for man's salvation," Big Peter
quickly assured him. "God saw the wickedness of men's hearts,
and He knew man could do nothing to save himself. So God sent
Jesus, His own Son, to earth to die on the cross. God accepts the
precious blood of Christ as an atonement for our sins. He died so
that we would not need to die eternally. Because He died, we can
be reconciled to God and enjoy eternity with Him."

"But what must I do to obtain this salvation for myself?"

"Just believe it and receive it," Mathes said simply.

"Is that all?" Henry sounded dubious.

" 'Believe on the Lord Jesus Christ, and thou shalt be saved.' "[70]

"Do you believe that Jesus Christ died for your sins?" Big Peter
probed gently.

"Yes," the young man whispered.

"Would you like to receive His gift of salvation, and take
Him as your Lord and Saviour? Turn your life over to Him. He

will cleanse you of your guilt before God by His life blood which He shed for you on Calvary, and give you the power to live a holy life."

"I'd like that."

And so there beside the Mur River, under the unsuspecting surveillance of the Spanish regiment, a searching soul was led to the Lord.

The young man prayed brokenly, confessing his sins and asking Jesus to be the Lord of his life. Then Brother Mathes prayed, asking God to grant courage and strength to this new believer and thanking Him for faithfully answering his mother's prayers.

The night was passing swiftly. Big Peter insisted that the young man take his precious notebook.

"Should I tell my uncle of my conversion?" he asked.

After some discussion, Mathes and Big Peter decided that it would be necessary for Henry to confess his wrong attitudes to his uncle and aunt and to ask their forgiveness.

"You have not been rebaptised yet," they counselled. "So your life will hardly be in danger."

"But I will not want to attend mass anymore," he pointed out.

It was agreed that Henry should try to complete his apprenticeship with his uncle, if at all possible; and then when he was free to leave (which would be in two months), he should make his way to Nikolsburg and seek out the brethren. In the meantime, he would feed on the portions of the Word in Big Peter's notebook and allow the Holy Spirit to guide him into all truth.

Henry lingered until the first streaks of dawn threatened to reveal his presence. Then, with fond good-byes and promises of prayer, he slipped away.

In spite of the sleepless night behind them, Peter and his friends stepped along briskly the next day, the thrill of the night's adventure making their feet light.

"To think that the Lord planned that we travel through here and find Henry just as he was about ready to leave," marvelled Andreas.

"And he had been waiting for us for years," Peter added.

"I wonder how many other longing souls the Lord has prepared for the evangelists in chains," Caspar commented.

Peter's mind ran ahead to the many miles of road they must travel on their way to the sea. He saw hundreds of people waiting along that road to hear the good news of salvation. He began to actually look forward to the next episode in this unconventional campaign.

He had a long time to wait.

At Bruck they had left the well-travelled trade route to follow the Mur River. Here majestic mountains rose steeply on either side of the valley. Small farms dotted the lower slopes and fertile valley floor, but there were few towns, and only local folks travelled the roads.

The January thaw ceased as quickly as it had begun, and in its place, a raw biting wind rushed off the mountains and buffeted the ragged band. The temperature sank well below freezing; and the men hunched their shoulders sideways against the wind, covering their noses first with one hand and then with the other to prevent frostbite. Progress was slow. Nights were interminable.

Peter was not sure which was worse—fighting and gasping against the wind or huddling together at night like so many blocks of ice. In his present misery, he almost forgot about their mission. His mind seemed frozen too. He tried to think of home, but he could not picture his mother's face clearly. It was too cold to sing, for the wind snatched the words away. It was even too cold to read at night, but the brethren never forgot to pray.

On the last night of January, the general found shelter for

them in a farmer's barn. The men were grateful to burrow into the straw, and the four cows and dozen sheep that shared their quarters warmed the building to a more tolerable level.

The next day being Sunday, the refreshed men requested permission to hold a worship service. It was almost like old times, Peter thought. The men sat in rows in the straw while the deacons exhorted.

During the first message, the farmer and his son entered the barn with pails in their hands. Michel Kramer talked to the accompaniment of the *zing-zing* of milk squirting into the pails. When they had finished milking, the farmer and his son remained on their milking stools. A short time later, the farmer's wife opened the door. Her husband beckoned her to be quiet. She sat on a feed bin. They stayed for the whole service while Brother Kramer spoke on Jonah.

Jonah had not wanted to go where the Lord sent him. But by an unusual and unpleasant experience, God brought Jonah to his senses. God was using them now, through much trial of the flesh, to do His work. For the benefit of the listening farmer's family and the soldiers who guarded all possible exits, he also pointed out how it does not pay to defy God. God wants our whole devotion. We must give ourselves over to His control. Like the call to Nineveh, God's call to us is to repent of our wicked works and accept His salvation.

While the brethren sang a hymn, their hosts slipped from the barn. The seed had been sown. They prayed that it would bring forth a hundredfold.

When the company moved on the next morning, they left four men behind. One was Brother Joseph. Ever since the news of the death of his little son, Brother Joseph had been despondent. He had no appetite and had become very weak. During the recent cold spell, he had been scarcely able to go on. The brethren were sad to see their companions left behind. A soldier remained to guard them, with instructions to travel on when they had recovered.

Peter was worried about his teacher. He hoped his discouragement would not overcome him. And he had wanted Brother Joseph to speak with Alfonso too. Now who would explain the plan of salvation to him, if he asked? Something seemed to have gone awry. Harassing thoughts of these circumstances whirled in his head. He could not imagine why Brother Joseph had to be the victim of special sorrows.

The wind had stopped, and although the air was still cold, they were able to sing again.

"Think we'll get to the sea before spring?" Lukas asked.

"Spring? Yes. It is February already, isn't it?" Peter was jolted from his musings.

"I don't see any signs of spring yet," said Lukas. "Looks more snowy than ever."

"That's because we're climbing higher," Caspar volunteered. "And we're leaving the river. Look."

They paused as long as their chained condition would allow, to glance below them where the ribbon of white grew smaller in the distance as it wound away to the east to join the Danube. They had turned directly south and were climbing higher into the mountains. Cultivated fields soon gave way to silent stands of conifers as they struggled upwards through deepening snow. They were still among the trees when night fell, so they spread pine branches for beds, and the soldiers built smoky fires out around the circle of men to ward off wild animals.

By the next evening, they had crossed the mountains and again made camp in the forest. By the light of the fire, Peter and Lukas calculated, with the aid of the map, that they must be close to Marburg, a substantial town by the Drave River.

It would be good to enter civilization again, Peter thought as he drifted off to sleep. Even if it meant being stared at. Maybe they could get back to their evangelistic efforts now. This rugged country had a wild beauty, but the potential souls to be saved that it afforded were few and far between.

A few hours later, the stillness of the night was shattered by a clamour of shouting and neighing. The prisoners sat up dazedly. Beyond the circle of light, the noise went on. Men shouted; armour clanked; tree branches crashed. The noise seemed to be moving away, along the path they had travelled earlier.

"Hey, look," Caspar whispered hoarsely. "No guards."

They all looked about. The ever-present soldiers were nowhere in sight.

"Where are they?" Peter stammered.

"They've gone," another voice declared.

"The guards are gone." The words sprang from more than one throat.

"We are delivered," someone sang out.

The commotion had almost moved out of earshot.

Prisoners were jumping to their feet. There was a general confusion.

"Let's go."

"We're free."

"They've all gone."

"Where are my shoes?" came from Caspar.

"But this doesn't make sense." Peter held back. "Where would they all disappear to in the middle of winter, on the mountain-side?"

"Don't stand there asking questions," Caspar said, pushing him impatiently. "Let's go."

"Where will we go?" Peter demanded, stubbornly standing his ground. "We'll leave an unmistakable trail in the snow."

The argument was short-lived.

With a crashing of boughs, several soldiers came trotting through the trees. Seeing the prisoners on their feet, they shouted, "Lie down."

Reluctantly, the men complied. Someone called boldly, "What happened?"

One soldier answered, "Some horse thieves tried to steal the horses. Go to sleep."

Horse thieves!

The young men were too excited to sleep.

Lukas sighed, "I almost thought we'd get away."

"When the Lord delivers us, I believe He'll do it efficiently," Peter declared. "We'd never have gotten anywhere in this snow."

"I wonder if the thieves got any horses?" Lukas pondered.

"They must be hard up if they'd come after them in the winter," Caspar said, yawning.

"Maybe they were Turks," suggested Andreas.

"Maybe."

The thick, fluffy snowflakes floating from the sky the next morning added to the disorder and confusion caused by the attempted robbery.

Alfonso was nowhere about. The fires went untended, and the men waited in vain for their ration of thin gruel. Fewer than usual soldiers stood guard around the prisoners.

"Where is everybody?" Caspar asked impatiently. "No breakfast, no fire, no soldiers. Are we going today, or aren't we?"

"There seems to be a lot of soldiers moving about, over under those trees." Andreas pointed beyond their own sheltering pine grove to where the soldiers had set up their camp.

"I was hoping they had gotten stolen along with their horses," Caspar quipped.

"How do you know any horses got stolen?" Lukas challenged.

"I don't."

"Let's go closer and see if we can figure out what's delaying them over there," Andreas suggested.

Normally, the men were given very little liberty. The two soldiers in charge of a band tried to keep their ten men close together. If they wandered away, they could expect a blow or, at the least, a curt order to stay put. Now, since neither of their guards were in sight, the four young men sidled cautiously through the snowflakes to the edge of the group of prisoners.

Just then a soldier appeared from behind a tree, followed by two chained prisoners. They passed directly in front of Peter. He started. "Jacob."

Jacob, the physician-cabinetmaker, paused. "It's you, Peter!" he exclaimed fondly. "How are you?"

"Fine, thanks," Peter assured him hastily. "Where are you going?"

"Some of the soldiers were injured in the fracas with the horse thieves. They want me to set a broken leg."

"Oh, could I help?" Peter asked eagerly.

The soldier, realizing he was no longer being followed, turned and gestured impatiently.

"These men can help set the leg," Jacob suggested courteously.

The man looked them over. He shrugged and turned towards the soldier's encampment. The four men hurried after Jacob and his partner. Peter had helped him set bones before, and he knew it took several strong men to restrain the patient during the agonizing process.

Near a blazing campfire, over which, Peter noted longingly, bubbled several kettles of porridge and a caldron of fragrant tea, six or eight men lay on pallets. No wonder the ranks of guards were thin this morning. It must have been quite a skirmish.

The business of the broken leg was attended to first. It took all four boys to hold the man down while Jacob tugged and pulled the fracture together. Then he skillfully bound it to a straight length of tree limb.

One soldier had fallen and been trampled by his horse. Jacob diagnosed several cracked ribs, and he bound the man's chest tightly with rags torn from a blanket. While he patched a head wound, Peter and Lukas looked for Alfonso.

They found him on the far side of the fire, nursing an ugly gash on his right thigh.

In reply to their concerned questions, he grinned sheepishly. "I not fight horse thieves; I fight trees." Using his hands to help communicate, he told how he had dashed off after the thieves, along with his companions; and in the dark, a sharp snag had ripped into his leg, ending his efforts for the cause. The others laughed with him. He seemed pleased that they had shown an interest in his welfare.

"Did they get any horses?" Lukas asked as Jacob poured warm water over Alfonso's leg.

Alfonso gritted his teeth and drew a sharp breath. "They get three horses. Two horses lost. Find them this morning." Beads of sweat stood on his forehead as the doctor picked dirt from the wound. "But we catch one bandit."

"You did?"

"Yah. We catch one horse robber. He dies today."

Jacob looked up. "You mean they will put the man to death?"

"Yah." Alfonso nodded. "Bad man. Must die."

Jacob hurriedly finished dressing the leg. "Where is this robber?"

Alfonso shrugged. "General Carlos know."

The elderly physician and his chain partner looked at each other. "You had better return," Jacob advised his young helpers. "We have other business to do."

The boys made their way back to the other prisoners. Peter had a feeling that if Jacob had anything to say in the matter, the horse thief might not die that day.

XX

Alfonso

"Marching is boring, but this is worse." Caspar yawned and stretched his free arm above his head.

"Wonder if the soldiers will recover sufficiently by tomorrow to go on," commented Andreas, who was whittling at a piece of pine he had broken from a tree.

"Wish I had a knife," grumbled Caspar.

"Bridgit gave me this knife a few days before the arrest." Andreas cradled the tool in his palm. "My mother brought it to me the day we left Falkenstein."

The others were silent, sympathizing with Andreas's heartache.

"I guess those woodchoppers got an eyeful this morning," chuckled Lukas, idly tossing chips of bark into the fire in front of them. "Imagine finding a large encampment of chained men deep in the forest on the mountainside."

"Their mouths almost hung open when we all began to sing," Andreas recalled. "I hope they caught the message of the song."

"It looked for a while as though they were going to turn and run," Caspar laughed. "They'll have a story to tell their families tonight."

Families. Peter felt glum. Where was his family? These comrades-in-chains seemed almost like his family now.

Later that afternoon, they watched two soldiers head down the trail, supporting the man with the broken leg, on a pack horse.

"Wonder where they're taking him," Lukas said.

"Maybe we aren't far from a town," Peter suggested.

They were not. The next morning they were roused early, and the convoy struggled through the snow onto the narrow roadway.

Seeing Alfonso's clumsy attempts to mount his horse, Peter and Lukas gave him a hand. Once seated, he glared at them with his old scorn; but then he smiled slightly and mumbled, "Thanks."

As they trailed down the winding pathway, Peter could see a double line strung out in front of him, dark blots moving against the fresh snow. General Carlos rode in front. Directly behind him walked a single prisoner—the horse thief, Peter guessed. Then he had not been executed the day before. What would become of him? Peter shuddered. He could expect little mercy. Theft was a serious crime, punishable by death. Poor man. But then, he reminded himself, they were all going to die too—on the ships. There was a difference though. They had a hope for the hereafter. This thief most likely did not.

After skirting a cliff whose bare granite face broke the monotony of whiteness, they saw the town in the valley, hugging both banks of a river. Cutting across a ploughed field and climbing over the low stone walls of a pasture, the company halted on the north shore of the river, half a mile downstream from the town. Two soldiers were dispatched to the town, the captured horse thief in tow.

"Poor man," Peter said, shaking his head.

Alfonso heard him. He turned sharply, "Why poor?"

"He will die."

The hardened young soldier shrugged. "So? He bad man. He die." He looked at Peter shrewdly. "You die too." Then, after a quick look around, he turned abruptly and slithered from the saddle. Leaning up against his horse, he looked earnestly at Peter and Lukas. "Why?" he demanded. "Why you want to be slave? Why you walk so far? Why you wear chains? Why you be kind to everyone—to me?" He waved his arms agitatedly.

Peter fumbled for words. How could he explain? "Jesus died for us," he began slowly. "We are all bad. I sinned, he sinned," he said, indicating Lukas. "You sinned."

Alfonso nodded puzzled agreement.

"So we must be punished. We must die. Like that robber. We must all die sometime. But if we die, being sinners, we will go to hell." He searched Alfonso's face for signs of comprehension.

The soldier nodded. He knew about hell.

"But Jesus died on the cross, a sacrifice for our sins; and if we believe He died for us, we need not go to hell. If we believe in Jesus and obey His words, we can go to heaven. We might all die on the ships, but we will go to heaven. If we say we don't believe in Jesus, we can go back home, but then we will go to hell when we die. We must obey God." Peter prayed that his testimony would make sense to Alfonso, in spite of the language barrier. The dark, troubled eyes before him seemed to understand, at least in part.

"How you all love so?" Alfonso blurted out. "I kick you. Shout. Be angry. You love. You love that bad man. How?"

"God loved us first," Peter replied, smiling. "God is love. We love God because He loves us. God's love in our hearts loves everyone."

"I not know love." Alfonso's tone was bitter. "My father not love me. My master not love. Other soldiers, not love. Nobody."

"Your father didn't love you?" Lukas probed.

"Nah!" Alfonso spat on the ground. "He had too many children. Me, he send away. Be servant to rich count."

"Your father sent you away?"

"Yah! My mother, she die. My father, poor man. I go live in big castle. Work. Work. Master kick me. Beat me. Yell."

"Didn't anybody ever care for you?"

Alfonso looked past them to the snow-capped peaks. "Yah. One girl. She like."

So there had been some romance in his life. Peter listened with interest.

Alfonso continued in a hard voice. "I be soldier. I go away. I come home. She gone. Married. She no care. Nobody."

No wonder he carried a chip on his shoulder. "Jesus loves you," Peter assured him. "Would you like to ask Him to take away your sins and put love into your heart?"

But Alfonso evaded the issue by changing the subject. "Where your home?"

"Steinborn," Lukas replied promptly. "Didn't you know that?"

"No." The soldier shook his head.

"Your mother, sister?" He looked at Peter. "Where they live now?"

"Moravia," said Peter. "I don't know where."

The soldiers had returned by now, minus the robber. They led a pack horse laden with newly purchased provisions. The company stepped cautiously across the frozen river and made their way along the far bank, back to the main road again.

They journeyed on through dense forests of heavy timber. Stacks of newly cut wood lined the roadway, and several times they heard the dull *chop-chop* of axes biting into wood or felt the ground tremble as a giant evergreen crashed to the forest floor.

They sang loudly in hopes that the message would reach the

ears of the woodcutters, but the sound was muffled by the soft snow and shaggy trees, and the music bounced back and rang in their own ears.

One evening when Alfonso distributed their black bread, he bent close to Peter. "You have something send you mother?"

Peter eyed him bewilderedly.

Alfonso tried again. "Maybe I go, find you home. When we get to sea," he explained quickly. "You send something. She know I am friend."

"He is saying that when we get to the end of this journey, he might try to find our families. If we send some token that they recognize, they will accept him," Andreas interpreted.

Alfonso smiled eagerly and nodded agreement. "You send something?" he repeated.

"He doesn't need proof. They'd believe him," Caspar grunted.

"It would be all right to try though."

"Here." Andreas held out his finely tooled knife. "Take this. Give it to Bridgit Hoffner. Tell her, 'Keep faith.'"

"Keep faith. Bridgit Hoffner," Alfonso repeated. He secreted the knife under the folds of his cloak and turned away.

"Why does he want it now?" Lukas was skeptical. "He has lots of time before we reach the sea."

"Do you think he will really go there?" Caspar too did not think much of the transaction. "You shouldn't have given him your knife, Andreas. He'll likely keep it, or sell it for a good price."

Andreas just smiled. "It won't do me any good if I'm a galley slave. And if it reaches Bridgit, she will know that I have kept the faith. I think, in light of his recent questions, Alfonso is close to the kingdom."

Back on the road again, they made an effort to draw Alfonso out concerning his plans. But he turned his head stubbornly and pretended not to hear. When they persisted, he shook his whip at them threateningly and scowled. It was hard to believe he had been so friendly a short time before.

"I'm sure it was all a sham," Lukas said, bending his head towards Peter and speaking quietly. "He's just hard up for money."

"I wonder if he owns anything," Peter returned. "The way those officials talked when they were trying to enlist us, a soldier makes lots of money."

"I doubt it," Lukas scoffed. "I wonder if he even owns that horse. I think I'll ask him sometime—but not now," he decided after glancing up at the stony face riding beside Peter.

The news that travelled along the chain concerning the horse thief cheered them all considerably. After several attempts, Jacob had bribed a soldier, with his pocket watch, to take him to where the robber was tied to a tree. Knowing his doom was sealed, the man had confessed his need and made his peace with God. They rejoiced that one more soul had benefited from their trials.

"Today or tomorrow we should reach Tiele," Peter announced the next morning, hastily consulting his worn map.

"And what will we find there?" Caspar smoothed the worst of the night's wrinkles from his coat.

"We'll be back on the main trade route again. See?" He pointed to the heavy line swinging in a curve, southward from Neustadt.

"Good," Lukas said. "We'll be out of this rugged country, and there will be more towns."

"That means more food," declared Caspar with satisfaction.

"And more people," Peter sighed, folding the map again. "I don't like going where there are people."

"There will be more souls to reach," Andreas reminded him.

They looked up at the approach of two men. One, to their

amazement, was General Carlos. He surveyed them sternly. "Where is Alfonso?"

"Alfonso?" Peter, Caspar, and Andreas repeated together.

"Alfonso?" echoed Lukas, looking about.

"Yes, the soldier." The general was impatient.

They all shrugged. "We don't know."

"They know." The other man, who was the soldier generally attached to the other end of their main chain, insisted. "Alfonso, he talk, talk to these men. They know."

"Is he gone?" Peter blurted.

"Gone," the other soldier affirmed.

"Tell us where he went," the general commanded.

Peter shook his head. Although he suspected where Alfonso might have gone, he really did not know. Was he heading for Moravia and the brethren there? But Moravia was a big country. They had not even told Alfonso to inquire at Nikolsburg for information. "I do not know," he stated honestly. "He did not tell us he was going."

Although the older soldier insisted that they were accomplices in Alfonso's disappearance, the general seemed satisfied with their ignorance, and soon moved on.

The procession finally got moving, but not before two soldiers had been sent galloping north along the road they had just travelled.

"They've sent someone after him," Peter thought. Oh, he hoped Alfonso could escape. For a soldier to abandon his duty was no light matter. He prayed fervently that Alfonso would find the brethren and, most of all, that he would experience the love of God in his own heart.

Oh, how he wished he could have gone along. They had been on the road now for five weeks, covering a little over two hundred miles. A lone rider on a good horse, barring accident or bad weather, could cover that mountain route in less than two weeks.

True to Peter's calculation, they reached Tiele that day. A sprawling crossroads town, Tiele was an untidy, noisy, crowded place. They rubbed shoulders with farmers and soldiers, merchants and travelling musicians, townswomen and officials, message boys and scribes, all bustling about their business. They even saw old Patlo again!

"Look!" Lukas pulled Peter's sleeve. "There's Patlo!"

Peter looked. He chuckled. "Sure is. Even has the right coat this time."

The unsuspecting peddler was struggling to lead a laden mule through a throng of schoolchildren. His violet-hued cloak was dirtier and more ragged than ever; his shoulders more stooped.

"The wrong mule though." Caspar had also spied the old vendor of various merchandise of unknown origin.

"Yes," Peter had to agree. Patlo's old mule was as bony and ancient as himself. This beast looked young and hardy, and stepped along effortlessly under its uneven load.

Many pamphlets were distributed before the evangelists in chains left Tiele for the highroad south. Only the Lord knew what would be the harvest from the seed sown there.

Another inn stable; another day's march. The hours dragged for Peter. He stole a sideways glance at Lukas. How he managed to keep so clean and neat under the circumstances, Peter could not understand. Even Lukas's coat hung smoothly from his shoulders.

Peter felt like a tramp. He knew he looked like one. Try as he might, he could not seem to keep his appearance as orderly as Lukas. Sometimes he felt his companion spent too much time fussing over how he looked. Who cared? Peter reasoned. Lukas would wash his handkerchief out every chance he had—whenever they knelt to drink from a stream or were handed a bowl of water. He was continually washing his face and smoothing his hair. Peter could not be bothered. Usually he was too tired to do more than gulp down his rations. He often dozed off during evening prayers.

Peter was staring sleepily into the fire while Andreas read from his notebook: " 'Wherein ye greatly rejoice, though now for a season, if need be, ye are in heaviness through manifold temptations: that the trial of your faith, being much more precious than of gold that perisheth, though it be tried with fire, might be found unto praise and honour and glory at the appearing of Jesus Christ.' "[71]

Peter certainly felt "in heaviness" tonight. These restraining chains, his aching feet, the cold and damp—it was all so futile. The appearing of Jesus Christ seemed remote.

Plop! Something landed in his lap. Inquisitively he picked it up. Philip, who had dropped it there, was watching him, a huge smile lighting his face. "What is it? A letter?" Peter turned the rolled paper over disbelievingly. "Whe-where did it come from?" he stammered.

Philip, still smiling broadly, handed a similar bundle to Caspar and to Andreas, who had ceased his reading on hearing Peter's voice. "From old Patlo, who else?"

"Patlo?" the younger men echoed. They looked at each other.

"So that *was* him!"

"Yes, that was him all right. He got himself a sturdier mule and took the more easterly route south, calculating to meet us here."

"He's not afraid of the Turks," chuckled Lukas.

"No, he is one himself, so he says," Caspar reminded them.

Peter had unfolded his letter, and it took only a moment of

scanning the fine writing to tell him it was from Ursula. Losing no time, he read eagerly:

Dear Brother,

Grace and peace to you in the Name of our Lord Jesus Christ, who through the eternal Spirit strengthens us and gives us grace to live in daily victory.

Patlo, the old peddler who used to visit us at Steinborn, has arrived here at the bruderhof and offered to transport letters to you. He feels confident he can find you by following the main routes south and making inquiries along the way. We owe much to the friendship of this strange man and pray that he will embrace the faith.

Uncle Guttenhann cautioned us not to mention our exact locality in case Patlo would be apprehended and the letters fall into the hands of the wrong authorities. I will say only that we have found refuge among the brethren at a large community. We are comfortable here and only long to have Father and you with us, but the Lord's will be done.

Perhaps I should tell you a little of our stay in the castle. Dear Sister Agathe! Remember how we used to talk about her? How ashamed I am when I think of those times. If it had not been for her, I am afraid it would have gone ill with us. That first terrible night, when we were locked in the tower, some soldiers tried to enter; but Sister Agathe stood sternly in the doorway and told them in no uncertain terms that such conduct was immoral and sinful. While they muttered angrily, she preached to them, calling them to repentance lest they fall into hellfire. The commotion drew the attention of their superior, and he ordered his men to leave us in peace.

Sister Agathe led us in daily prayers and inspired us to remain in good spirits. It was she who persuaded the castellan that it would be advantageous to put us to work in the kitchen and chambers. She demanded an audience with him and, to our amazement, got it. (You know how she is.) She herself worked tirelessly and also kept constant check on all of us to see that we were unmolested.

I spent most of the days peeling potatoes and chopping cabbage in the kitchen. It was I who recognised the beggar woman who whined at the outdoor cooking hut. She looked truly pitiful. The first note written by the brethren was given into my keeping, so you can imagine how nervous I was with that little wad of paper in my pocket. I didn't know how I would get it to Sister Boewen, but fortunately the head cook accepted my suggestion that I give a pail of potato peelings to that beggar to stop her whining. The note went along with the peelings.

Then, for reasons unknown to us, we were again locked in the tower. The entire experience was a trial of faith for all of us. At home, we girls used to talk of the new fabric we had for a dress, or we'd discuss which young men were most handsome or the details of the next wedding or a different way to cook chicken. Now we encouraged each other to overcome our discouragement by meditating on Christ's example; we recalled the sufferings and triumphs of saints in years gone by, and we spoke much of heaven. We learned to set our affection on things above and not on things on earth, because we discovered that they can disappear overnight. Only those things that are eternal endure. We confessed our sins one to another and prayed often for you brethren and those at home. Although we were given enough to eat, we suffered from cold.

We were happily surprised to be unexpectedly released, and lost no time finding our way home. In the darkness, I stumbled on a rock and turned my ankle. It was very painful for several days, and I was unable to walk. But it is better now. It was so wonderful to be home, although we sorrowed to learn of your fate. It is still hard to believe that you are far away, destined to be slaves on a ship. But we rejoice that you are counted worthy to suffer for His sake. And be of good cheer. Grandfather Boewen, that dear old saint, reminds us almost daily that he is sure of your return. He says the Holy Spirit has given him the assurance that this trial is of the Lord and that you will not all perish. To this end he insists that we pray and wait for your return. We will be anxious to hear from Patlo in the event he finds you.

But I have wandered from my story. Our provisions in Steinborn were low. The marshal and his soldiers had seized all the accessible food, and we had only that which was in the secret storehouses. The cattle that had been taken up the mountain gave very little milk, so they were slaughtered. Uncle Guttenhann felt it was impractical for us to remain there any longer.

Mother and I with the two younger children were a part of the first group to leave. We were able to hire sleighs and horses from the people of Steinborn. I should mention that several times we found gifts of bread or milk on the doorstep of the dining hall where we were all staying. They did not dare to aid us openly, but it seems the villagers felt kindly towards us. It appears that our years there were not in vain. Uncle Guttenhann was also able to sell some of the tools and furniture that had escaped the clutches of the soldiers. The remainder we took with us.

And, Peter, just think! I had to drive one wagon. Can you imagine? I, who was always afraid of horses! There was no other way. The others in our sleigh all had small children to care for. I was very apprehensive at first; and of course we were scarcely away from Steinborn before my horse shied, reared, and tumbled us all in the snow. I was as terrified as the horse, but with the help of the other women, we were able to calm him and get the sleigh back on the road. After that, it seemed that the worst had already happened; and I was not so frightened.

We had an otherwise uneventful trip to Nikolsburg, where we were met by Brother Riedemann. He directed us here. The later parties were sent to other bruderhofs.

I am busy helping in the kindergarten here. There are seventy-two children, so fifteen teachers are required. The children are so precious with their eager questions and quaint observations. They are so teachable. We can learn so many lessons from them. They trust us to meet their needs and direct their activities, just as we should trust our heavenly Father to provide for us.

Mother helps in the kitchen or laundry as the case may be. She is cheerful, but she is thinner, and I know she misses you and Father greatly.

Maria says to tell you she has lost a tooth. She is saving it in a cup to show you when you come back. She does not realise that you may never come back; she only knows you have gone on a long journey.

And really, Peter, you always did want to travel. Are you seeing all the faraway places you longed to visit? I know you didn't imagine it quite this way, but God's ways are unsearchable. Can you keep good courage? A reward is awaiting the faithful. This life is but a vapour. Soon it will be past. Much better it is to die for the faith than to die in our sins.

Bridgit is here and thinks often of Andreas and of her wedding that wasn't to be. She has a heavy heart, I am sure, but she is so cheerful and selfless. There have been two weddings here since we arrived, and she has given the brides the lovely bedding and linens she had prepared for her own home. She busies herself stitching clothing for the children and embroidering tablecloths to brighten the homes of others.

Now I have a special message for you to deliver. Are you able to talk with Caspar? Hulda Reimer asked me to tell you to tell him that she is praying for him. She is too modest to write to him personally and does not want to be bold, but I know she is fond of him. I had not known they were special friends; had you?

I commend you now into God's keeping. I long for the return of all of you, but most of all I desire that you remain true to the One who has called us from darkness into His marvellous light that we may meet again, if not here, then over there where there is no more sorrow or tears, sickness or pain.

Mother is writing to Father and will tell you about George.

Your loving sister,
Ursula

The next two days sped by as the men shared, reviewed, and discussed the news from home. Caspar had had a long and welcome letter of encouragement from his parents. Peter had found no opportunity to relay Hulda's message, so he bided his time, not wishing to embarrass his cousin by a public announcement.

Andreas marched along as in a dream, his letter from Bridgit read over and over, lying in a pocket near his heart. Lukas's father had shared the news from his wife with his son.

Big Peter's letter had told of George's death. He had passed away on the journey to Moravia and had been laid to rest on a hillside where several infants had been buried earlier. His last days were fraught with pain, and he had gone joyfully to meet his Maker.

Peter was glad that George could at last be well and strong.

"You walk like an old man." Caspar's teasing voice interrupted Peter's thoughts.

Peter did not bother to answer. All morning Caspar had been making not-too-subtle taunts about how old Peter looked.

At breakfast he had peered over the rim of his bowl and remarked that Peter looked older this morning.

Peter figured they all looked older with their shaggy beards and ragged clothing, so he had not taken the comment seriously. He had learned from experience not to take Caspar too seriously all of the time.

But then, when they lined up for chaining, Caspar had made some remark about Peter's joints creaking louder than usual. This time he had managed to answer that maybe his cousin's hearing was failing.

But at this latest allusion to oldness, he was sure he had heard Lukas snicker. What was going on here? He threw what was supposed to be a withering glance over his shoulder at his pesky cousin. Even Andreas was grinning broadly at his discomfiture.

While Peter was casting about for an adroit response, Andreas finally came to the rescue. "Happy Birthday," he said.

Birthday? Sure! It was his birthday! He was twenty years old today. It was hard to keep track of time. Twenty. He had surely looked forward to being twenty. Somehow he had felt that once a person dropped the "teen" from his age, he would have reached some sort of landmark.

"How does it feel to be twenty?" Lukas, who was still a teenager, asked.

"I don't know. Ask me in a few days when I've gotten used to it."

Actually he felt like turning twenty was an anticlimax. The past two months had matured him far more thoroughly than a birthday ever could.

Twenty years. Would these past twenty years constitute his whole life span, or would the Lord grant him twenty more? He wished he knew.

Alfonso's place had been taken by a silent, unbending older soldier. In the excitement of the letters, Peter had almost forgotten his former guard. But when he saw the two who had ridden off in pursuit of the deserter return one evening, their horses' heads hanging from exhaustion, he knew Alfonso was safe.

XXI

Encounters in Carniola

"A letter is to be written and given to old Patlo tomorrow." The prisoners were sitting in the hayloft above an inn stable in Stein. Andreas had just returned from dragging Caspar from one group to another in his eagerness to discover whether there was any way to get a message to Bridgit.

"How are they going to accomplish that?" scoffed Lukas, looking up from his reading.

Caspar and Andreas lowered themselves onto the hay. "Back in Tiele, Patlo indicated that he would meet us here in Stein. Brother Jacob is going to request permission to purchase some liniments and herbs for potions. Hopefully he can deal with Patlo."

"Hopefully," grunted Lukas skeptically.

"Are you writing?" Peter asked Andreas.

"I want to, but I have no pen or paper," Andreas replied despairingly.

"Let's go see if anyone has something we could improvise for writing material." Caspar unfolded himself, and the two of them went off on their search.

Peter and Lukas were left alone in their corner, but not for long. A head and shoulders emerged through an opening in the loft floor, and a stableboy with a pitchfork heaved himself through. He was followed by another. Rather self-consciously, they proceeded to fork hay through the hole.

Peter watched them for a time. They were country lads, possibly fifteen or sixteen years old. They seemed to be in a hurry to finish their chore and escape the watchful eyes of the prisoners. Suddenly Peter nudged Lukas. "Let's be evangelists."

Lukas looked sideways at him. "How? What shall we say?"

"We could start by giving them some literature."

Lukas agreed, so with friendly smiles, the partners-in-chains approached the two boys.

"Hello." Peter tried to put warmth into his greeting.

The boys leaned on their forks and stared, not sure whether to answer.

"Are you almost done working for the day?" Peter tried again. One boy nodded. The other answered, "Yah."

"Can you read?" Lukas asked them.

"Read?" The boys looked at each other in puzzlement. Then they both nodded.

"Here are some papers for you to read." The young evangelists offered their pamphlets. "They will tell you how to find real peace and joy."

The stableboys hesitated. Plainly they were a mite suspicious of these queer lodgers.

Angry shouts rose from the stable below. The boys jumped. Quickly they snatched the papers and stuffed them into their pockets. Then they forked hay furiously for a few minutes before disappearing down the ladder to their duties below.

"Well," sighed Lukas. "We didn't get very far there."

"The seed is cast forth," Peter consoled him. "It will bring forth, some thirty, some sixty, and some an hundredfold."

They were almost through the town of Stein the next day

before they encountered Patlo. Their column had come to a halt in a narrow street between two tall buildings. Shouts echoed in the confined space, and it was evident that some atypical distraction was impeding their progress.

Caspar stepped up onto a doorstep to see better. Craning his neck, he reported excitedly, "I see old Patlo's purple cloak up there."

"Wonder what the old fellow is up to now," Lukas chuckled.

"What's he doing?" Peter demanded.

"I can't see. . . . Oh, now the general's horse moved. It looks like . . . yes, Patlo's mule is lying down in the middle of the road . . ."

"Sounds familiar," Peter said.

" . . . and Patlo is beating it with a thin stick and yelling at it to get up."

Peter and Lukas tried standing on a doorstep across the street from Caspar, but they were just too short to see over all the other heads bobbing up and down in front of them in attempts to see the action.

Caspar kept up a running commentary for their benefit. "Now Patlo is shaking his head and throwing up his hands in exasperation. General Carlos is angry. He's ordering some soldiers to move the mule. . . . They are pushing from behind while Patlo pulls in front. . . . No good."

"Next step—Patlo will try to sell them something," Andreas predicted to Peter and Lukas.

" . . . Now the general is sitting and thinking what to do next. . . . Oh, Patlo is opening a sack. . . . There, he's showing the general something."

"I told you so," Andreas chuckled.

" . . . The general is shaking his head angrily. Patlo is talking fast and waving his arms. . . . There, Brother Jacob is speaking to his guard. . . . His guard is riding forward to the general. . . . He's speaking to him."

"Patlo staged this purposely," Peter stated. "What's happening now?" He prodded Caspar, who had ceased his recital of events.

"The soldier is unlinking Brother Jacob and taking him and his partner up to the mule. . . . Patlo is opening more bundles. . . . Jacob is opening jars and sniffing salves.

"See if you can see when he slips the letter to him," begged Andreas.

Caspar stretched on one leg. "Oh, now the general moved. I can't see them."

In a short time, the transaction was completed; and with surprising ease, the stubborn beast was prevailed upon to stand up and step aside. As the prisoners filed by, Peter distinctly saw the old peddler wink, although his dark, wrinkled face remained impassive.

Peter inhaled great gulps of crisp, fresh air. He was relieved to again be away from the stifling smells and the crowds of the town. Trees grew to the top of these rounded mountains of the province of Carniola. Brightly painted farm buildings nestled against gently rolling foothills. In summer, he thought this area would be an artist's palette of shades of green, bordered by the blue sky. Unfortunately, it was unlikely it would ever be his privilege to see it in summertime.

An hour later, the stillness of the snow-clad landscape was interrupted by the rhythmic clatter of galloping horses. The horses swiftly gained on the walking men and whirled past them, their flying hooves spraying mud and snow as they went. But instead of disappearing into the distance, the three riders reined in and stopped to speak with the general at the head of the column, while the remainder of the soldiers and prisoners stood waiting.

Presently the general rode back along the column with the three newcomers. He ordered the men to close ranks as he wished to speak. When they were clustered in a tight semicircle around the horses, he addressed them:

"These men are bailiffs from Stein. They have received complaints from several citizens that some prisoners were distributing seditious material in their town." His face showed disapproval. "You are aware that this is forbidden. They have warrants to arrest those who are guilty of such actions."

Peter's mouth went dry. His stomach lurched sickeningly.

"Arrest?" muttered Lukas. "How can they arrest us? We are already in chains."

"All those who were engaged in conversation or passing printed material to the citizens in Stein must return with these bailiffs and face prosecution."

There was a stir among the prisoners as they all looked at each other.

"Raise your hand if you were involved." The general was clearly annoyed at this delay.

Almost every hand was raised. The Christians, committed to sharing their salvation with their fellow men, seized every opportunity to do so. The evening in Stein had been no exception.

The general scowled in annoyance. He turned inquiringly to the bailiffs. After a brief conference, he announced, "Since they cannot try all of you, they will be satisfied with twenty representatives. Are there any volunteers?"

Peter hesitated. All he had done was pass out one small paper. What could they do to them? They were already in chains. They could, he guessed, throw them into prison here and separate them from their brethren. They could even—he turned cold at the thought—execute them right on the spot. Those flames and the anguished screams of the victims he had seen at Nikolsburg danced before his eyes.

Several older men had volunteered already. Surely more would volunteer. The older men would know better how to answer. They would not expect those new in the faith to suffer for the rest. He felt Lukas's eyes on him. He turned.

"Let's," Lukas whispered hoarsely.

As one, the two young men raised their hands.

There were too many volunteers, but because Peter and Lukas stood near the general, they were among those singled out to follow the bailiffs back to Stein.

Some hours later they stood again in a dark-panelled courtroom before an austere-faced judge. The bailiffs stood ready to accuse their captives; and two court clerks, quills in hand, were prepared to record the transactions.

One clerk read the charge: "It has been brought to the attention of the court of Stein, in the province of Carniola, that certain chained prisoners, while within the borders of this diocese, have preached and promulgated heresies forbidden by command of the king. The aforesaid crime being punishable by death, the offenders have been apprehended and now face sentence."

The judge nodded, and the clerk took his seat.

The twenty chained brethren stood meekly before the judge. He peered at them sternly. Turning to the bailiffs, he asked, "What is the evidence?"

"Your Honour,"—one man stepped forward to place a printed pamphlet on the desk—"this was handed to a serving maid at an inn last evening."

Another bailiff spoke up. "I saw, with my own eyes, some of these men speaking to some goatherds at the public fountain this morning."

The judge was turning the paper over and over in his hand. Were they to be given no chance to defend themselves? Not that it would do any good, Peter reflected, recalling the travesty of a trial in Vienna.

The judge scanned a few lines on the paper. His lips hardened into a thin line. "The Gospel of John," he hissed mockingly. He tossed the paper to a clerk. "Keep that for the records." Folding his white hands deliberately, he regarded the motley prisoners coolly. "Printing of the Scriptures is forbidden. The ordained men of the church are the only ones capable of interpreting the Scriptures. The Bible in the hands of the common folk becomes a tool of the devil. We tolerate no heretics in this diocese." He paused to reflect a moment.

What would the verdict be? Peter felt faint. His head whirled. He was already virtually condemned to death on the galleys, but he had been able to push that destiny into the future. Now it might be all over here, today.

One bailiff stepped forward. "Your Honour, it has been our custom to execute by fire those who teach against the church," he began eagerly.

"Yes, yes," the judge replied testily. "But these men are under sentence from the court in Vienna already."

"Forty lashes," he declared with finality. "To be administered in the public square. Sentence to be carried out immediately."

"Forty lashes! Relief that they were to escape the flames mingled with consternation at the ordeal facing them. Public whippings were not only humiliating but they also often left the victims so battered and bruised that they were unable to walk unaided.

A short time later the men stood without their coats, facing the crowd that had gathered at the summons of a town crier. A public flogging was an interesting diversion, especially during the uneventful winter months. This one would be particularly so because the convicted were strangers and there were so many that four executioners flexed their arms and swung their whips in preparation for the sport. At the sound of the bugle, the mob cheered and the beating began.

The first blow made Peter gasp and sent him staggering forward. Daggers of searing pain shot through his back. Again and again the blows fell. In spite of the cold, his back felt as though it were on fire. Could he bear it?

Then, into his mind flashed a picture of his Lord, who "was in all points tempted like as we are, yet without sin,"[72] enduring the very same experience before Pilate. The jeers of the bloodthirsty mob faded as the blows fell relentlessly on Peter's bleeding back. He was forced to his knees, but praying earnestly, he bore the pain stoically and did not cry out. At last it was over.

He lay on the cobbles in a heap, Lukas beside him. Gradually the voices of the crowd penetrated his dimmed senses. His lacerated back burned like fire. Faces swam together and blurred into blackness.

The prisoners were left where they lay, and it was some time before they had recovered sufficiently to pick themselves up and limp painfully after the Spanish soldiers who had returned for them. Their shirts had been reduced to shreds; and in spite of the cold, Peter could not bear the weight of his coat, so he wore it back to front, leaving his back exposed.

No one remembered much of that walk through the darkness to where their comrades were waiting. Peter was tempted to think evil of the bailiffs and judges who had inflicted such misery on them. Through the long, pain-filled night, he at times wished he had never handed the fateful paper to that stableboy. But then the Spirit would comfort him that he had done his duty and kept the Great Commission. Maybe, he reflected through his pain, someone would find true joy and peace as a result of their missionary endeavors in Stein.

Brother Jacob was permitted to treat those who had been

flogged. While he rubbed soothing ointment into their wounds, he told them news that lent meaning to their suffering.

"Last night before you returned, two men came to speak with us," he related. "One was a priest from a village west of here. The other had seen the public beating and told him of it. This priest has been studying his Latin Bible and has become disillusioned with the church. He has secretly shared his discoveries with some of his parishioners. They would like to form a pure church patterned after the New Testament example. When he heard that a group had been punished for supposedly spreading religious heresy, he determined to speak with us and ask for help."

"What can we do?" Peter asked through teeth clenched in suffering.

"The brethren discussed many points of doctrine with him. He knew little about adult baptism but listened with an open mind to our exhortation. He promised to return again tonight and speak with us further."

So there was to be a harvest from the seed sown in Stein. Peter rejoiced even as he limped along the highroad. The Spirit of God was working in the hearts of men, leading to the truth those who sincerely sought Him.

The New Testament church was born in suffering and thrived under the persecution of Nero and other godless rulers. Even so, the sixteenth-century church was growing and spreading, bathed in the blood of the saints.

That night the seeking priest and four of his followers let themselves down through a hole in the roof of the barn where the prisoners were sleeping, and the brethren spent hours praying with and instructing them. Before dawn the priest departed, having determined to abandon his office in the church and launch out in faith to teach the New Testament.

The brethren encouraged him to write letters to the bruderhofs in Moravia, requesting assistance from their leaders, and this he promised to do. A new church was born that night in a ramshackle barn in Carniola.

Two stormy days later, Peter's back was still smarting, although the wounds were healing quickly under Jacob's ministrations. Along with his salve, the elderly physician also dispensed words of encouragement and comfort.

"Thou therefore endure hardness, as a good soldier of Jesus Christ."[73] Those words were conveyed by a seasoned warrior who had shown long-suffering and patience in persecution, to a young man like Peter himself. Like Timothy, he too had known the Holy Scriptures from a child, but now he was under test for his faith.

Paul had said, "Wherein I suffer trouble, as an evil doer, even unto bonds; but the word of God is not bound."[74] How true, Peter mused as they tramped off the miles. He thought of the growing multitude that had been touched by the Word through their bonds: Alfonso, Henry, the shepherds at Neustadt, the horse thief, the councillors in Vienna, the people at Schöttwein, the priest and followers at Carniola, not to mention many stable hands, market vendors, fellow travellers, and farmers who had accepted the printed Word. God only knew the far-reaching effect of their unique evangelistic endeavor.

Peter stretched his legs towards the warmth of the open fireplace in the large, crowded dining room of a country tavern.

"This is real comfort," Caspar, beside him, exulted. "It's not too often we get to sit inside."

"We aren't exactly in the seats of honour," Peter pointed out.

Thirty of General Carlos's charges perched on narrow benches, around the walls of the noisy room. Their guards, several travellers, and a throng of roughly dressed countrymen sat at the tables that occupied most of the floor space.

Men laughed loudly and called to one another with coarse jokes and much table thumping and hip slapping. A half-dozen harried waitresses darted to and fro, attempting to serve the demands of their customers.

Another rowdy group entered and noisily made their way to the few remaining tables. They were better dressed than their fellow countrymen and were young men. Possibly students, Peter guessed. They lost no time in shouting for service. Three of the younger waitresses answered their summons. The men teased them boldly, and the girls blushed and giggled coquettishly, enjoying the attention.

Presently the students, if such they were, called out to the other serving girls to join them. One waitress set down a full platter and, with a twitch of her full skirts, answered the summons. But one young lady did not. Her reluctance and decency stood out in contrast to the unseemly conduct of her peers.

Peter studied her curiously from under half-closed lids. He noticed that the remaining waitress was an older woman, and she seemed to shadow the younger one. She was never more than a few steps from her. They worked together, it seemed.

The younger girl had a round, honest-looking face framed by wavy brown hair. For her size she could almost be Ursula. She moved about gracefully, attending to the needs of the customers but not responding to their rude advances. Whenever a particularly crude man called for something, the older woman would quickly come to his assistance. She had the same plain, open face, although her forehead was creased with lines of care, and she moved heavily as though very weary. They must be related, Peter decided. Either mother and daughter or else sisters. But what were such decent women doing in a place like this? He watched with revulsion as an intoxicated man reached for the girl, but then breathed a sigh of relief to see her older companion step quickly between them.

He forgot the two women when hot soup was brought to them. It had been a long time since he had eaten a warm meal, and even longer since he had eaten in a warm room.

"They get the meat, and we get the bones," Lukas grumbled, stirring in his soup for some scraps of meat.

"Just be thankful it's warm and not rotten," Peter chided. It was rather disheartening to see the soldiers gulping huge mouthfuls of roast chicken and drowning white potatoes in rich gravy, but then a prisoner could expect no better.

Peter could not keep his mind off that one young woman, however. When she gathered their empty bowls, their eyes met for a moment, and she smiled a shy but kind smile at him. She really did remind him of Ursula, and her eyes were blue. Who was she? Why was she here? How could she remain so untainted by this evil environment?

Even after they had been led out into the cold again and were huddled in an empty corner of the stable, Peter could not forget that girl. Her smile seemed to float in the air above him. He could not sleep. He told himself he was not really interested in her but that her presence there was a mystery and he was just curious.

He still could not sleep.

Then, in the darkened stable, he heard a rustling sound. Someone was prowling about. Peter sat up, not disturbing Lukas, who snored on. Two figures approached the sleeping men. No one else seemed to be awake.

"Who goes there?" Peter called out in a hoarse whisper.

"It is Lisle Roettgen and her daughter, Barbel," answered a woman's voice. "We are serving women from the inn. We would like to question you about your faith."

Peter nudged his father, who lay near him, as was their custom whenever possible. Although their faces were obscured, he was sure the intruders were that mystery girl and apparently her mother.

Big Peter opened his eyes, and Peter explained the situation. These nighttime encounters were becoming routine, so Big Peter and Mathes Legeder cordially invited the two women to sit down on a feed bin near them.

Lisle, the older woman, explained, "I am a widow. My husband died when my daughter here was only three years old. Because I had no means of support, I was given into the custody of my husband's brother, the owner of this tavern. He is a very unscrupulous man, and there is much evil in this place. But I had to work for my keep; and when Barbel was old enough, her uncle forced her to serve his customers also. I tremble daily for her safety, but thus far the Virgin Mary has heard my prayers."

Peter's gaze rested involuntarily on the girl's face. Her eyes were large in the moonlight. She looked small and defenseless. He wished there were something he could do to protect her. But he was chained . . .

Lisle hurried on. "My husband was a good man, not like his brother. He was very religious—kept the Ten Commandments faithfully, attended mass regularly, said his prayers twice daily, and paid his church dues without complaining. But when he died"—she buried her face in her hands—"the priest had given him the last rites, and we thought he was gone. But then," she continued, lifting her head and drawing a shuddering breath, "he opened his eyes, looked about wildly, and said, 'It's not enough.' Those were his last words."

"How awful," Peter thought sympathetically.

"Since then," the widow continued, "I have used every penny I find left on the tables to buy indulgences for his soul. I pray to all the saints, and yet his final words 'It's not enough' haunt me.

I am afraid it's not enough. But what more can I do?" she pleaded desperately.

"You are right," Mathes' steady voice agreed. "It is not enough. 'For the law having a shadow of good things to come, and not the very image of the things, can never with those sacrifices which they offered year by year continually make the comers thereunto perfect. . . . For it is not possible that the blood of bulls and of goats should take away sins.'[75] All the Old Testament sacrifices and adherence to the Law could not cleanse from sin. They had to go through the motions again and again. No number of confessions or prayers can save us."

"Then keeping the commandments and confessing to the priests is not enough?" Lisle repeated earnestly.

"No," Mathes answered, shaking his head.

"What more can I do?"

"If we had a light, I could show you that chapter in Hebrews."

Barbel slipped from her seat and disappeared into the shadows. She was back shortly with a small candle.

Mathes thumbed through his notebook and then handed it to the woman so she could read for herself. Lisle and Barbel bent their heads over the book together, letting the tallow from the candle drip onto the page. "Read verse ten," he directed.

Lisle read slowly, " 'By the which will we are sanctified through the offering of the body of Jesus Christ once for all.' "[76]

"Jesus Christ offered Himself as the supreme sacrifice for the sins of all mankind; and His death, because He was the perfect Lamb of God, took away the sins of the world."

"Yes, I knew that." Lisle sounded puzzled. "But what does that have to do with my problem? Do I not still have to go to the priest? Only the priest can intercede for me. I am only a simple woman. I cannot approach God in my own merits."

"Read on," the deacon encouraged her.

" 'And every priest standeth daily ministering and offering oftentimes the same sacrifices, which can never take away sins: but this man, after he had offered one sacrifice for sins for ever, sat down on the right hand of God; from henceforth expecting till his enemies be made his footstool. For by one offering he hath perfected for ever them that are sanctified.' "[77]

"You see, Lisle," Big Peter broke in, "Jesus is seated at the right hand of God, interceding for us. Even the Old Testament priests could not entirely erase the sins of the people. Jesus said, 'I am the way, the truth, and the life: no man cometh unto the Father, but by me.'[78] And in 1 Timothy we read, 'For there is one God, and one mediator between God and men, the man Christ Jesus.' "[79]

"Peter told the Jews, 'Neither is there salvation in any other: for there is none other name under heaven given among men, whereby we must be saved.' "[80]

"So then my husband was right when he said, 'It's not enough.' " Lisle's eyes, in the candlelight, were troubled. "If the priests cannot forgive sin and if keeping the commandments is no merit, how shall a Christian live?"

Mathes took the book from her and read, " 'This is the covenant that I will make with them after those days, saith the Lord, I will put my laws into their hearts, and in their minds will I write them. . . .' "[81]

"God has given us the Holy Spirit," Big Peter explained. "When we invite Jesus Christ to become Lord of our lives, when we receive the provision He has made for our salvation, He forgives our sins. It says there"—he pointed to the notebook—" 'And their sins and iniquities will I remember no more.'[82] Then he puts into us a new heart, one that is under the control of the Holy Spirit. 'Therefore if any man be in Christ, he is a new creature: old things are passed away; behold, all things are become new.' "[83]

Mathes read, " 'And having an high priest over the house of God; let us draw near with a true heart in full assurance of faith, having our hearts sprinkled from an evil conscience, and our bodies washed with pure water.'[84] By faith we can draw near to God, and He will hear our cry."

It was quiet in the stable for a few minutes. Then Lisle stood. She took a deep breath. "I thank you for your instruction. What you say is assuredly the truth."

"Would you not like to ask Jesus into your heart right now?" pleaded Mathes.

Lisle hesitated. Then she shook her head. "I need time to think of what you have said. What would I do? Where would I go? My brother-in-law would be furious."

"Leave that in the hands of God," Big Peter encouraged her. "Now is the day of salvation. Do not put it off," he urged. "And you?" he turned towards the girl, who had not spoken but who had followed the discussion with interest.

"I—I think I would like to have Jesus as my Saviour," she replied in a low voice. "But Mother?" She glanced anxiously at her mother.

"No." Mathes shook his head. "Every person must answer for himself to God. 'The wages of sin is death.'[85] Do you see yourself as a sinner before God?"

The girl looked away. "Yes," she whispered.

"Do you believe that Jesus Christ died for your sins and that He has the power to save your soul?"

She nodded.

Her mother stood by, not interfering.

"Won't you ask him to come into your life, now?"

"How?" Barbel lifted tear-filled eyes.

"Just talk to Him. Tell Him you believe He died for you. Ask Him to cleanse you from sin. Then thank Him for forgiving your sins and giving you eternal life. Ask him to take control of your life and to lead you in paths of righteousness."

And there, in the shadowy barn, surrounded by sleeping prisoners, Barbel prayed her first halting prayer.

Peter rejoiced for her, and as she asked for God's leading in her life, he prayed the same for himself.

Lisle, although she rejoiced at her daughter's radiant face and expressions of peace and joy, still felt she wanted to pray and ponder. She promised to speak with the brethren before they were led away the next morning.

Peter lay awake for a long time after the two women had glided silently from the stable. Barbel's glowing face floated above him. He told himself he was only overly excited because a new soul had been born into the kingdom. If only . . . but, he tossed restlessly. What was the use in dreaming?

XXII

On to the Sea

"Hey, Peter!" Lukas's voice in his ear and a jerk on his left arm penetrated Peter's dreams. He opened one eye groggily and then closed it against the brightness steaming through the open stable door.

"Get up." Lukas jerked impatiently at the chain that joined them. "We have a holiday today. Are you going to sleep it away?"

Peter groaned. He felt like he could sleep all day. A holiday? He looked sleepily at Lukas, who was meticulously picking tiny shreds of straw from his coat. "What holiday?"

Lukas continued to pick straws. "A messenger came from the inn down the road where the other men stayed and said that most of the soldiers there ate some bad food last night and are too sick to travel. So we'll have a day of rest."

Peter sat up. A day to stay here! Barbel! He would see her again. Then furtively he looked around to see if anyone had heard his thoughts.

He began picking straw from his own coat. It was filthy, he noted with revulsion. He scraped with a dirty fingernail at some caked mud. Why had he never noticed before how grimy his hands looked?

He followed Lukas to the water trough, where other brethren

were splashing water on their faces, glad for the chance to wash. Normally Peter completed his own toilet in a hurry and waited impatiently for Lukas to scrub his neck and ears with his unbelievably clean handkerchief and smooth his black hair. This morning Lukas waited on him. He even withdrew his handkerchief but quickly replaced it, deciding that to use it would do more harm than good. He did his best with his bare hands to make himself presentable. As for his hair—he sighed as he attempted in vain to run his fingers through the matted locks. Barbel would never look at him anyway, not after seeing that handsome Lukas who was so neat and clean. He wished he had paid more attention to his appearance before this. But had she not smiled at him last night when she took his bowl? But then, she had smiled at Andreas and Caspar too.

Peter strolled with Lukas to the open stable door, his head down.

In the narrow courtyard, the men were standing in clusters. Peter heard Lisle's name mentioned. The conversion of the previous night was under discussion. Peter listened along with his companions, not revealing that he had been a witness to the event.

As they ate their breakfast, seated again on the narrow benches against the wall inside the inn, Peter could not keep his eyes from Barbel. She followed her mother about with a light step. The smile never faded from her face. When she took his bowl, her eyes lit up in recognition. "You were there last night," she said softly. All Peter could do was nod. She moved on. Had anyone heard? Lukas, beside him, had been talking to Caspar, so apparently the exchange had gone unnoticed. Not that it mattered, Peter scolded himself. There could never be anything between them. He was doomed. He had no future here.

They spent the remainder of the day standing in the winter sunshine in the courtyard or reposing on the straw in the barn.

For a group of condemned convicts, they were amazingly cheerful, Peter thought moodily. Animated conversation of their adventures in soul winning mingled with recitations of Scripture and discussions of Bible doctrines.

A letter was composed to be sent to Moravia at the first opportunity, informing the churches of the priest and followers near Stein. Andreas, having acquired quill and paper, was endeavoring to pen a few lines to Bridgit while Caspar pestered him with his old jocosity.

"Can't you do something about this cousin of yours?" the frustrated Andreas appealed to Peter. "You'd think he was fastened to me, the way he keeps looking over my shoulder."

Peter suddenly remembered that he had never told Caspar about Hulda's message. "Well," he drawled, "I almost forgot, but Ursula said that someone else had sent greetings to Caspar."

The rangy Caspar looked startled. "What was that?"

"Oh, nothing much." Peter waved his hand. "Ursula just said that someone wanted to send you greetings, but"—he wrinkled his forehead—"let's see if I can remember now who it was."

"You, you . . ." Caspar reached for him.

"Hold on," Andreas pleaded. "Don't drag me into your frays."

Caspar had to be content with shaking Peter's shoulder. "Come on," he begged. "You still have the letter, don't you?" He reached for Peter's coat.

At last Peter yielded up the letter, and Caspar was content to sit subdued beside Andreas.

Several times during the long day, Peter caught glimpses of Barbel tossing grain to the chickens behind the shed, carrying a huge pail of potatoes into the kitchen, throwing slops onto the pile beside the kitchen door. He wished he knew her better and could speak with her. She seemed to be a serious girl and a hard worker by all appearances.

That evening the prisoners gathered in the stable to sing and pray together. Because he was watching for them, Peter noticed Lisle and Barbel slip through a crack in the door and seat themselves in the shadows of an empty horse stall.

Brother Mathes spoke on Jesus, the Bread of Life. Then several others gave their testimonies.

One older brother who, Peter knew, had forsaken his family to follow Christ, quoted, " 'He that loveth father or mother more than me is not worthy of me. . . . And he that taketh not his cross, and followeth after me is not worthy of me.' "[86]

The forsaking, and the cross, seemed a very high price to Peter just now. Why could he not dream and plan for the future? These confining chains. His eyes sought out Barbel. Had she been looking his way? Surely not. Surely he had only imagined it.

That night Lisle told of how she had prayed the night before and had finally yielded her heart to the Lord. "Now what shall I do?" she asked.

After some discussion, the brethren advised her to contact the group of believers near Stein. If necessary, she and Barbel could leave the inn, and the church near Stein would provide for them. Even though uncertainty and probably hardship lay ahead for these two new Christians, they rejoiced in their new-found salvation and looked to their heavenly Father to guide them.

Peter had hoped that the soldiers would still be ill the next morning. Not that he enjoyed the thought of their suffering, but he did not want to move on. The command was given however, and preparations were made to leave. Reluctantly he swallowed his tasteless porridge and succumbed to being chained into line.

As the column filed through the gate and around the corner of the wall, Peter's downcast eyes caught a flash of blue. He looked up, startled, to Barbel and behind her Lisle, standing against the stone wall. Barbel's blue eyes looked straight at him. "Good-bye," she said softly. "God bless you."

Had she spoken to him? They were past now, and Peter was afraid to turn and look back. If only they would have met under different circumstances. If only he were an ordinary traveller. If only they could live unmolested and safe in a bruderhof. If only . . . but what was the use? This was reality—this wearying marching, these dragging chains, the cold and dirt and rotten food and ever-present soldiers. Then—the ships. His gloomy thoughts tramped along with his feet down the road to the south.

A day and night later found the company camped on a ledge overlooking a foaming, rushing river. "The Save," Peter informed his friends.

"Why isn't it frozen?" Lukas asked.

"We are farther south now. Haven't you noticed that it isn't as cold?"

"I just thought we were getting tougher," Lukas quipped.

"And it is almost spring," Andreas pointed out. He was attempting, unsuccessfully, to tie his shredded shoelaces together with more knots.

Spring! What was spring? It seemed as though it had been cold forever. Peter watched the white water churning eastward towards its confluence with the Danube. If only he could float along with it.

As if reading his mind, Lukas blurted out, "Couldn't we lash together a raft and float down that river?"

The others watched the water far below. Lately they had spent a great deal of time discussing escape plans. They were so well guarded. Even though they were left untethered at night, except for the chains that joined the pairs, there were always guards on duty. The soldiers slept in shifts.

There might have been opportunities to escape even then. Various other individuals had found their way around the guards.

Granted, some had had to use bribery to gain access to the prisoners. But there were always those clumsy chains. And then they
would surely be missed in the daily count and a search party
would be sent.

Then too there was loyalty. Peter dreamed of escaping and
fleeing back to Carniola, where he could find Barbel; and together
they would make their way home. But Peter knew he would never
feel right about securing liberty while his brethren were still in
bonds. No, as his father and others of the men said, it would have
to be all, or none. Most still had the faith that God would deliver
them, but Peter felt it was a large order. They were expecting a
lot from God. Then instantly he chided himself for his lack of faith.

It took a long time before a suitable fording spot was found,
and they were only able to travel a few miles the next day. Peter
did not really care. Each step took him farther from Barbel and
closer to his doom.

Suggestions of spring greeted them every day. Birds sang in
the tree branches along the path. The snowbanks dwindled, and
water ran everywhere. At places the trail became soggy and treacherous. The sun shone warm on their backs.

"Soon we should be at Laibach," Big Peter commented as they
lingered around a fire one evening.

How old his father looked—so thin and weary. He had always
been a picture of strength and health. The march had taken its
physical toll on all of them.

"There were some Anabaptists there at one time."

"Really?" The young men looked at him with interest.

"I thought we were travelling through totally unevangelized
lands," Peter said.

"Not really." Big Peter shook his head. "Dedicated evangelists
have travelled far and wide, but King Ferdinand's strong-armed
resistance has wiped out much of their labours. A few converts

are often made here and there, but then they are put to death—and the faith dies with them."

"Like Henry's parents."

"Yes. Only that seed of faith survived in Henry. Sometimes, because of severe persecution, the new believers recant."

"There aren't many like that, are there?" asked Caspar.

"Sad to say, yes," sighed his uncle. "Many are those who start out but, for fear and favour of men, fall back and lose their eternal reward."

"I didn't realise that." Peter was surprised.

"We don't often speak of them," his father explained. "It is the heroes of faith, the saints who endured, who are spoken of and sung about. 'For the earth which drinketh in the rain that cometh oft upon it, and bringeth forth herbs meet for them by whom it is dressed, receiveth blessing from God: but that which beareth thorns and briers is rejected, and is nigh unto cursing; whose end is to be burned.'[87] And that burning," he stated solemnly, "is an eternal burning, far more to be feared than a burning of the body. 'For God is not unrighteous to forget your work and labour of love.'[88] Hebrews 11:13 says, 'These all died in faith, not having received the promises, but having seen them afar off.' So don't despair. Keep trusting God for your needs each day."

"What about Laibach? You were saying there had been some Anabaptists there." Andreas brought the conversation back to its starting point.

"Yes, the Philippite brethren with us say they knew a minister who had fled from there because of persecution. That is all they know of the place. It is doubtful there are any believers there now."

Laibach was another crossroads town, situated in the Alpine foothills. From there, roads led south to the sea or west to Italy and European centres. The day they arrived there, the city was teeming with people dressed in colourful holiday clothes.

"Do you suppose all these people are worshippers?" Lukas asked as the prisoners made slow progress along the edge of the street next to the buildings. It was the Lord's Day.

"They aren't acting very worshipful," Caspar observed.

People danced gaily on the street corners, and children darted through the crowds, waving colourful cloth streamers and shouting merrily.

"Must be a festival of some sort," Peter concluded.

In the noisy throng, the ragged prisoners, squeezed against the wall, went largely unnoticed. The soldiers were forced to dismount and lead their horses. They inched their way towards the city's main street, but here their progress was halted altogether. Loud cheers, waving arms, and shrieks of delight filled the air. The crowd parted momentarily, and above the tumult Peter heard the blare of trumpets and beat of drums.

"It's a parade." Lukas craned his neck to see.

Then, above the heads, a garish monstrosity moved jerkily across the square. More floats followed, some bearing replicas of demons, and others of saints. After these models, a huge wooden cross decorated with garlands of spring flowers bobbed along while the people bowed, threw kisses, or held out imploring hands.

"Idolatry!" Caspar breathed in Peter's ear. "All in the name of religion."

"Pagan rites adopted by the church," Andreas murmured. "This is what we are saved from, friends."

When the procession had passed, followed by the noisy crowd, General Carlos's company were able to move on unhindered. They encountered no fellow believers, nor did they see any evidence of such in Laibach. What had become of them remained a mystery. Perhaps they had recanted.

Peter's thoughts wandered to Martin and his father. Martin

seemed far away and long ago. Where were they now? The letter had said they were given into the service of some baron. They had not been reunited with their families after all. Had they clung to their faith? Young men like Martin generally served as squires with a view to becoming soldiers someday. Peter was glad he had chosen to suffer affliction with the people of God. It was hard, but at least they had God on their side.

They were on the last leg of their journey. The mountains had receded into the distance, and their way led across a fertile, gently rolling plain. Here flocks of sheep, shaggy with winter wool, grazed in seas of lush grass. Cows, their bells clanking metallically, plodded home for milking; farmers followed the plows, leaving heavy rolls of black earth in their wake; fat feather ticks spilled from upper-story windows as housewives aired the bedding in the spring sunshine.

Opportunities to share the Good News were limited. Occasionally they heard some familiar German tones, but most of the words were strange to their ears. Peter listened, fascinated, to the bartering in marketplaces and banter of stableboys in the inns. How anyone could make sense out of such gibberish was beyond him. It was unnerving to know that thoughts were being communicated within his hearing that were incomprehensible to him. If Brother Joseph were here, he would understand. He knew so many languages.

Where was Brother Joseph?

They had heard nothing from the schoolmaster since he had been left behind to recover at the mountain farm. Had he passed away? Or had he somehow escaped and returned home? Maybe they would never know.

The marvels of the awakening spring were largely lost on Peter. He thought he had long ago become reconciled to the hardships of the march and to his impending agonizing demise on the ships. But his encounter with Barbel had thrown him into an inner turmoil. He wanted to be true and faithful. He still acknowledged the higher calling to which all other interests had to succumb. And yet . . . if only . . . Sometimes he felt like kicking himself. He had never been interested in girls before. Oh, being a realist, he had supposed he would eventually find someone he appreciated and would settle down to make a home. But he had had those dreams of travelling and preaching too. Marriage had seemed a long way down the road. There was plenty of time for that.

Now here he was . . . no future . . . no hope for tomorrow . . . a condemned slave—and he could not stop thinking about Barbel.

He had never thought much about what kind of young lady he would want for a wife. His gregarious cousin had introduced the subject occasionally. Caspar declared he would find a girl who was strong and robust, capable of stooking sheaves and handling animals. None of these dainty little butterflies for him. Andreas, of course, had chosen; and Peter supposed that Bridgit was all right. She was skillful with her fingers and had a sweet, unselfish disposition. She was rather quiet though. Peter was sure that if he, who found small talk burdensome, had to spend too many evenings with another reticent person, communication would be unanimated and negligible.

Ursula, now—he always felt comfortable with her. Her laughter bubbled easily, and she generally found the silver lining to any cloud. Discreet enough for propriety, she was always eager to share news or discoveries with her family and friends. Barbel, in the brief glimpse he had of her, had seemed much the same.

He admired the way she had consistently avoided the advances of the rude customers. Her attire and manner had been very modest. Yet she had had enough mettle to take a stand for Christ before her mother and had had the benevolence to speak encouragement to him. He wondered where she was now. Had the unscrupulous uncle locked them up or turned them over to the authorities? Maybe she was facing a death sentence or suffering torture. He closed his mind to such thoughts and prayed instead that they had found their way safely to the newly formed church near Stein.

That night as he lay awake under the stars, he heard Andreas stirring restlessly beside him. Suddenly he felt that he must confide in someone. Andreas would understand.

"Andreas," he called softly.

"Huh?"

"You awake?"

"Um-hum."

"How do you stand it? I mean—when you think of Bridgit and of never seeing her again; how can you go on being so content?"

Andreas was silent for so long Peter was afraid he had gone back to sleep. At last he admitted, "It is a struggle. But I've committed her into God's hands. I believe that He cares for her more than I do."

"But don't you nearly burst sometimes for wishing you could be together again?"

"Yes—I do. But I cling to the knowledge that God's way is best. And I bolster my faith by hoping that it is true, as Brother Michel steadfastly believes, that we will yet be delivered."

"But we are nearly there!" Peter protested. "Once we're chained in the hold, I'm sure all hope will be gone."

"But we aren't chained in the hold yet, and I'm sure God could deliver us even then," reminded Andreas gently. "Remember Abraham's temptation?"

"Yes."

"God told him to offer Isaac, and He let him walk all that way to Mount Moriah with servants and provisions, climb that mountain, and actually lift the knife to slay his only son, before He stopped him. All that time Abraham had no assurance that God would spare Isaac except the promise that his seed would be as the sand. He had faith that, as Hebrews says, God could and would, if necessary, raise Isaac from the dead. I keep thinking of that. Maybe God is waiting till the last minute to reward our faith. There may be some searching soul to reach yet."

"There are other Bible examples of that, aren't there?"

Andreas thought for a time. "The priests had to step into the waters of Jordan before they parted."

"Noah spent one hundred twenty years building an ark and loaded it with animals before a drop of rain was ever seen on the earth." Peter ran mentally through Hebrews 11.

So although he did not reveal his secret heart to his confidant, Peter was a little comforted. Reluctantly, he laid these new and tender hopes on the altar of sacrifice, trusting his heavenly Father to shape his life as He would.

The long tramp continued. On and on they walked, sweating now in their winter coats, yet not wishing to remove them for the raggedness of the shirts underneath. Some walked barefoot, their shoes having disintegrated.

Through farming hamlets and luxuriant vineyards, where new leaves hid the supporting fences; around hills, plush with stands of sprouted grain; and over quiet streams on quaint wooden bridges trudged the evangelists in chains.

The soldiers, eager to end their stint of duty, became more talkative and quickened the pace of march. At last came a day when they crested a hill and caught a glimpse of sapphire against the azure blue of the sky, where the land met the horizon.

The sea. The soldiers gave a cheer, and except for the chains binding them to their prisoners, would have dashed away in their exhilaration.

They hurried on, the sapphire line growing ever wider and spreading as far as they could see to the east and west.

Even though the sea spelled disaster to them, Peter felt the current of excitement that rippled along the chains. Scarcely any of them had seen, or ever hoped to see, the Adriatic. Now here they were. The very air seemed different. It smelled like . . . Peter could not say what. Just like . . . like . . . water—a bit like the air after a heavy rain.

Then they were standing on the cliff above the shore. Sea and sky. Nothing but the sun-dappled water as far as the eye could see, except for a narrow band of brown at the bottom of the picture.

And there, its stout stone walls set down, it seemed, right into the water, lay the small port of Trieste, their destination.

Surrounded on three sides by a wall, the waves lapped up against the buildings on the fourth. A large rectangular fortification on the east corner attracted Peter's attention. With its wooden ramparts, this must be a keep. It reminded him of Falkenstein and his prison experience there. Would they be put in prison here?

But the ships. Where were the ships? Anxiously he scanned the shoreline and the water beyond. A dozen wooden fishing boats were tied to their moorings to the east of the town. The beach was festooned with yards of fishing nets spread to dry. Here and there the blue of the sea was dotted with more small boats—but there were no ships.

Peter's hopes rose. Maybe there was a mistake. Maybe no warships docked here. It certainly was not a large harbour.

The breeze carried the smell of fish and moist wood to them as they negotiated the steep path down the cliff. Then they were outside the gates of Trieste, where they were forced to stay all that afternoon and night. The soldiers murmured angrily at the delay and retaliated by kicking and pushing their charges.

More uncertainty. What would become of them next? General Carlos had gained admittance to the city and did not reappear before dark.

Strains of hymns bounced back from the high walls before them that night and were swallowed up by the brisk sea winds.

The next morning, in a small hall of justice, General Carlos officially delivered his eighty-four Anabaptist prisoners into the hands of the mayor of Trieste.

XXIII

Our God, Whom We Serve, Is Able to Deliver Us

In prison again!

Weeks of incarceration at Falkenstein had not hardened Peter to prison life. Compared to this, the castle dungeon had been comfortable. The brethren were packed into a cell built for half their number. The damp dirt floor quickly became mud under their feet. Water dripped from the walls. And no wonder. If they were in the fortification they had seen from the cliff top, it was probable that the sea lapped against one wall of their prison.

Stone ledges around the walls afforded space to lie down, but this privilege had to be enjoyed in relays. The smell of the sea filtered in through one tiny barred opening high in the wall. Caspar had volunteered to climb on Peter's shoulders to see what was outside this window, but so far he had not figured out how to accomplish the feat with Andreas hanging on.

Twice daily the key turned in the lock, and the door opened wide enough for several hard loaves of bread and a bucket of water to be handed in. There was no washing now, not even for Lukas. Peter's shrunken stomach ached naggingly, and when it was his turn to stand in the mud, he found his legs turning to jelly after several hours.

Days came and went. How long would they be kept in these deplorable conditions? Were they to be put on ships after all? In their distress, the men turned often to their precious notebooks and found comfort in the promises of God. Hopes of seeing home and loved ones began to grow dim, and they centered their thoughts on heaven and their eternal reward. Each one did his part to encourage others, and together they prayed and sought the Lord.

Peter stood back to back with his father, leafing through his worn notebook. He had read it from cover to cover twice in the last week. Soon he would know the whole thing by heart. Psalm 22 was a favourite of his these days. "My God, my God, why hast thou forsaken me? why art thou so far from helping me, and from the words of my roaring? . . . Our fathers trusted in thee: they trusted, and thou didst deliver them. . . . Be not far from me; for trouble is near; for there is none to help. . . . My strength is dried up like a potsherd; and my tongue cleaveth to my jaws. . . ."[89]

That was an accurate description of their present condition. "Be not thou far from me, O LORD: O my strength, haste thee to help me. . . . Ye that fear the LORD, praise him. . . . For he hath not despised nor abhorred the affliction of the afflicted; neither hath he hid his face from him; but when he cried unto him, he heard."[90]

Sometimes Peter was tempted to wonder whether their prayers ever penetrated the dripping roof above their heads. Would God ever deliver them? Their situation was worsening daily. Those with no shoes were suffering the most. When the men sat on the ledges, more of them could rest, but each one was still granted a few hours to lie down.

"Listen to this," Mathes Legeder, also reading from his notebook, quoted, " 'If we abandon Christ and His Holy Word, we fall into the wrath of God. If we remain firm in His Holy Word, then we face the sword.' I don't recall who said that, but I have it copied here. It is a choice all men must make. Most, unknowingly, choose the first, but I would rather face persecution at the hands of men than face an angry God some day."

The days and nights blended together. Time was marked by the arrival of food, and turns of lying, sitting, and standing. Peter could not have said how many days they had been in this foul hole, but Mathes Legeder knew when it was the Lord's Day, and he proposed a worship service with the participation of all.

The three deacons, with their partners, sat on a ledge while the others sat or stood facing them. Peter studied their faces from his position a few feet away. Old Michel Blauer had been white-haired ever since Peter knew him, but now his once-bushy locks were thin and straggly. His head had settled down between thin shoulders that were permanently bowed. Yet he had walked all this way. He reminded Peter of a twisted old pine he had once seen on a mountain. Denuded of needles, it had stood stubbornly against the prevailing winds.

Mathes Legeder. Some accused him of being too pushy and impulsive. But what would they have done without him during these months of hardship? It was he who saw to it that rations were divided fairly; it was he who kept track of time and places; it was he who negotiated with the general for special attention for the sick. Bossy he might be, but he always had the well-being of others in mind. Peter felt he had mellowed somewhat. His tone of voice was kinder, and he was less prone to prod and hurry others along.

Michel Kramer had aged too. His hair was heavily streaked with grey, and his lean face was even leaner. But his eyes still surveyed the congregation with serenity and compassion. The loss of his two eldest sons, who had left on a missionary journey never to be heard from again, and of George, had only made the gentle man more sympathetic and compassionate. Peter was happy to see him stand to begin the service.

He told simply and briefly the story of the three Hebrew youths. Alone and in a strange land, they refused to bow before the idol that King Nebuchadnezzar had erected. Michel challenged his cellmates with the answer those three Hebrews gave the king when he held before them the sentence of death in the fiery furnace if they refused to obey his command. They said, "If it be so, our God whom we serve is able to deliver us from the burning fiery furnace, and he will deliver us out of thine hand, O king."[91]

"Many of us have persistently believed that God would deliver us from this trial, yet we have journeyed all this way and now wait here in this vile prison. Do we still trust that He can save us, or have we given up hope? These young men were in the very mouth of the furnace, yet they could answer this great monarch with utter confidence in their God.

"Now I want you to notice what they said further." In a ringing voice, he read, " 'But if not, be it known unto thee, O king, that we will not serve thy gods, nor worship the golden image which thou hast set up.' "[92]

The deacon lowered his book. "Why do you suppose they added that hypothesis? Did they doubt that God could come to their aid? No, my friends—not for a minute. But being the children of God, they knew that in His wisdom, God might choose to let them perish at this time and in this way, to manifest His glory. And so they submitted themselves to His power, not questioning His ability as the omniscient One.

"Then, with the knowledge that God might not choose to deliver them, why did they still answer that they would not worship the golden image Nebuchadnezzar had set up?" He paused significantly. "Because it was wrong.

"My brethren, it may be that we will be offered another chance to prove our allegiance to the king by accepting their communion wafers or confessing to a priest. But even in the face of death, we must refuse—not because we are certain God will deliver us, but because it is wrong."

Next, Michel Blauer stood unsteadily before his flock. He did not preach. He endorsed the preceding message and added, "Dearly beloved, it is true that we must hold to the truth at all costs, as our brother has said, yet the Lord has given me continual assurance that we will return to our homes and loved ones. I feel our deliverance is near at hand. Let us lift up holy hands without wrath and doubting. Continually, in my dreams, I have seen an angel hovering over us. Indeed, God has said He will send angels to guard our footsteps. Just last night I saw an angel standing in this open doorway." Michel Blauer indicated the door that was shut and locked."

A strange thrill ran through Peter. He knew some of the men felt that the aged deacon was becoming senile. They all loved and respected him; but much as they wanted to believe in his visions, the more practical members were not counting on their realization.

Mathes Legeder rose, straight and strong as ever, his dark eyes snapping from under a luxuriant growth of black hair. "The Lord has led me to remind us of the apostle Paul. This renowned travelling evangelist had his narrow escapes too. He lists his experiences in the second letter to the Corinthians, mentioning stripes, imprisonments, stonings, beatings, shipwrecks, and perils by robbers, false brethren, and his own countrymen. He too was hungry, cold, and sick. But he concludes this colourful catalogue: 'I take pleasure in infirmities, in reproaches, in necessities, in persecutions, in distresses for Christ's sake: for when I am weak, then am I strong.'[93]

"The Lord had told him, 'My grace is sufficient for thee: for my strength is made perfect in weakness.'[94] I would like to claim the grace of God for all of us. Our own adventures in bonds bear some semblance to those endured by Paul. We have seen how the Lord has turned our helplessness and loss into gain for His kingdom. Let us go on, steadfast in faith, trusting Him to keep us in His will."

Twelve days in "the pit," as they dubbed their murky accommodations, had left most of the men weak and suffering from coughs or ague. Without General Carlos and his supplies, there was little Brother Jacob could do to relieve their symptoms other than prescribe more time on the stone ledge where it was drier.

It was with immense relief then on that twelfth afternoon, that the men responded to the invitation of a jailor to follow him from the cell. Stumbling down the corridor, apprehensions and hopes mingled in Peter's mind. Where were they going? Surely anything would be better than "the pit." But, then, maybe they were being led to the ships.

The hallway led to a large open area. While the men blinked in the sunlight, metallic clangs rang out. What was happening?

"They're removing our chains," Lukas whispered disbelievingly.

It was true. Several blacksmiths were attacking the iron wristbands that had plagued them for so long. Peter gladly bore the heavy blows of the hammer as the chisel cut into the iron. Then he was free.

Peter lifted his arm, and it flew up to shoulder height. It felt weightless. He looked at Lukas. For the first time in over two months, he could step somewhere without taking Lukas along. He tried it. He moved ten feet and then looked back to see if his friend was coming. Lukas, also free, hurried to his side.

"We've been together so long, I doubt if we can function separately," he joked.

Everywhere men were swinging their arms and praising God aloud. The pile of chains in the corner of the courtyard grew higher and higher.

But what did it all mean? Had they been unshackled prior to being released, or had these chains been discarded for new ones to be given on some ship? Peter feared the latter possibility was more likely.

To their disappointment, when the last chain had been tossed on the heap with a metallic rattle, the same jailor conducted them back to "the pit."

The cell buzzed with conversation. Speculations as to why they had been unchained and exclamations of joy at their freedom of movement mingled with lamentations for their impending doom on the galleys.

Peter said nothing. It was better not to think. Thinking opened the mind to Satan's forces. Better to just trust and take one moment at a time.

What was that man doing?

A squat, square-shouldered Philippite was crouching beside the door, his eye to the keyhole. Was he trying to look through the keyhole?

Peter inched nearer. The man took his eye from the latch and probed at it with his fingers. Finally he stood up, looked about, and clapped his hands. Those nearest him stopped talking. When he had the attention of a few, the man said, "I am a locksmith. I have made locks similar to the one on this door. If I had the proper tools, I think I could pick this lock and open the door."

His announcement was greeted with gasps of surprise. Hope swelled in Peter's chest. He remembered the angel Michel Blauer claimed to have seen in the open doorway. Could it be?

But an instrument was needed. Everyone looked expectantly at everyone else.

"What do we have?"

"Do we have anything?"

"A knife?"

A knife was passed quickly to the man. He bent to try it but shook his head. "Too wide," he said. "I need something smaller."

A pen nib was tried next, but it was too short.

Peter almost groaned. Wasn't there something?

They tried fastening the pen nib into the knife handle. The nib went in farther but hadn't the strength to move the necessary pieces.

"My needles!" A shoemaker pushed his way to the door, waving two sturdy needles, one having a curve at the end. "The general gave us these to mend shoes and forgot to take them back. Will they do?"

"Just the thing." The locksmith selected the curved needle and bent to work on the lock.

"Pray, brethren," Mathes Legeder exhorted.

And pray they did—desperately—while the man twisted and turned the small instrument in the lock.

Then suddenly the door was open—wide open.

They all stood immobilized, too amazed to move.

"The Lord has delivered us," Michel Blauer said tearfully. "Let us thank Him."

"We aren't free yet," reminded Mathes Legeder. "Send someone to spy out the hallway and courtyard. See if there are guards about."

By this time night had fallen and it was dark in the cell. A man crept furtively down the hall, and his footsteps faded out of hearing.

Very shortly he was back. "It is hard to see, but there seems to be no one about. The yard is deserted. The pile of chains is lying there still. Perhaps we could use them to scale the wall."

There was no time to lose. With admonitions to move noiselessly, the men glided like shadows from the pit, down the corridor, and into the open courtyard.

Peter looked up at the high stone walls. How could they scale them? What lay on the other side? Surely they could be seen. His hands shook with suppressed excitement.

Already some men had stooped against a wall so that others could mount their shoulders. Some set to work at the chains, tying them clumsily together. The rattling of chains grated on Peter's ears. They were so noisy! He nervously watched a dark archway across the courtyard.

The man on top of the human pyramid peered over the wall. "The sea is right below us. We can drop right into the water."

"But how deep is it?" someone asked.

"We'll have to take that chance."

"Here, hand those chains up."

Peter stared at that dark archway. Was that a light? It was! Someone was coming! He opened his mouth to call a warning, but it was too late. A man with a lantern stepped into the courtyard.

The prisoners froze in their places.

A second man followed the first from the archway. The lantern bearer spoke to him over his shoulder.

Then the lantern glow revealed the first of the escaped men. The man with the lantern stopped abruptly, his mouth dropping open in amazement. The one behind him stared and then opened his mouth to shout. But the first quickly put a hand over his mouth.

They were dressed in civilian clothes now, but Peter recognized them as two of the Spanish soldiers.

All was lost. There would be no escape now. The eighty-four of them could easily tackle two men, but Christians do not do such things.

Then, amazingly, the first soldier snuffed out his light. In the darkness they could hear him approaching. He spoke slowly, "You good men. Your God helps you. I tell you how to go." He walked quickly to the corner of the wall behind the pile of chains. "Here. You go over wall here. There is a tower, but guard can't see you here. Go into water. Tide is out now. Walk in water to east, past town. Now I go. All the saints help you." And before they could thank him, the two Spanish soldiers had retreated the way they had come.

Their gratitude and thanksgiving threatened to overflow audibly, but silence was imperative, and this was the time for action.

Three men clambered up a human ladder and perched on top of the wall in the corner the guard had indicated. The clumsy chain ropes were handed up and lowered over the wall. After several men fastened the ends of the chains securely in the courtyard, the three on the wall disappeared, and a muffled splashing announced their arrival in the water on the other side.

One after another, the men shinnied up the improvised ropes. Peter knew he had lost strength in the last weeks, but with the urgency of desperation, he was up and over the wall. He gasped as the chest-deep cold water swirled about him. Already he could see a line of dark shapes ahead of him, bobbing along the wall and disappearing into the darkness. He hoped he could find his father.

With one hand clutching the wall and the other arm waving to keep his balance on the slippery rocks underfoot, Peter waded forward. His body quickly became impervious to the cold water, but his teeth continued to chatter with excitement. At any moment, he expected to hear a shout from the guard tower.

He had almost reached the end of the wall. He raised his head. He was at the base of the tower now! Every ripple sounded like a tremendous splash! At the corner of the wall, a dark form whispered, "Walk out where it is deeper and follow the rest."

Apprehensively Peter left the security of the wall and stepped after the head that bobbed in front of him. "Good thing the waves are not so high tonight," he thought. "God must have sent the clouds to shut out the moonlight for us to—" A-ah! His foot slipped on a stone and he went down.

The cold water closed over him! He floundered wildly! Was he to perish here in the Adriatic in such an ignominious way? "Help me, God!"

Peter felt a firm grip on his arm, and he regained his footing. He choked and gasped while his rescuer supported him.

"Let's go." Peter never knew who had snatched him from a watery grave.

Past the fishing boats tied at the wharves, past the huts of the fishermen huddled darkly on the shore. On and on Peter struggled, his longing for freedom overpowering his fear of the black water that numbed his body and threatened to squeeze the breath from his chest. On and on. It seemed as though he had been in the water for hours.

He could see nothing beyond the two disembodied heads before him. Behind—he turned for a backward glance—were two more heads. The town, the high walls, and the guard tower had all been swallowed up in the darkness.

At last the head in front veered to the left, and some shoulders rose to meet it. Gratefully, Peter waded into shallower water. The waves carried him rapidly towards the sandy beach.

A strip of sand lay between the water and the cliff. As Peter crawled out of the water, he could see dark, bent-over figures scuttling towards the safety of that cliff.

Weighed down by his dripping garments, his feet sinking in the wet sand, Peter felt as though he was running on one spot, but at last he reached the group of men huddled in the shelter of an overhanging rock.

When he saw Big Peter's large frame emerge from the darkness, he wasted no time in joining his father. Together they watched for Caspar.

We are free! free! free! The words sang in Peter's head. What did it matter that he was wet, dirty, thin, and ragged? He was free! When everyone was accounted for, Brother Michel Blauer led them in a prayer of thanksgiving. No one questioned his visions now. The doubters had been humbled before the faith of this seasoned saint. His prayer was simple and brief: "O Lord, Thou who hearest the cries of Thy people, Thou who rememberest them in their affliction and deliverest them from all their enemies, we thank Thee. We thank Thee for this experience and for the many souls who have turned to Thee through it. May Thy kingdom increase mightily. We praise Thee now for bringing us out of the very jaws of death by a miracle. May we ever be yielded to Thy will as we turn our faces towards home and loved ones. . . ."

Home and loved ones! Peter had not thought beyond their immediate escape. Home and loved ones—Mother, Maria, Ursula, the baby. He would see them again. But when he recalled the miles upon miles of hills and valleys and rivers and mountains that lay between them and home, his heart sank. How would they ever get there? All that way!

They would inevitably be pursued. How could eighty-four men travel four hundred miles undetected? What would they eat? Where would they stay? And they were all so weak. He was not in as poor shape as some, but the thought of retracing the arduous journey filled him with despair.

What was the use? They would never make it anyway.

Brother Mathes Legeder was organizing briskly with some of his old aplomb. "We will travel by various routes and at different times," he directed. "I feel we have an obligation to those souls we encountered along our way."

Heads nodded in agreement.

Twenty men, including Brother Kramer, Andreas, and his Philippite friend Johan, were advised to follow the shoreline of the Adriatic Sea eastward for some distance and then head north in groups of three or four. They would be travelling through new territory, so they were commissioned to preach whenever opportunity arose. Theirs was a dangerous route, lying near the lines of invading Turks.

Peter's earnest prayer followed Andreas as the first group slipped away into the darkness. Oh, that God would lead him safely home to his waiting bride.

The dividing and instructing went on. One by one Peter saw his comrades-in-chains turn their faces towards home. Lukas and his father, among others, were to follow the sea westward before turning north. Philip, the harness maker, and a dozen companions volunteered to remain hidden in the area, giving the others a chance to get a head start and so put distance between them. Two or three casual travellers could escape detection where a large group could not.

All were instructed to preach or teach as the Lord opened the way, but they agreed that they were not to take unnecessary risks. They did have family responsibilities and felt that the God, who had led them this far, would also bring them home to Moravia.

Plans were made to contact the new believers in the towns along their route. Peter could scarcely conceal his joy when his father offered to visit the brethren at Carniola. He would see Barbel again! All the dreams and longing that he thought he had successfully buried came flooding back. Would Barbel and her mother be with the Carniola church? Somehow he felt confident they would.

He could see himself already, relating to her the details of their thrilling escape. He would tell her how he had not been able to forget her, but then he had finally surrendered her future and his to the Lord.

But what if she was not even interested in him? He pushed the nagging doubts aside. After all, she had said "Good-bye" and

"God bless you" especially to him that day they left the inn.

Caspar and Big Peter moved away from the group, and Peter followed. As they worked their way laboriously up the escarpment by clinging to knotted branches of scrubby bushes that poked themselves up through the rock, Peter felt strong and confident again. God would provide. He fed the sparrows; He would feed them too. It was spring. They would not suffer from the cold any longer. As for their rags, perhaps the brethren at Carniola could remedy that, but for now it was enough to be free. Puffing and panting, Peter hauled himself up after Caspar.

At last they rolled over the top of the cliff. They lay still for a time, catching their breath.

The moon had risen, although its brilliance was partly obscured by clouds. Peter stood up and looked back to the southwest, where the black water rippled up against the pile of blocks that was Trieste. Only a few hours ago, they had all been locked inside these walls. With his right hand, he absent-mindedly fingered the scabs and calluses on his left wrist. Those dreadful chains, which had hampered them day and night for two and a half months, had been the instruments of their liberation.

" 'How unsearchable are his judgments, and his ways past finding out!' "[95] he murmured.

"Look!" Caspar whispered hoarsely.

The clouds had parted. Peter's gaze followed Caspar's pointing finger out across the moonlight-spangled waves to the horizon. There were three great ships, their white sails floating against the dark sky like giant gulls, and their dark hulls riding low in the water.

"Admiral Doria's warships!" breathed Peter in awe.

"That is why our chains were removed earlier tonight," Big Peter said. "God's timing is always perfect. By tomorrow we would have been on those ships."

Peter stared long at the ships bobbing against the sky. The brethren had been snatched from the door of the furnace and out of the lion's mouth, and the Red Sea had parted before them just in time.

One of the ships turned lazily, and in the moonlight, Peter could see the long-handled oars bristling from its sides. He shuddered. Almost he had been doomed to . . .

A hand clutched his sleeve. "Come on, Peter. Let's go," Caspar urged.

With one last backward glance, Peter turned and trudged through the bushes after his father and cousin.

It was a long way home.